PRELUDE TO THE KINGDOM

Prelude to the Kingdom

MORMON DESERT CONQUEST
A Chapter in American Cooperative Experience

By
GUSTIVE O. LARSON

Publishers
MARSHALL JONES COMPANY
Francestown   New Hampshire

Printed in the United States of America

To
MY FATHER

Preface

IN days when America's spiritual fire burned more brightly, men dared to believe that God had work for them to do. None became more obsessed with a sense of divine commission than did the Mormons in the second quarter of the nineteenth century. Like other contemporary groups, these modern "Saints" undertook to lay the foundations for "the Kingdom of God" as a prelude to Christ's millennial reign. The spiritual kingdom was to have an earthly counterpart. The principles of Christian brotherhood were to find expression through temporal engagements.

Such a Kingdom required concentration of membership into one place, and "the Gathering," as it was called, became an important part of the "latter day" program. The Perpetual Emigrating Fund Company became the machinery of a great cooperative immigration movement. Through its direct and indirect assistance a hundred thousand people were rescued from economic slavery to be planted in the furrows of opportunity in the valleys of the Great Basin.

The enterprise succeeded out of all proportion to the promise of circumstance. It was a victory won through unity of effort. Today in a world which has become cooperative conscious in its quest for social and economic security, the Mormon experiment affords a significant background. It should be called upon to reveal the elements of its success formula. At least three of these were: (1) A strong spiritual incentive, (2) a group consciousness which merged individual and community interest, and (3) a will and aptitude for working together for mutual benefit. While the gathering is not regarded as a finished movement, its narration in these pages closes with the year 1887, when the Emigrating Fund Company was officially dissolved. The concluding chapters trace survival of the cooperative spirit in our own day under greatly changed circumstances.

In the face of prevailing charges that organized religion is failing to save men from social calamity, these chapters suggest certain definite possibilities to the contrary. The story depicts a people, with all their human weaknesses, seriously engaged in building the Kingdom of God on a seven day week foundation. To them there were no sharp distinctions between temporalities and spiritualities. They drew extra strength to build canals, conquer the deserts, and to manufacture necessities from the vision of a great spiritual enterprise. They had an intense feeling of divine vocation and a sense of trusteeship with reference to material possessions.

The spirit of sacrifice was conspicuous in the Mormon experience. Enthusiasm for the Kingdom dictated that immediate wants should wait upon the future and that personal desires be sublimated to group welfare. Thus a single announcement from the pulpit of authority sent hundreds of men annually with necessary outfits on a thousand mile journey to bring in the immigrants, and uprooted thousands of families to relocate in new areas of the ever expanding empire.

The will and the capacity for working together characterized the Latter-day Saints in their social and economic experiments in Ohio and Missouri. The Perpetual Emigrating Fund was conceived in the Mormon conflicts of Missouri and Illinois and came into being some years later when the Church leadership in Salt Lake Valley called upon the members to fulfill their pledge of cooperation. The same cooperative temper prompted defensive measures in commerce and mercantilism and sustained the development of home industries.

These chapters do not pretend to offer a history of the Latter-day Saints Church nor any systematic account of Utah's settlement. They skim lightly over Mormon beginnings in the East to present the modern "Saints" finally at work in their Great Basin laboratory. The writer has exercised freedom in selecting such incidents and episodes as he has felt would accomplish his purpose in revealing the spirit and method of "the gathering" and the "building of the Kingdom." He has sought to reflect these through original sources, letting them tell their own story. This has been done through liberal quotations from contemporary records and correspondence. He has also used Mormon terminology quite freely. A Mormon himself, he recognizes the danger of bias, but has attempted to present the story objectively as one of the significant movements in American westward expansion.

Among those to whom the writer is indebted for assistance in the preparation of these chapters are staff members of the L.D.S. Library in Salt Lake City. Also, the late Dr. Andrew L. Neff, under whose guidance the author first made a study of Mormon immigration activities. He is grateful to Dr. John A. Widtsoe for his encouraging suggestions and for the Foreword and to Ezra T. Benson for helpful criticism and contact with his wide experience in the field of modern cooperative enterprise; to A. Hamer Reiser and William R. Palmer for reading the manuscript in various stages of preparation and for their helpful contributions; to Allen H. Lundgren for the illustrations and last but not least, to Virginia B. Larson, for secretarial assistance and many constructive suggestions as the work progressed.

THE AUTHOR

CONTENTS

Foreword

I T was man or the desert! That was the challenge facing
the Mormon pioneers on July 24, 1847. Gloriously, the
battle was won by man. From the experimental beginning
in the Great Salt Lake Valley, have grown millions of homes,
covering the defiant desert. Song and happy laughter,
churches and schools, farms and factories, have displaced
the coyote's call, and the expanse of colorless sage.

This epoch making story beggars, as a whole, the skill of a
writer. It is too much, in its details, like a vast tapestry. Its
completeness will be best understood as the different parts
are set forth one by one in separate studies.

This has been done in this excellent, readable book. Director Gustive O. Larson presents here a study, from the labors
of many years, of one of the most human intriguing phases
of the pioneer toil — the Perpetual Emigration Fund, which
in many respects represented the very soul of the people.

A religious impulse led to Mormon settlement in the Far
West. Others of the faith, in this and other countries, desired to cast their fortunes with their fellow believers. And,
they were welcome. The desert could not be tamed without
man power. But the distances were great, and many were
poor. Then those in the desert, in their poverty, came to
the rescue. Thus grew the flow of converts to the "valleys
of the mountains." From these recruits, communities of
civilized people were reared, and supplied with the necessities and comforts of life. The pilgrims who trailed over
two thousand miles of weary desert, at last emerged victors,
and showed what wonders may be achieved when many labor
together in brotherly love. It is a story to soften the heart.

How this was done Director Larson sets forth skillfully in
PRELUDE TO THE KINGDOM. While he traces con-

sistently the thread of cooperation, which brought many emigrants to the chosen land, he does not stop there. He follows the converts into the occupations and industries through which they built their "kingdom," making of the book a brief history of the whole western movement. And the author does not wholly look back, for he carries the story in another form, fitting a new day into the present L.D.S. Church welfare program.

In this study, principles are laid bare, which must be adopted everywhere if peace and prosperity are to cover the earth. It is a book for the day — for this day with its many and disturbing problems. It is a book that can be read profitably.

JOHN A. WIDTSOE

PRELUDE TO THE KINGDOM

1

Introductory

THE early nineteenth century, rich in social experiments and prolific in new religious creeds gave birth to what became popularly known as Mormonism. The new religion shared with contemporary offspring some definite characteristics of the period — political, religious and economic.

The political mood of the youthful nation was one of intense nationalism. Behind the slogan of "manifest destiny" was a general conviction that America had been reserved for the development of free institutions. Said the Rappite Manifesto, "In America nothing hinders the Society from practising its belief. It is a special providence that this land became a republic."

Closely linked with this political doctrine was the spirit of millennialism. Great religious revivals stirred the border states with the imminence of the millennium. The Campbellites (Disciples) and Adventists date from this period. Of the latter group the Millerites were particularly obsessed with expectancy of Christ's immediate return.

Economic disorganization with attendant evils, generated communistic experiments of both foreign and American origin. The Labadists, Ephratists, Rappites, and Shakers, not to mention scores of others, labored zealously to build the Kingdom of God as a fitting prelude to Christ's return.

"Oh presumptuous man," wrote one of their leaders, "You view the treasures of Heaven as a common stock; why not consider then the treasures of Earth in the same light? It is reasonable to suppose that he who cannot learn to share with his brother in this life will not easily do so in the World to Come and that no one need expect to find happiness in a heavenly society of men unless he first learn and practice the social virtues here among his fellow creatures[1]."

It remained for Robert Owen who came to America in 1824, to win national attention for nonreligious communistic experiments. From platform and press he popularized his doctrine of universal brotherhood and economic reform. In his mind the day of private property was coming to a close. Backing his message with money he purchased New Harmony, Indiana, from the Rappites in 1825. The colony began on a basis of equality, all dressing alike and sharing equally in everything. There were no restrictions of color or creed.

Numerous other colonies of the Owen pattern appeared in and around Ohio. But they were short lived. Owenism, in practise, closed with this confession from its founder: "I had hoped that fifty years of political liberty had prepared the American people to govern themselves advantageously. I supplied land, houses, and the use of capital . . . but I find that the habits of the individual system were so powerful that these leases have been, with a few exceptions, applied for individual purposes and individual gain. . . . This proves that families, trained in the individual system, have not acquired those moral characteristics of forbearance and charity necessary for confidence and harmony[2]."

Other experiments followed. But it was significant that the only Utopian ventures which enjoyed any degree of success were those which joined religious with economic idealism.

Mormonism had its beginning in this national, millennial, and Utopian atmosphere. It had the stamp of each upon it. But it differed sufficiently to cut its own channel through the maze of contemporary isms and escape into the open west as a distinct product. Its sense of mission relative to locating God's latter-day Kingdom in a land specifically reserved for it characterized an intensely real "Zion building" program. These chapters attempt to trace development of the formula by which the Mormons, in pursuit of this objective, made a substantial contribution to American expansion. Following is an introduction to its origins.

The Mormon story relates how the religious turmoil of his day set fourteen year old Joseph Smith to serious contemplation. In the spring of 1820, he resorted to prayer in the woods near his home and was rewarded with a vision. Two celestial visitors whom he designated the Father and the Son, appeared, announcing the apostate condition of all Christian creeds and the need for restoration of the original. Here, he was told, lay his "Mission" if he should qualify.

Ten years followed, years of preparation interspersed with other "visitations" which culminated in the coming forth of the Book of Mormon[3] and in the announced restitution of the lost authority of the Priesthood. Now the youthful prophet was ready for the commission to organize, or more accurately from the Mormon point of view, to restore, the Christian Church in its original pattern and power. The official organization of the "Church of Jesus Christ of Latter-day Saints" was effected in a log house conveniently near Lake Seneca in Western New York State on April 6, 1830.

Six young men in their twenties were selected from a little band of believers to give the movement corporate existence according to legal requirement. These six included three of the Smith family, farmers all, two Whitmers, also farmers, and Oliver Cowdery, itinerant school teacher. The prophet who was then twenty-four and Cowdery, most closely associated with him in the production of the Book of Mormon, were accepted as presiding elders of the Church. Soon Lake Seneca became the scene of numerous baptisms.

Joseph Smith, in spite of his youth already had something of those qualities which commanded the loyalty of thousands who later flocked to his standard and divided men into camps of those who either loved or hated him intensely. Weighing over two hundred pounds he stood six feet tall — strong, athletic, blonde, with a frank, open countenance. "A man of commanding appearance," wrote Boston's mayor, Josiah Quincy, when he met the Mormon leader at the height of his career in Nauvoo, Illinois.

Among those who were soon to feel the power of that personality and play leading roles in the dramatic scenes of the "restoration" were Sidney Rigdon, Edward Partridge, Orson Hyde, and Parley P. Pratt, drawn from the ranks of the strongly millennialist Disciples; John Taylor and Brigham Young from the Methodists, Heber C. Kimball from the Baptists, and Orson Pratt, Wilford Woodruff, Lorenzo Snow and Willard Richards, unaffiliated with any religious denominations.

These men of whom only four (Brigham Young included) were older than their leader, came, with one exception, from old American stock in Vermont, Massachusetts, Connecticut, New York, and Ohio. They included four preachers, a miller, potter, physician, merchant, farmer philosopher, college student, and last a carpenter-glazier who, as Joseph's successor, was to become best known of them all.

The direct challenge of the "prophet of Palmyra" to established religious creeds won for him a lifetime of bitter opposition and persecution. But he seemed to thrive on it and there was not lacking response to the announcement of the "restoration." Two months after the Church was organized ninety members attended its first conference. In the fall missionaries, passing through Ohio on their way west to carry the message to the Indians in Missouri, added another two hundred converts. Early in 1831, this number had swelled to over a thousand. This favorable response not only presaged the future onrush of membership, but also served to draw Mormon headquarters out of New York State into Ohio.

The religious body expanded from within to meet requirements of its rapid growth until it could boast "the same organization which existed in the Primitive Church[4]." Numerous "revelations" became the heritage of these modern

"Saints" and these were compiled into what became known
as the Book of Doctrine and Covenants. In the general pattern of the organization thus developed during the first half
dozen years of its existence, the prophet president appeared
as exclusive oracle through which Divine Will would be
made known. But a theo-democracy was preserved through
provisions which required membership approval before any
revelation or official announcement became binding upon
the Church.

It became increasingly evident, as the infant Church attempted to plant itself simultaneously in Ohio and Missouri,
that the founder's conception of "the restoration" included
the establishment of a complete new social order. It shared
with contemporary religious Utopias the ambition to literally build the Kingdom of God on earth. The "select" who
would respond to the warning voice of the "latter-day" missionaries would be gathered together into one place to escape
the calamities awaiting the wicked. There they would build
"the Kingdom" preparatory to Christ's millennial reign.

In the plan the American Continent held a favored position. The Book of Mormon recorded ancient prophecy
to the effect that it was "a choice land above all other lands,
a chosen land of the Lord. . . . wherefore the remnant of the
House of Joseph shall be built upon this land, and it shall
be the land of their inheritance and they shall build up a
holy city like unto Jerusalem of old[5]."

Indeed in the mind of the Mormon prophet everything
pertaining to America's discovery and colonization had been
divinely directed in order to preserve the continent as a
stronghold of human liberty where Zion might rise again.
Thus the Lord had spoken; "Therefore it is not right that
any man should be in bondage one to another. And for
this purpose have I established the constitution of this land,
by the hands of wise men, whom I have raised up unto this
very purpose, and redeemed the land by the shedding of
blood[6]."

Their Zion building program was not the only Mormon concept which harked back to ancient scriptures[7]. In 1836, the first Latter-day Saint "temple" was dedicated in Kirtland, Ohio. This structure, which still stands as a monument to Mormon origins, served as the sacred rendezvous where heavenly "keys" were committed into human hands. In rapid succession, records the Doctrine and Covenants[8], the prophet enjoyed four celestial visitations. The temple itself received divine approval through the appearance of the risen Lord; the Prophet Elijah, whose return was predicted by Malachi, came to "turn the hearts of the fathers to their children and the hearts of the children to their fathers[9];" the ancient covenant by which Israel became a chosen people "through whose seed all families of the earth should be blessed[10]" was renewed with the Latter-day Saints; and finally, Moses appeared to restore the keys for the "gathering" of scattered Israel.

Unusual claims these, to divine intervention, but the results which sprang therefrom were no less spectacular. Out of that spiritual pageant came some of the foundation stones of Mormon philosophy, the motivating principles of its whole constructive program. Temple building and temple services, involving extensive genealogical research, became a distinguishing characteristic of the Latter-day Saints.

However, the operation of the two remaining "keys" had a more direct bearing on the present story. The "covenant" idea and the consciousness of being "chosen" in the service of God had been the mainspring of ancient Israel's spiritual progress. The effect was no less stimulating upon this latter-day people who became fired with a conviction that they were divinely designated as modern successors to that covenant. They were recipients of the privileges and responsibilities of a "chosen people."

Finally, the prophetic assurance of Israel's "gathering" passed from the realm of abstraction to a concrete program through Mormon consciousness of personal responsibility for bringing it about. Following their prophet's announcement of Moses' visitation in the temple and his delivery of the "keys of the gathering of scattered Israel," the Latter-day Saints felt an inescapable course marked out for them. This concept of "the gathering" as one of the basic planks in the platform of a modern "chosen people," led to positive action with results unique in the annals of history.

1   Calverton, V. F., Where Angels Dared To Tread, pp. 78-80.
2   Ibid, pp. 195-196.
3   Wallace, Henry A., at New York Times Book Fair: (1937) "Of all American religious books of the nineteenth century it seems probable 'The Book of Mormon' was the most powerful. It reached perhaps only one percent of the people of the United States, but it affected this one percent so powerfully and lastingly that all the people of the United States have been affected, especially by its contribution in opening up one of our great frontiers."
4   Mormon "Articles of Faith," No. 6. A Bishopric of three was followed by a First Presidency of equal number, a Patriarch, a Quorum of Twelve Apostles, and a Quorum of Seventy.
5   Book of Mormon, Ether 13:2,8.
6   Doctrine & Covenants, 101: 79-80.
7   Mormon "Articles of Faith," No. 10.
    Whitney, Orson F., Popular History of Utah, p. 41, "Joseph Smith's concept of the community, while subsequent in annunciation to the theories of Robert Owen and the French Socialists was not inspired by Modern Socialism and its methods. His ideas were ancient and Biblical, not modern and secular; they were of Moses and Joshua, rather than of Owen and St. Simon."
8   Doctrine and Covenants, Section 110.
9   Malachi, 4:56.
10 Genesis, 12.

2

The Mormon Utopia

SOON after Joseph Smith followed his missionaries into Ohio in 1831, he found himself surrounded by a thousand converts in and around Kirtland. Sidney Rigdon, with most of his Campbellite flock had come into the Mormon fold. They continued, after apostolic fashion, to live as one family — holding property in common. In view of the Mormon claim to restoration of primitive Christianity, it came as a surprise to "the Family" that Joseph disapproved. Not long thereafter however, he announced, as divine revelation, the principles of a new order. These unfolded in significant contrast to most of the communistic experiments of the day — both religious and secular.

The Mormon plan, known as "The Law of Consecration[1]," reflected Joseph Smith's developing religious philosophy. Basically it assumed that the human personality was God's first concern and all things were measured in relation to their effect upon its welfare and progress. "This is my work and my glory to bring to pass the immortality and eternal life of man[2]," the Lord announced in Mormon scripture. Another favorite quotation, "Men are that they might have joy[3]," prefaced the doctrine that man, pre-earth spiritual offspring of God, comes into mortality to "work out his salvation" through obedience to divine law. He will be "saved no faster than he gains knowledge[4]." The "eternal progress" of man in this mortal state is inescapably affected by his physical world. A healthy social and economic environment is vital to the development of both body and spirit. Hence the Mormon health code known as the "word of wisdom[5]," and constant stress upon educational values[6], man's free agency[7], and equality of opportunity[8].

Gross inequalities of wealth with resultant evils brought the poor as well as the rich under condemnation:

> "Wo unto you rich men that will not give of your substance to the poor, for your riches will canker your souls; wo unto you poor men, whose hearts are not contrite and whose bellies are not satisfied, and whose hands are not stayed from laying hold upon other mens goods, whose eyes are full of greediness, and who will not labor with your own hands."

> "Nevertheless in your temporal things you shall be equal, and this not grudgingly, otherwise the abundance of the manifestations of the Spirit will be withheld.

> "For if ye are not equal in earthly things ye cannot be equal in obtaining heavenly things[9]."

The Mormon economy was projected upon this religious foundation. It assumed the existence of enough land and resources for all — and that every man had a right to a livelihood. If in each community there were not enough of the common necessities of life for everyone, then it was because the few deprived the many. The "Law of Consecration" aimed to avoid this through the following principles which would preserve individual initiative in a collective society:

1. The earth belongs to the Lord. In recognition of this principle all properties held by members were deeded over to the Bishop. This was called the "consecration" of property.

2. Man is a steward over his possessions which are known as "inheritances." The Bishop deeded back to the members the same property or as much of it as represented his real needs which he received as his "portion" or "stewardship." This he held as private property to use or dispose of as he pleased.

3. Surplus property (beyond his real needs) and surplus production beyond the requirements for reasonable comfort belong to the "Bishop's storehouse." Any part of a member's property not returned to him after "consecrating" it to the bishop became common property of the church for distri-

bution as inheritances to the poor. All surplus production beyond real need was turned into the Bishop's storehouse on a strictly voluntary basis.

4. Distribution of inheritances and goods from the common storehouse were to be made by the Bishop to the needy "according to his family, according to his circumstances, and his wants and needs."

5. Private ownership remained the fundamental principle of the plan and each member was encouraged to labor in honesty and frugality to make his private property produce a living.

The plan sought to minimize evils incident to great inequality of wealth, and of poverty in the midst of plenty. But in so doing it would preserve the advantages of individual initiative, private ownership, and the incentive of reward for effort. Individual welfare was dependent upon industry; group welfare was promoted through surpluses turned to the common treasury.

The Law of Consecration was closely identified with the building of the "City of Zion."

"And with one heart and with one mind, gather up your riches that ye may purchase an inheritance which shall hereafter be appointed unto you. And it shall be called the New Jerusalem, a land of peace, a city of refuge, a place of safety for the Saints of the Most High God; and the Glory of the Lord shall be there and the terror of the Lord shall be there, inasmuch that the wicked will not come unto it, and it shall be called Zion[10]."

This ideal was to be realized on the American frontier. The prophet's first reference to location of the "New Jerusalem" came in September of 1830, when he recorded, "Behold, I say unto you that it shall be on the borders of the Lamanites (Indians)[11]." Soon thereafter Mormon missionaries to the Indians in Missouri sent back glowing reports of that country, and the following spring, Smith, together with thirty others, arrived at Independence, Jackson County, Missouri.

Here, it was determined, should be the center of "Zion" and Joseph proceeded to designate it so officially, and lay plans for its development.

> "Hearken, oh ye elders of my Church, saith the Lord your God, who have assembled yourselves together, according to my commandments, in this land, which is the land of Missouri, which is the land which I have appointed and consecrated for the gathering of the Saints wherefore this is the land of promise, and the place of the city of Zion . . . . it is wisdom that the land should be purchased by the Saints; . . . and also every tract bordering by the prairies, inasmuch as my disciples are enabled to buy lands. Behold this is wisdom, that they may obtain it for an everlasting inheritance[12]."

The foregoing was accompanied by the naming of certain men to serve in specific preliminary capacities; namely, Sidney Gilbert "to receive moneys, to be an agent unto the Church to buy land in all the regions round about, inasmuch as can be done in righteousness and as wisdom shall direct;". Edward Partridge was to continue as Bishop in Zion "and divide unto the Saints their inheritance;" William W. Phelps "to be established as a printer unto the Church." . . . "And thus let those of whom I have spoken be planted in the land of Zion as speedily as can be, with their families, to do those things even as I have spoken[13]." These officers of the new Zion were soon to be supported by the influx of carefully chosen man-power; "And again inasmuch as there is land obtained let there be workmen sent forth of all kinds unto this land to labor for the Saints of God[14]."

The first permanent group of "Saints" arrived in Jackson County on August 2, 1831. Religious fervor governed the immediate proceedings, Twelve men representing the twelve tribes of Israel carried the first log for the first house. Then Sidney Rigdon faced the new arrivals:

> "Do you receive this land for your inheritance with thankful hearts from the Lord"
>
> "We do," came in chorus.

"Do you pledge yourselves to keep the law of God on this land which you never kept in your own lands?"

"We do."

"Do you pledge yourselves to see that others of your brethren who shall come hither keep the laws of God"

"We do."

The assemblage knelt in prayer while Rigdon dedicated the land for the gathering of the Saints. Rising, he said, "I now pronounce this land consecrated and dedicated unto the Lord for a possession and inheritance for the Saints, and for all faithful servants of the Lord to the remotest ages of time, in the name of Jesus Christ, having authority from Him. Amen."

Detailed plans for the City of Zion were delayed until it was too late to apply them in Jackson County. But they formed the general pattern of Mormon settlements of the future as here summarized:

"The plan provided that all the people should live in the city; that the city should be one mile square; that the blocks should contain ten acres, cut into half acre lots, allowing 20 houses to the block; that the streets should be 8 rods wide, and intersect each other at right angles and run north and south and east and west; that the middle tier of blocks should be 50 percent wider than the others (these were to be used for schools, churches and other public buildings); that stables and barns should be outside the city; that farm lands should be laid off north and south of the city; that no lot should contain more than one house; that all houses should be set back 25 feet from the street, etc.,[15]"

Under this plan the farmer, as well as the merchant and mechanic, would live in the city. Together with his family he would enjoy the educational and cultural advantages of group life. The home would no longer be isolated and would share in the same comforts and refinements as those of the business or professional man. Visioning the future the prophet appended the lengthy specifications with the comment, "When this square is laid off and supplied, lay off another in the same way, and so fill up the world in these last days and let every man live in the city, for this is the City of Zion."

The designation of Missouri as the Land of Zion had a powerful, magnetic effect upon the Mormon converts. So intense became the desire of all to gather to Jackson County that the Mormon leaders, both in Missouri and Ohio, had great difficulty in regulating the western movement so as not to upset the Zion program at the very beginning. The following reflects the difficult problem of "boosting" Zion while at the same time restricting and regulating emigration to it:

> "Let all these things be done in order, and let the privileges of the lands be made known from time to time by the Bishop or the Agent of the Church. And let the work of the gathering be not in haste, nor by flight; but let it be done as it shall be counselled by the elders of the Church at the conferences, according to the knowledge which they shall receive from time to time[16]."

> "And now behold this is the will of the Lord your God concerning his saints that they should assemble themselves together unto the land of Zion, not in haste lest there should be confusion, which bringeth pestilence[17]."

Two other problems presented themselves. The first was the lack of purchasing power by the newcomers and the second was the reluctance on the part of the old-timers to sell. Although the territory may have been literally the "Land of Zion" to the "Saints" it remained just plain Missouri to the Missourians. An increasing flow of the religionists into Jackson County was cause for alarm. Their industry and their cooperative enterprise was disturbing to the frontiersmen. Social and religious differences aroused suspicions and aggravated relations between them. Political jealousies, uneasiness over the slave issue, the peculiar Mormon interest in the Indians, their claims to special divine favor as a religious group, and irresponsible announcements that the land was reserved as a Latter-day Saint inheritance, all contributed toward a crisis. The Mormons were ruthlessly expelled from their promised land in 1833[18].

During the next three years the exiles lived in Clay County, hoping ultimately to return to their lands in Jackson County. Every avenue for solution of their problem was explored except one — they could not consider selling their sacred "inheritances in Zion." Under these circumstances came a communication from the prophet in Ohio in which he explained their dilemma as a result of unfaithfulness on their own part, commanded them to gather anew, and predicted final victory for the Saints and the redemption of Zion.

> "Therefore let your hearts be comforted concerning Zion: be still and know that I am God. Zion shall not be moved out of her place notwithstanding her children are scattered. They that remain and are pure in heart shall return, and come to their inheritances, they and their children with songs of everlasting joy, to build up the waste places of Zion; . . . Neither shall there be any other place appointed than that which I have appointed for the work of the gathering of my saints. Until the day cometh when there is found no room for them; and then I have other places which I will appoint unto them, and they shall be called Stakes[19] for the curtains, or the strength of Zion[20]."

The Mormons failed, however, to regain their Jackson County inheritances and reluctantly vacated Clay County to find more permanent homes farther north. In Caldwell and adjacent counties, twelve to fifteen thousand of them gathered from 1836 to 1838, exiles from Zion, but not forgetful of her. The refugees were only allotted three years in Caldwell County before the pent up forces of mobocracy broke upon them in all their fury. Expulsion from the state in midwinter of 1838-39 was effected under the extremities of social hatred. An exterminating order from the Governor loosed all restraints of law and a Mississippi crossing into Illinois became one of desperation. The sacrifice of two million dollars worth of property was the least part of their suffering.

That this ill wind could blow anybody good would have been hard to believe by the beleaguered "Saints." But pressure from without develops group solidarity and as they passed through the fire of persecution another link in the chain of cooperation was forged. Joseph Smith had been court martialed and condemned to be shot. Refusal of a high ranking official to execute the order left the prophet languishing in a Missouri prison. In this emergency Brigham Young stepped forward to assume command. Fraternal ties were already strong in the group and added to this was the absolute necessity for remaining in a body if the original plans for Zion building were to be consummated. Therefore Brigham acted to prevent scattering of the flock beyond the limits of effective cooperative effort.

A general meeting of those who fled from Missouri, was called on January 29, 1839, at which, it is recorded, "On motion of President Brigham Young it was resolved that we this day enter into a covenant to stand by and assist each other to the utmost of our abilities in removing from this state and that we will never desert the poor who are worthy, till they shall be out of reach of the exterminating order of General Clark, acting for and in the name of the State[21]." The following covenant was then subscribed to by two hundred and thirteen names:

"We whose names are hereunder written do each for ourselves individually, covenant to stand by and assist each other to the utmost of our abilities in removing from the state in compliance with the authority of the state; and we do hereby acknowledge ourselves firmly bound to the extent of all our available property, to be disposed of by a committee, who shall be appointed for that purpose for providing means for the removing of the poor and destitute, who shall be considered worthy, from this country, till there shall not be one left who desires to remove from the state; with this proviso that no individual shall be deprived of the right of disposal of his own property for the above purpose, or of having the control of it, or as much of it as shall be necessary for the removing of his own family, and to be

entitled to the over-plus after the work is effected; and furthermore, said committee shall give receipts for all property
and an account for expenditure of the same[22]."

A committee of seven was named to administer the property in accord with the above. Agents were sent ahead
toward the Mississippi to cache grain at intervals for the use
of the refugees. Contracts for their ferriage across the river
insured final deliverance from their enemies. No sooner
had these essentials been arranged than Brigham fled to
Illinois to escape mob vengeance. Here he was joined by
Joseph Smith on April 22, 1839.

The tax burdened citizens of Illinois welcomed the exiles
with open arms and during the next six years the Mormons
repeated their community building at Nauvoo. Efforts to
reclaim property in Missouri failed, and return to Zion became a matter of the more distant future. The "other places"
which the Lord had "appointed unto them which should be
called Stakes" must of necessity receive first attention. Zion
now expanded to include all America to accommodate the
changed circumstances while Independence remained the
hub or "Center State" of the enlarged pattern. Wrote Joseph
Smith in April, 1844:

> "You know there has been great discussion in relation to
> Zion — where it is and where the gathering of the dispen-
> sation is . . . The whole of America is Zion itself from North
> to South, as is described by the prophets, who declare that
> it is the Zion where the mountain of the Lord would be,
> and that it should be in the center of the land."
>
> He explained further:
>
> "I have received instructions from the Lord that from
> henceforth wherever the elders of Israel shall build up
> churches and branches unto the Lord throughout the States,
> there shall be a stake of Zion. In the Great Cities of Boston,
> New York, etc. there shall be stakes."

The Law of Consecration was left behind in Missouri but
the program of building a spiritual Kingdom with temporal
foundations, and under a sense of divine guidance con-

tinued. The spirit of consecration found new expression in
a "law of tithing," instituted in 1838 and cooperative enterprise soon built the largest city in Illinois. Nauvoo, however, was destined to become only a stepping stone in the
westward march of the Latter-day Saints. Their Missouri
troubles pursued them to Illinois and the exodus of 1846
became a search for a place more suited to their purposes of
Zion building. That place they were to find far beyond the
borders of civilization in the valleys of the Great Basin.

1 The term, United Order, has often been used loosely to identify all the
   Mormon social-economic experiments. However the system in use in
   Joseph Smith's day was referred to as the "Law of Consecration" or the
   "Order of Stewardships." Later, as a part of a reform movement in
   Utah, Brigham Young referred to the varying system as "United Order."
   For more detailed discussion see, Geddes, United Order Among the
   Mormons; Palmer, William R., United Orders, in Improvement Era,
   Dec., Jan., Feb., 1942-43; Fox, F. Y., United Order, Improvement Era,
   July, 1944; and Clark, J. R. Jr., L. D. S. Church Conference Report,
   April, 1942.
2 Pearl of Great Price, Moses I:39.
3 Book of Mormon, 2 Nephi II:25.
4 Smith, Joseph, History of L. D. S. Church, Vol. IV, p 588 and Doctrine &
   Covenants, Sec. 130:18.
5 Doctrine & Covenants, Section 89.
   The Mormon health code, known as the Word of Wisdom, reflected
   the warning voices of Joseph Smith's day against the evils of tobacco,
   alcohol and "hot drinks." As Against this negative aspect it urged
   the use of certain wholesome food products and ended with a promise:
   "And all Saints who remember to keep and do these sayings, walking
   in obedience to the commandments, shall receive health in their
   navel and marrow to their bones; and shall find wisdom and great
   treasures of knowledge, even hidden treasures; and shall run and not
   be weary and shall walk and not faint; and I the Lord give unto them
   a promise that the destroying angel shall pass by them as the children
   of Israel and not slay them."
6 Just as maintenance of physical health became a part of Mormon religion,
   so education of the mind took on spiritual significance. The following
   illustrate the Mormon concept of salvation as a process already in motion:
   "Whatever principles of intelligence we attain unto in this life, it will
   rise with us in the resurrection.
   "And if a person gains more knowledge and intelligence in this life,
   through his diligence and obedience than another, he will have so
   much the advantage in the world to come." (Doctrine & Covenants,
   Sec. 130:18-19.)
7 "Remember that you are free to act for yourselves — to choose the way to
   everlasting death or the way of eternal life." Expanding this theme

from the Book of Mormon, Joseph Smith wrote, "All persons are entitled to their agency for God has ordained it so. He has constituted mankind moral agents and given them power to choose good or evil." Thus free man stands responsible for his own progress.

8 The development of lay leadership in the Mormon group and its "Universal priesthood" which allows all worthy male members to officiate according to graded advancement provided equality of opportunity.

9 Doctrine & Covenants, Sec. 56:16, 17, Sec. 70:14 and 18:6.

10 Doctrine & Covenants, 45:65-67.

11   "   "   28:9.

12   "   "   57:1-5.

13   "   "   57:14-15.

14   "   "   58:54.

15 Nelson, Lowry, The Mormon Village, Summary, 1930.

16 Doctrine & Covenants, Section 58:55-56.

17   "   "   "   63:24.

18 Geddes, Joseph A., The United Order Among the Mormons, p. 61.

"One closely associated with the bishop in Missouri wrote at a later date: 'Money was to be sent up to the bishop, and as fast as lands were purchased and preparations made, the bishop was to let it be known that the Church might be gathered in. But this regulation was not attended to for the Church got crazy to go up to Zion as it was then called. The rich were afraid to send up their money to purchase land, and the poor crowded up in numbers, without having any places provided, contrary to the advice of the bishop and others until the old citizens began to be highly displeased. They saw their country filling up with emigrants, principally poor. They disliked their religion and saw also, that if left alone, they would in a short time become a majority, and of course, rule the country. The Church kept increasing and the old citizens became more and more dissatisfied, and from time to time offered to sell their farms and possessions, but the Mormons, though desirous, were too poor to purchase them.' "

Also Bancroft, H. H., History of Utah, p. 97.

"The prophet had declared that Zion should be established and should put down her enemies under her feet. Why then should they hesitate to proclaim their anticipations. They boasted openly that they should possess the whole country and that the unbelievers should be rooted out from the land."

And Mackay, Charles, The Mormons or the Latter-day Saints, pp. 72-74, "The manner in which the Mormons behaved in their Zion was not calculated to make friends. The superiority they assumed gave offense, and the rumors that were spread by some false friends, who had been turned out of the Church for misconduct excited against them an intense feeling of alarm and hatred. They were accused of communism . . . joined to the odium unjustly cast upon them for these reasons, they talked so imprudently of their determination to possess the whole state of Missouri and to suffer no one to live in it who would not conform to their faith, that a party was secretly formed against them of which the object was nothing less than their total and immediate expulsion from their promised Zion. It is also probable that the more indolent Missourians gazed with jealous eyes as the new-comers exhibited that agricultural thrift which has always characterized them as a people."

19 Isaiah 54:2,3. "Enlarge the place of thy tent, and let them stretch forth the curtains of thine habitations; spare not, lengthen the cords, and strengthen thy stakes; For thou shalt break forth on the right hand and on the left; and thy seed shall inherit the gentiles and make the desolate cities to be inhabited."

20 Doctrine & Covenants, Section 101:16-21.

21 History of the Church, Period I, Volume III, pp. 249-250.

22 Tullidge, Edward W., History of Salt Lake City., p. 636.

3

The Gathering

NEVER did religion grip a people in the vise of reality more than the "restoration" gripped the followers of Joseph Smith. And few have drawn greater strength to achieve than they did under a sense of actual participation in a divine "latter day" program.

The building of the Kingdom was dependent upon concentration of membership into one place and this principle, already referred to, was called "the gathering[1]." Nordic peoples held a preferred place in the enterprise through being identified with the "blood of Israel." However, the term broadly interpreted, included all who were "adopted" into the brotherhood through conversion to the faith. These, the world over, were warned to escape from "Babylon" and flee to "Zion." "Wherefore the decree has gone forth from the Father that they shall be gathered in unto one place upon the face of this land, to prepare their hearts and be prepared in all things against the day when tribulation and desolation are sent forth upon the wicked[2]." "And the glory of the Lord shall be there, and the terror of the Lord also shall be there, insomuch that the wicked will not come unto it, and it shall be called Zion. . . . And there shall be gathered unto it out of every nation under heaven. . . .[3]"

Many there were to whom "the Kingdom" made its appeal. Haunted by fear in a precarious social and economic world and comforted little by religion whose only lift was the promise of better things hereafter, thousands welcomed the prospects of tasting the abundant life in mortality. They welcomed participation in a tangible program directed toward its achievement. The fear of "tribulation and desolation" made them long for the security which was promised through fellowship in an organized force for righteousness. The building of the Kingdom challenged them as a cooperative quest for salvation. Social insecurity in many lands contributed heavily to "the gathering" in the half century following Mormon settlement in Nauvoo and in the Great Basin.

Hand in hand with the principle of Gathering went another distinctive feature of Mormonism — that of extensive proselyting. Rapid growth in membership resulted from the labors of an ever increasing number of zealous missionaries. Church expansion presented a continuous cycle of missionary winning convert who in turn became the missionary. Having found the "Pearl of Great Price" each convert was not only willing to sacrifice all else to attain it but was anxious to share it with his friends. From the ranks of the new disciples rose occasional ambassadors of exceptional strength whose harvest of converts were numbered by hundreds and by thousands. Among these appeared such names as Brigham Young, Heber C. Kimball, Wilford Woodruff, John Taylor, the Pratt brothers, the Richards, the Snows, and many others.

Throughout the length and breadth of the land they carried the message of "the Restoration" — to the Southern States, to New England, to Canada. Sometimes it appeared as if certain neighborhoods were waiting for their announcement and on more than one occasion whole congregations turned to them for baptism. Excerpts from the Woodruff diary reflect the spirit and progress of these scripture fulfilling emissaries. Concerning his activities on the Fox Islands, off the coast of Maine, in late 1837, he wrote, "We continued to baptize the people of North Island until we baptized every person who owned an interest in the Baptist meeting house. I then followed Mr. Douglas home to South Island and preached the Gospel to members of his church, and baptized nearly all of them.

"One day Elder Hale and I ascended to the top of the granite rock on South Island for prayer and supplication. . . Elder Hale read the sixteenth chapter of Jeremiah, where mention is made of the hunters and fishers that God would send in the last days to gather Israel. We were indeed upon the island of the sea standing upon a rock where we could survey the gallant ships. . . . And what had brought us here? To search out the blood of Ephraim, the honest and meek of the earth, and gather them from these islands, rocks, holes, and caves of the earth unto Zion. . . . After spending most of the day in praise and thanksgiving, we descended to the settlement and held a meeting with the people[4]."

The sequel to this auspicious beginning is told in two isolated entries in the Spring and late Fall of 1838; "I called the people together and exhorted them to sell their property and prepare to accompany me to the land of Zion. I had labored hard for many days for the temporal and spiritual welfare of the inhabitants of those islands and the Lord had blessed my labors and given me many souls as seals of my ministry, for which I felt to praise Him; and now I felt to labor quite as zealously to gather out those who had embraced the Gospel, and lead them to Zion. . . .[5]

"Thus ended my journey of two months and sixteen days. I had led the Fox Island Saints to the west through all the perils of a journey of nearly two thousand miles in the midst of sickness and great severity of weather. In the Spring I took my family and removed to Quincy, Illinois, where I could mingle with my brethren; and I felt to praise God for His protecting care over me and my family in all my afflictions[6]."

The secret of Mormon missionary success was an intense conviction that the Lord had charged them with a tremendous responsibility. No sacrifice was too great for the establishment of the Kingdom. Listen to the words of their Prophet:

"A great and marvelous work is about to come forth unto the children of men. Behold the field is white already to harvest, therefore whoso desireth to reap, let him thrust in his sickle with his might, and reap while the day lasts, that he may treasure up for his soul everlasting salvation in the Kingdom of God[7]."

The waves of the "restoration" spread in ever widening circles to cross the boundaries of neighborhood, state, and nation and finally lapped the shores of distant continents. "Send forth the Elders of my church unto the nations which are afar off; unto the islands of the sea; send forth unto foreign lands; call upon all nations, first upon the Gentiles, and then upon the Jews. And behold and lo, this shall be their cry, and the voice of the Lord unto all people; go ye forth unto the land of Zion, that the borders of my people may be enlarged, and that her stakes may be strengthened, and that Zion may go forth unto the regions round about. . . . Let them therefore who are among the Gentiles flee unto Zion. . . go ye out from among the nations even from Babylon, from the midst of wickedness which is spiritual Babylon[8]."

Prior to 1837, proselyting was confined to the United States and Canada, but that year brought a significant overseas expansion. Early success in Canada had resulted in picking up family threads which led to England and in 1837 Heber C. Kimball, with six others, was sent to "open the doors of salvation to that nation." Ten days after landing on Britain's shore the little party performed a number of baptisms. In eight months before returning home two thousand converts had been won for the cause, of whom Kimball personally baptized fifteen hundred.

Two years later the same Woodruff of Fox Island success reported a single year's activity in England as follows: "I travelled 4,469 miles, held 230 meetings, established 53 places for preaching, and planted 47 churches and jointly organized them. . . . The baptisms of the year were 336 persons under my own hands, . . . I baptized 57 preachers mostly those connected with the United Brethren, also two clerks of the Church of England." He concluded his summary of 1840 with reference to raising funds for various purposes including "to assist 200 Saints to emigrate to Nauvoo[9]."

A decade later, when the Mormons were already well established in England, the gospel of the "Kingdom" was ready for its invasion of Continental Europe.

Four hundred and sixty-two "Latter-day Saints" tramped American soil as missionaries without financial remuneration of any kind before the opening of the British Mission. Five hundred and seventy-seven labored in America and England prior to Mormon settlement of Nauvoo, and during the six year period while the Mormons remained in Illinois, (1840-1846) one thousand, two hundred and twenty of their number left their newly established homes to carry the message of deliverance to the States and England.

Although there was immediate response to proselyting in England in 1837, converts were not urged at that time to come to America, for "Zion" was not yet prepared to absorb them. In 1840, however, after Nauvoo had become the Church headquarters, the missionary movement became a part of the great program of "Gathering." Excerpts from the diary of another successful missionary reveal its modest beginnings in 1840:

> "Between the middle of September and my own embarkation in October, I chartered three vessels for New Orleans, and filled them with the migrating Saints, viz:
>
> "The *Sidney* with one hundred and eighty souls; the *Medford*, with two hundred and fourteen souls; and the *Henry* with one hundred and fifty-seven.
>
> I next chartered the *Emerald*, on which I placed about two hundred and fifty passengers, including myself and family[10]."

Still later, when the Mormons were settled in the Great

Basin, missionary activity came to be identified for more than a half century, with emigration to Utah.

1 Tullidge, Edward W., History of Salt Lake City, p. 663, comments: "It was in the design of Joseph Smith at the very opening of the Latter-day dispensation to construct for his followers a new social system as well as to reveal a "new" spiritual religion as taught in patriarchal ages and by Jesus. Blending thus the genius and institutions of the Patriarchal and Gospel dispensations the Mormon Church grew up as the spiritual and temporal halves of a divine plan and government. Hence a "gathering" dispensation became both to the prophet and followers as a signature of their "new covenant" and a gathering place was the very base of their millennial work. There was needed a Mormon Zion and a constant flow of emigration, in fine, a well sustained system of Mormon colonization, to evolve and consummate the prophet's plan."
2 Doctrine and Covenants, Section 29:8.
3 Doctrine and Covenants, Section 45:67-69.
4 Cowley, Mathias F., Life of Wilford Woodruff, pp. 79-80.
5 Cowley, Mathias F., Life of Wilford Woodruff, p. 88.
6 Cowley, Mathias F., Life of Wilford Woodruff, p. 98.
7 Doctrine and Covenants, Section 6:1-3.
8 Doctrine and Covenants, Section 133:8-9; 12-14.
9 Cowley, Mathias F., Life of Wilford Woodruff, p. 34.
10 Pratt, Parley P., Autobiography, p. 36.

4

The Basin

WHILE Mormonism was unfolding itself on the American frontiers, the land which was to serve as laboratory for its "Zion building" program was being explored and won for the United States in the far West. Coincidently it was one of Joseph Smith's New York neighbors, by the same family name, who played a principal role in its conquest. These two Smiths more than a century ago reached out across the continent to lay the foundations for an empire in the Great Basin. The same decade gave them birth in neighboring villages but despite their dovetailed contribution to the development of the west, they remained strangers to each other. Only once their trails ran close together. On that occasion Joseph, the prophet, arrived in Independence, Missouri, sixty days too late to meet the trapper, Jedediah Smith, before his final journey into the wilderness. For the purposes of this chapter Jedediah is called into service to represent his entire trapping fraternity.

The two Smiths were eminently successful in their respective fields. Nevertheless they moved in the shadow of more prominent national figures. Jedediah was recognized as a superior mountain man by his associates, but his name did not travel beyond the trading frontier. Joseph, although hailed as a prophet by ten thousand followers in a stormy Missouri period, and by twice that number during a no less turbulent Illinois career, scarcely claimed the national spotlight. It was the illustrious John C. Fremont, following two decades later, in the trails of Jedediah, who was named the "Pathfinder" and missed the White House by a narrow margin. It was Joseph's friend Stephen A. Douglas, to whom the Mormon prophet gave the nickname "Little Giant[1]," whose voice rang in the halls of Congress, and sought the nation's highest office. Yet this same Douglas said in Washington that if he could command the following of Joseph Smith, he would gladly lead it west to found a commonwealth.

The trapper preceded the prophet to the frontier on the Mississippi by a scant decade. From Independence, in 1823, he plunged into the wilderness with Henry W. Ashley's mountain men. For seven years the Great Basin was his home. Joseph, remaining in New York, penetrated the spiritual jungle of that formative period, and emerged with a new religion. In the same year (1830) that Jedediah returned to St. Louis, after exploring the mysteries of the Basin, Joseph effected the organization which was destined to settle it.

The Great Basin includes the area between the Rockies and the Sierra Nevada Mountains which refuses drainage to the sea. The Snake River on the north, and the Colorado on the South and East, escape its borders unfed by Basin tributaries. Its triangular form, extending nine hundred miles, north and south, is almost as large as the Ohio River Valley, and has given birth, politically, to Nevada, half of Utah, and parts of Idaho, Oregon, and California. Once the waves of an extensive inland sea lapped the foothills of the Wasatch Range which forms the eastern rim. But centuries diminished the water's surface until at length its remnant formed a sheet of concentrated brine. This salty sea of 2400 square miles, remained the Basin's most distinctive physical feature.

The region presented a vast, forbidding desert. Its endless sage cast a dull gray haze across the valleys. These were bordered by dark green junipers covering the foothills of the surrounding mountains. On the higher levels, quaking aspen and conifers reached upward toward rocky peaks above. Out of these mountains into the neighboring fringes of green flowed the principal streams which made human existence possible. Stronger native tribes roamed the more desirable areas leaving the open desert to "digger" Indians, who subsisted largely on roots and rodents. The Shoshonies in the northern Wasatch and Uintah ranges warred against the Utes and Piutes who occupied the central and southern portions.

Spanish civilization had moved northward in the 16th and 17th centuries to throw a line of settlements up the Rio Grande Valley on the east and another up the Pacific coast west of the Basin. Between these two the Colorado River presented a barrier which diverted Spanish commerce northward to penetrate the southern reaches of the Basin. Beginning in the last quarter of the 18th century caravans of trade shuttled increasingly back and forth between Santa Fe and the Pacific coast settlements.

Except for this Spanish intrusion upon its southern borders the Basin remained an unsolved mystery far into the nineteenth century. West of the Rockies, Mexican California stretched indefinitely northward, and Russian Alaska extended southward. Between the two, American and British claims had been established. The American claim to Oregon, of which the northern Basin was something of a hinterland, rested upon Gray's discovery, Lewis and Clark's exploration, and Astor's settlement. Against these the British presented equal claim and, following the War of 1812, it was agreed by the two nations to hold the country jointly without prejudice to the rights of either. So the field was open to American and British exploitation.

The first invasion under this arrangement came from the north. The Northwesters penetrated the Upper Green River country, reaching with their traps, into the Northern Basin. News of wealth in furs stirred deeper interest in the West. The Hudson Bay Company moved into position on the Columbia to work the fur bearing streams of the interior. Washington paid little heed but private interests in America were ready to contest this British advance. After 1823 aggressive forces of both nations met frequently in the mountains.

Prominent among these Americans were many originally associated with the Rocky Mountain Fur Company, organized by William H. Ashly and Andrew Henry. They included Jedediah S. Smith, the Sublette brothers, James Bridger, Thomas Fitzpatrick, Etienne Provost, David E. Jackson, Robert Campbell, James P. Beckwourth and others. During the winter of 1824-25 while the others invaded the region of the Great Salt Lake and its contributing streams, Smith attached himself to a party of Britishers and lived with them as an unwelcome guest on the lower Columbia. Returning in the Spring, close upon the heels of his rival, Peter Skeen Ogden, he came upon the Salt Lake soon after its original discovery by Bridger. That same Spring Ashley descended the Green River around the east end of the Uintah Range, continuing as far south as the Spanish Trail and returned to meet his trappers on the headwaters of the Bear, the Weber and Provo Rivers. The following year, after a fortune had been made in furs, he sold out his interests to Smith, Sublette and Jackson.

During the next five years Jedediah made the first overland journey between the American trapping frontier and the Spanish settlements in California; recrossed the Sierra Nevadas and the desert to his old haunts on the Great Salt Lake. Upon his return he noted in his diary, "Those who may chance to read this at a distance from the scene may perhaps be surprised that the sight of this lake, surrounded by a wilderness of more than 2,000 miles diameter, excited in me those feelings known to the traveller, who after long and perilous journeying, comes again in view of his home. But so it was with me for I had travelled so much in the vicinity of the Salt Lake that it had become my home of the wilderness[2]."

Smith returned to California only to escape an Indian ambush and throw himself upon the mercy of his Hudson

Bay competitors at Vancouver. Here he learned of the British resolve to "keep every damned Yankee east of the Rockies." After rejoining his associates in the fall of 1829, he trapped the upper reaches of the Missouri in keeping with an unwilling agreement to confine operations to waters east of the Divide. It looked as if Jedediah's "wilderness home" would be shared between England and Mexico unless new American forces arrived to hold the region of his explorations.

Upon returning to Missouri in 1830, Jedediah added much to the accumulating information about the Great Basin area lying west of the Rockies. Such information in the form of trappers journals, maps, newspaper items, etc., was studied seriously by many who shared a growing interest in the West.

Jedediah was killed the following year by Indians on the Santa Fe Trail. The partnership of Smith, Sublette and Jackson passed to close associates, including Thomas Fitzpatrick and James Bridger. When his trapping days were over, Fitzpatrick turned the wealth of his experience to government reconnaissance. Among those he served as guide was John C. Fremont in his explorations of the West. Bridger continued to follow traps for several years, then served as guide, and finally marked the close of the trapper's heyday when he built a fort in the Green River country in 1843. Here he remained to see, in 1846, companies of California emigrants swing off from the Oregon Trail to find a shorter route through the Wasatch and around the south end of the Great Salt Lake. In this effort names like Hastings, Harlan, Reed and Donner became associated with trail blazing, triumph and tragedy. The following year and increasingly thereafter, Bridger saw the Mormons pour through the South Pass and settle in the Valley of the Great Salt Lake.

1 Peoria Daily Transcript, Sept. 13, 1858. Peoria, Ill., Public Library.
2 Sullivan, The Travels of Jedediah Smith, A Documentary Outline, p. 23.

5

Nauvoo

THE Missouri misfortunes of the Mormons had tossed them into a horseshoe bulge on the east bank of the Mississippi. Here for six years (1839-46) they rested "as a stone in a sling" preparatory to being hurled into the promised land "just where the Lord wanted His people to gather." The City of Nauvoo poised on the river bank displaying beauty and enterprise out of all proportion to its frontier surroundings. Politically it was an independent city state. Its temple spire rose above a population of nearly 20,000 while Chicago yet remained a trading post.

The Mormon capitol emerged from a swamp to present some practical phases of modern Zion building to many a surprised traveler. American newspapers in 1843 circulated widely a typical account written by an English observer. Said he,

"The city is of great dimensions, laid out in beautiful order; the streets are wide, and cross each other at right angles, which will add greatly to its order and magnificence when finished. The City rises on a gentle incline from the rolling Mississippi. At your side is the temple, the wonder of the world; round about and beneath, you may behold handsome stores, large mansions, and fine cottages interspersed with varied scenery. At the foot of the town rolls the noble Mississippi, bearing upon its bosom the numerous sea-ships which are conveying the Mormons from all parts of the world to their home. I have seen them landed and I have seen them welcomed to their homes with the tears of joy and the gladdening smile to share the embrace all around. . . .

"The inhabitants seem to be a wonderfully enterprising

people. The walls of the temple have been raised considerably this summer: it is calculated when finished to be the glory of Illinois. They are endeavoring to establish manufactories in the city. They have enclosed large farms on the prairie ground, on which they have raised corn, wheat, hemp, etc. and all this they have accomplished within the short space of four years. I do not believe there is another people in existence who could have made such improvements in the same length of time under the same circumstances. And allow me to remark, that there are some here who have lately emigrated to this place, who have built themselves large and convenient houses in the town; others on their farms on the prairie, who if they had remained at home, might have continued to live in rented houses all their days and never once have entertained the idea of building one for themselves at their own expense[1]."

Here was the City of Zion in projection and the spirit of Zion in operation! A methodist minister, Mr. Samuel A. Prior observed that same year, "The place is alive with business, much more so than any place I have visited since the hard times commenced. I sought in vain for anything that bore the marks of immorality, but was both astonished and highly pleased at my ill success. I could see no loungers about the streets nor any drunkards about the taverns. . . . I heard not an oath in the place, saw not a gloomy countenance; All were cheerful, polite and industrious[2]."

In view of good prospects for a permanent settlement in Illinois, Mormon proselyting was renewed with vigor, both in the states and abroad. Brigham Young was sent to preside over the British Mission, together with most of his associates in the "Quorum of the Twelve."

And now it was time for "the Gathering" to commence in earnest. Joseph Smith and his two counsellors, who constituted a "First Presidency" wrote early in September 1840, to the "Saints scattered abroad:" "Having through the kindness of our God been delivered from destruction, and having secured a location upon which we have again commenced operations for the good of his people, we feel disposed to go

forward and unite our energies for the upbuilding of the Kingdom. . . . The work which has to be accomplished in the last days is one of vast importance, and will call into action the energy, skill, talent and ability of the Saints so that it may roll forth with that glory and majesty described by the Prophet; and will consequently require the concentration of the Saints to accomplish the works of such magnitude and grandeur.

"The work of the gathering spoken of in the scriptures will be necessary to bring about the glories of the last dispensation. It is probably unnecessary to press this subject on the Saints as we believe the spirit of it is manifest, and its necessity obvious to every considerate mind. . . . To those who feel thus interested, and can assist in this great work, we say let them come to this place."

There was immediate response to this and subsequent calls for concentration of membership in Illinois. Wagon caravans came overland from the States and Canada while shiploads of Saints crossed the Atlantic to push up the Mississippi toward Nauvoo. Heber C. Kimball wrote on July 15, 1841: "On Friday last, seventy saints came to Nauvoo, led by Lorenzo Barnes from Chester Co., Pennsylvania; they travelled in wagons, living in tents by the way. On the next day a company came in wagons from Canada, all in good spirits, and in the course of two or three days all obtained places to live in. The saints are coming in from all parts of this continent daily and hourly, and the work is spreading in all of this land[3]."

On March 27, 1842, Joseph Smith recorded: "I witnessed the landing of one hundred and seventy English Saints from the Steamer Ariel under the presidency of Lyman Wight; also about three thousand dollars worth of goods for the Temple and Nauvoo House." Again on April 12, the following year, he wrote: "About five p.m. the steamer 'Maid of Iowa' hauled up at the Nauvoo House landing, and discharged about 200 Saints, in charge of Elders Parley P.

Pratt and Levi Richards. These had been detained at St. Louis, Alton, Chester and other places through the winter having left Liverpool last fall. Dan Jones, captain of the 'Maid of Iowa,' was baptized a few weeks since; he has been eleven days coming from St. Louis being detained by ice. I was present at the landing and first on board the steamer, . . . I could not refrain from shedding tears; so many of my friends and acquaintances arriving in one day (another company had arrived the same day) kept me very busy receiving their congratulations and answering their questions. I was rejoicing to meet them in such good health and fine spirits; for they were equal to any that had ever come to Nauvoo[4]."

In this fashion early Mormon converts continued to pour into Nauvoo, always greeted by a large assemblage of their brotherhood when they arrived at the landing. Wrote one William Kay, who had charge of an English company, while they waited at New Orleans for transfer to the River Steamer on March 9, 1844, " . . . We have this morning the steamer alongside us, and intended gathering our baggage on board today. I assure you we rejoiced exceedingly at the sight of the steamer, which was the Maid of Iowa, and at the thought of going up in a vessel belonging to the Church, and commanded by an Elder of the Church, Brother Dan Jones[5]."

Thirty-two companies in all, including approximately five thousand British converts, sailed from England bound for Nauvoo during the years from 1840 to 1846. But even this brief moment of success was sowed with seeds of disruption. Treachery within accompanied ominous rumblings from outside the Mormon ranks. Even journalistic eulogy ended with a note of warning. The New York Sun, on September 4, 1843 wrote: "This Joe Smith must be set down as an extra-ordinary character, a prophet-hero, as Carlyle might call him. He is one of the great men of this age, and in future history will rank with those, who, in one way or other, have stamped their impress strongly on society.

"Nothing can be more plebeian, in seeming, than this Joe Smith. Little of dignity is there in his cognomen; but few in this age have have done such deeds, and performed such apparent miracles. It is no small thing in the blaze of this nineteenth century, to give to men a new revelation, found a new religion, establish new forms of worship, to build a city, with new laws, institutions and orders of architecture, to establish ecclesiastical, civil and military jurisdiction, found colleges, send out missionaries and make proselytes in two hemispheres; yet all this has been done by Joe Smith, and that against every sort of opposition, ridicule, and persecution. This sect has its martyrs also, and the spirit in which they were imprisoned and murdered, in Missouri, does not appear to have differed much from that which has attended religious persecutions in all ages of the world.

"That Joe Smith, the founder of the Mormons is a man of great talent — a deep thinker, an eloquent speaker; an able writer, and a man of great mental power, no one can doubt who has watched his career. That his followers are deceived, we all believe; but, should the inherent corruptions of Mormonism fail to develop themselves sufficiently to convince its followers of their error, where will the thing end? A great military despotism is growing up in the fertile west, increasing faster, in proportion, than the surrounding population, spreading its influence around, and marshalling multitudes under its banners causing serious alarm to every patriot[6]."

Joseph Smith, in the hope of securing federal support in the Mormon case against their Missouri enemies, went to Washington. President Van Buren closed a reluctant interview with the pathetic political confession, "Your cause is just but I can do nothing for you." Further unrewarded efforts to gain a sympathetic ear in Washington sent the prophet back to Nauvoo with a new interest in the West. Already in Missouri the troubled "saints" had heard much about the trappers' paradise. They had devoured eagerly the valuable information brought back to the frontiers by the trapping fraternity. One of their publications, the Evening and Morning Star had chronicled the adventures of Captain Bonneville beyond the Rocky Mountains, and reported the return of Sublette with wealth in beaver furs[7].

Smith's interest in the West developed in proportion to increasing pressure from his enemies. In August of 1842, his feelings took the form of "prophecy." Having crossed the river with a number of friends to witness installation proceedings of the local Masonic Order at Montrose, he waited under the bowery of the block school house. A barrel of cold water refreshed the little group. As Joseph gazed upon a sparkling glass of water it seemed to bring suggestions of a crystal mountain stream. As if longing for escape he said, "The saints will continue to suffer much affliction and will be driven to the Rocky Mountains. Many of you will apostatize. . . . and die at the hands of enemies . . . but some of you will live to go and assist in making settlements and build cities and see the saints become a mighty people in the midst of the Rocky Mountains[8]." On a later occasion the ill fated leader knelt on the floor of the Masonic Hall in Nauvoo to sketch with a piece of chalk the general location of what he called the Great Salt Lake Basin and mapped the course to it[9].

The Mormon prophet sought fulfillment of his utterance in the coming months. Perhaps he envisioned his mountain empire when he drilled the Nauvoo Legion on the public square. One May day in 1842, Judge Stephen A. Douglas adjourned his court to watch the celebrated Legion on parade and joined with Lieutenant General Smith in reviewing two thousand well-trained men. This independent body of militia assumed significance as it grew to number five thousand volunteers.

Then in November 1843, Smith turned to politics. Aware that his following controlled the balance of the Illinois vote, he wrote prospective presidential candidates relative to redress for Mormon losses in Missouri. Henry Clay suggested, in reply, that they "find redress in Oregon." Finding no sign of sympathy with the Mormon cause, Joseph's followers nominated him, in state convention, for President of the United States. By this means the Mormon leader sought to get his views before the people. Among those views he favored early occupation of "Oregon."

On February 23, 1844, Joseph organized the Western Exploration Company to search out a possible refuge for the Mormons in Oregon or California[10]. Seventy-five men were to go equipped to make the survey. But he still hoped for cooperation with the Government. On March 26, he directed an "ordinance" to Congress. It read in part, "Whereas, Oregon is without any organized government; . . . and whereas, it is necessary that the emigrants to that newly settled territory should receive protection; . . . and whereas, Joseph Smith has offered . . . to open the vast regions of the west and south to our enlightened and enterprising yeomanry: to protect them in their researches; to secure them in their locations; and thus strengthen the government and enlarge her borders; . . . (therefore) Be it ordained by the Senate and the House . . . in Congress assembled, that Joseph Smith, of the city of Nauvoo, in the state of Illinois, is hereby authorized and empowered to raise a company of one thousand armed volunteers in the United States and Territories, for the purposes specified in the foregoing preamble, and to execute the same. . . .[11]" Apparently the Nauvoo Legion was not drilling without purpose.

Orson Hyde, who carried the memorial to Washington, reported back in substance; "Do not expect congressional action; Oregon held under joint treaty with England; appearance of armed force would arouse British opposition; all agree however, that we are authorized to go already without government sanction; if we are to go, the sooner the better in order to secure advantage of priority rights; Judge Douglas has given me a map of Oregon; also Freemont's Journal which I am sending to you with his compliments. Douglas says he can direct Mr. Smith to several gentlemen in California; when he comes to Illinois he will visit Mr. Smith[12]."

Hostility toward the Latter-day Saints in Illinois broke wide open when the press of a bitter anti-Mormon paper was destroyed after its first issue appeared. The prophet was warned to flee across the Mississippi. On June 23, the diary of Willard Richards states, "At daybreak arrived on the Iowa side of the river. Sent Orin P. Rockwell back to Nauvoo with instructions to return the next night with horses for Joseph and Hyrum, pass them over the river in the night secretly and be ready to start for the Great Basin in the Rocky Mountains[13]."

But the youthful leader who had dared incorporate "the Kingdom," and whose hands had steered its initial course upon the open sea of American ideas, was not destined to continue at the helm. Like another who sought deliverance of his people, Joseph was permitted only a glimpse of the promised land before another rose to lead them in.

Smith was persuaded to give himself up for trial. Under a pledge of legal protection from Governor Ford he was taken to Carthage to await proceedings. When the Governor's party withdrew, a masked mob attacked the jail killing both Joseph and his brother. They fell victims of prophet-hating intolerance.

1   Cannon, Geo. Q., The Life of Joseph Smith, p. 348.
2   S. Mucker, History of the Mormons, pp. 152-155.
3   Jensen, Andrew, XII Contributor, p. 446.
4   Jensen, Andrew, Contributor XII. 449.
5   Ibid.
6   Deseret News, August 28, 1943.
7   Neff, Andrew L., History of Utah, p. 33.
8   History of the Church, Vol. V, p. 85.
9   This statement is based on a personal account by Stephen H. Goddard as recorded in L.D.S. Journal History for July 26, 1897.
10 History of the L.D.S. Church, Period I. Vol. VI, p. 224.
11 History of the L.D.S. Church, Period I. Vol. VI, pp. 275-277.
12 History of the L.D.S. Church, Period I. Vol. VI, pp. 373-375.
13 History of the L.D.S. Church, Period I. Vol. VI, p. 548.

6

Escape

IT was hoped, by friends and enemies alike, that the removal of Joseph Smith from the Mormon scene would pour oil on the troubled waters in Illinois. The "Quorum of Twelve," under the direction of Brigham Young, acted promptly to assure the scattered saints that Nauvoo would continue the program launched by their martyred leader. Their call to gather at Nauvoo reflected the practical blending of temporalities and spiritualities in the building of the Kingdom. " . . . Let it be distinctly understood that the City of Nauvoo and the temple of our Lord are to continue to be built up according to the pattern which has been commenced, and which has progressed with such rapidity thus far.

"The city must be built up and supported by the gathering of those who have capital and are willing to lay it out for the erection of every branch of industry and manufacture which are necessary for the employment and support of the poor, or of those who depend wholly on their labor; while farmers, who have capital, must come and purchase farms in the adjoining country and improve and cultivate the same. In this way all may enjoy plenty, and our infant city may grow and flourish and be strengthened an hundred fold; and unless this is done it is impossible for the gathering to progress, because those who have no other dependence cannot live together without industry and employment.

"Therefore, let capitalists hasten here, that they may be assured we have nerves, sinews, fingers, skill and ingenuity sufficient in our midst to carry on the necessary branches of industry[1]."

However, old conflicts soon flared up anew and as the pressure against the Mormons increased, the Rocky Mountains again beckoned them. The Nauvoo Neighbor published at least fifty descriptive articles on the West for its eager Mormon readers[2]. Freemont's reports appeared serially, concluding with an account of his experiences at the Great Salt Lake. Responsible leaders with Young at their head devoted more than one session in the Nauvoo Temple to reading from Freemont's Journal[3]. Also, as the confusion of bloodthirsty mobs crowded in on them, the Church leaders became more diligent in examining "maps with reference to selecting a location for the Saints west of the Rocky Mountains, and reading various works written by travellers in those regions[4]."

It is not within the scope of these pages to review the conflicts which culminated in the Nauvoo crisis of the winter of 1845-46. Suffice it to say that already in the fall of 1845, the Mormons faced the inevitable with a determination to leave Nauvoo the following spring. A race developed to bring the temple to completion before the final gong of the exodus should sound. Such apparent inconsistency of effort could only be understood by the initiated, who felt that if they could but once enter the sacred chambers of the temple to partake of its blessings, any and all sacrifice would have been justified.

In October the building was sufficiently advanced to accommodate a general conference of the people. Here the leaders, upon whom the responsibilities of the Prophet Joseph had fallen, presented, philosophically, the impending retreat to the wilderness. Parley P. Pratt, referring to the heavy expense and labor involved in the purchase of lands and erection of beautiful buildings, including the temple, raised the question — "Why is it that we have been at all this outlay and expense and then are called to leave it?"

Sacrifice, he pointed out, had always been required of the
people of God, and if such were now to be made let it be a
worthy one.

"We do not want to leave a desolate place to be a reproach
to us but something that will be a monument to those who
may visit the place of our industry diligence and virtue. . . .
The Lord has another purpose to bring about and to fulfill.
We know that the great work of God must all the while be
on the increase and grow greater. The people must enlarge
in numbers and extend their borders; they cannot always
live in one city, nor in one country; . . . The Lord designs
to lead us to a wider field of action, where there will be
more room for the Saints to grow and increase, and where
there will be no one to say we crowd them, and we can
enjoy the pure principles of liberty and equal rights. . . .
One small nursery may produce many thousands of fruit
trees, while they are small. But as they expand toward
maturity they must needs be transplanted, in order to have
room to grow and produce the natural fruits. It is so with
us. We want a country where we have room to expand, and
to put in requisition all our energies and the enterprise and
talents of a numerous, intelligent, and increasing people[5]."

Said Heber C. Kimball, outspoken apostle snatched from
the potters trade, "I am glad the time of our exodus is come.
I have looked for it for years. . . . We want to take you to a
land where a white man's foot never trod, nor a lion's whelps,
nor the devil's; and there we can enjoy it, with no one to
molest and make us afraid; and we will bid all the nations
welcome whether Pagans, Catholics, or Protestants. . . . Let
us become passive as clay in the hands of the potter: if we
don't we will be cut from the wheel and thrown back in the
mill again. A third speaker added, "We calculate to go the
same people we are now; preserving the same principles which
have caused us to grow and expand as we have done. . . . and
however much the people may seem disposed to not go, the
sails are set, the wind is fair, and we are bound to weather

the point, whether we will or not; for we are not at the helm[7]. . . . "

Finally, Brigham Young, leader of the Quorum of the Twelve and soon to be chosen President of the Church, crystalized into action the prevailing sentiments by a motion that in the exodus "we take all the Saints with us, to the extent of our ability, that is, our influence and property." Being duly seconded by Kimball, the motion won unanimous support of those present. Brigham then continued, "If you will be faithful to your covenant, I will now prophesy that the great God will shower down means upon this people to accomplish it to the very letter. I thank God that the time has come so much sooner than I expected, that the scripture is being fulfilled, 'My people shall be willing in the day of my power;' and I almost feel to thank our friends abroad for hastening it on now[8]."

The Mormons labored under two major obsessions during the Fall and Winter of 1846. The first was the completion of the Temple, the second, preparations for leaving it. These two were interwoven closely in the general circular of the "Presiding Brethren" on October 8, 1845, to the membership scattered through the country:

"Beloved brethren: You will perceive the foregoing interesting minutes of the conference . . . not only the unparalleled union of the great body of Saints convened but also that of a crisis of extraordinary and thrilling interest has arrived. . . . It is our design to remove all the Saints as early next spring as the first appearance of thrifty vegetation. In the meantime the utmost diligence of all the brethren at this place and abroad will be requisite for our removal and to complete the unfinished part of the Lord's House, preparatory to dedication by the next General Conference. The font and other parts of the Temple will be in readiness in a few days to commence the administration of holy ordinances of endowments for which the faithful have long diligently labored and fervently prayed desiring above all things to see the beauty of the Lord and inquire in His Holy Temple. We therefore invite the Saints abroad generally so to arrange their affairs as to come with their families in sufficient time to receive their endowments, and aid in giving the last finish to the House of the Lord previous to the great emigration of the Church in the Spring. . . . Therefore dispose of your properties and inheritance, and interests for available means such as money, wagons, oxen, cows, mules and a few good horses adapted to journeying and scanty feed. Also for durable fabrics suitable for apparel and tents; and some other necessary articles of merchandise. Wake up, wake up, dear brethren, we exhort you, from the Mississippi to the Atlantic, and from Canada to Florida, to the present glorious emergency in which the God of Heaven has placed you to prove your faith by your works preparatory to a rich endowment in the Temple of the Lord. . . . "[9]

Behind the outward drama of threats, arrests and trials, mobbings, and burnings, the "Saints" streamed into the Temple sanctuary during the Winter to "receive their endowments." In the meantime the entire city was transformed into a gigantic outfitting center. "During the winter of 1845-46 the Mormons made prodigious preparations for removal," wrote Governor Ford of Illinois, "All the homes in Nauvoo and even the temple (shops) were converted into workships; and before spring more than twelve thousand wagons were in readiness. The people from all parts of the country flocked to Nauvoo to purchase houses and farms, which were sold extremely low, lower than the prices at a sheriff's sale, for money, wagons, horses, oxen, cattle, and other articles of personal property which might be needed by the Mormons in their exodus into the wilderness[10]."

On February 8, 1846, Brigham recorded, "I met with the Council of the Twelve in the southeast corner room of the attic of the Temple. We knelt around the altar and dedicated the building to the Most High. We asked His blessing upon our intended move to the West; also asked Him to enable us some day to finish the Temple, and dedicate it to Him, and we would dedicate it in His hands to do as He pleased; and to preserve the building as a monument to Joseph Smith. We asked the Lord to accept the labors of His servants in this land. We then left the Temple[11]."

So violent became the opposition and so bitterly did law defying groups harass the Mormons that the contemplated Spring exodus became a February escape into the merciful arms of an Iowa winter. In the words of the Historian Bancroft, "And now putting upon their animals and vehicles such of their household effects as they could carry, in small detachments the migratory Saints began to leave Nauvoo. Before them was the ice-bound river, and beyond that the wilderness[12]."

1   Jensen, Andrew, in Contributor XII, p. 404.
    Also Linforth, James, Route from Liverpool to the Valley of the Great Salt Lake, p. 2.
2   Neff, Dr. Andrew L., History of Utah, p. 35.
3   History of L.D.S. Church, Period I, Volume VII, pp. 548, 556.
4   History of L.D.S. Church, Period I, Volume VII, pp. 558.
5   History of L.D.S. Church, Period I, Volume VII, pp. 463-464.
6   History of L.D.S. Church, Period I, Volume VII, pp. 467.
7   History of L.D.S. Church, Period I, Volume VII, pp. 468.
8   History of L.D.S. Church, Period I, Volume VII, pp. 465.
9   History of L.D.S. Church, Period I, Volume VII, pp. 478-480.
10 Ford's History of Illinois, page 412.
11 History of the L.D.S. Church, Period I, Volume VII, 580.
12 History of the L.D.S. Church, Period I, Volume VII, 580.

7

Developing Solidarity

THE wheels of "Zion's Camp" cut deep into Iowa mud as they rolled toward the Missouri. This was Brother Brigham's company and in its wake followed most of those who had made their escape from Nauvoo. The Exodus forced upon them unexpectedly early, found many of them wholly unprepared for the new experience. Wrote Eliza R. Snow, a woman of culture:

"We had been preceded by thousands, and I was informed that on the first night of the encampment, nine children were born into the world and from that time, as we journeyed onward, mothers gave birth to offspring under almost every variety of circumstance imaginable except those to which they were accustomed; some in tents, others in wagons — in rainstorms and snowstorms. . . .

"Let it be remembered that the mothers of these wilderness born babies were not savages accustomed to roam the forest and brave the storm and tempest. . . . Most of them were born and educated in the eastern states. . . . There they had embraced the Gospel, and for the sake of their religion, had gathered with the Saints. . . . There (Nauvoo) they had lovely homes, decorated with flowers and enriched with choice fruit trees just beginning to yield plentifully.

"To these homes, without lease or sale, they had just bade a final adieu, and with what little of their substance could be packed into one, two, and in some instances, three wagons, had started out desert-ward for — where? To this question the only response at the time was, God knows[1]."

Men and women rise above circumstances when motivated by strong convictions. These suffering folk did little complaining. Were they not in the hands of God? John Taylor, writing to the converts in England (who waited their turn to come to Zion) passed from recounting their sufferings to explain:

> "It is true that in our journeying we do not possess all the luxuries and delicacies of old established countries and cities but we have abundance of staple commodities. . . . We feel contented and happy in the wilderness. The God of Israel is with us — union and peace prevail; and as we journey as did Abraham of old, with our flocks and herds to a distant land, we feel that like him, we are doing the will of our Heavenly Father and relying upon His word and promises; and having His blessing, we feel that we are children of the same promise and hope, and that the Great Jehovah is our God[2]."

Thus sustained they could not fail.

Fortunate too, were these modern "saints" in their leadership. Brigham Young, loyal Scotch-Irish disciple of Joseph Smith, assumed command not only by right of seniority but by the very power of his personality. He was sturdy, puritan and practical. During the next thirty years the fortunes of the Saints were to be in his hands. The poor would feel his helping hand; the slothful feel the crushing weight of his righteous wrath. He was equal to the occasion on the plains of Iowa. He wrote:

> "I propose that we proceed to the purchase (of lands) on Grand River, Iowa, and fence in a field of two miles square, build about 20 log cabins, plow some land and put in spring crops and thus spend our time until the weather settles; select men and families to take care of our improvements and the rest proceed westward. . . . Then those who follow can tarry on Grand River or go on to the Missouri bottoms and other places where there will be plenty of feed for their cattle, and tarry through the winter, and come on another season as soon as they can make their way through[3]."

Seven years previously Brigham had assumed command of a bewildered band of refugees in Missouri. He had brought order out of chaos and rescue through cooperative effort. The pledge of cooperation signed by the Mormons in Missouri was renewed in the "Temple Covenant" at Nauvoo. That covenant was the only hope for thousands of adherents who, too poor to equip themselves, tugged desperately at the economic fetters which held them fast in the doomed city. Without assistance they would be lost to the group. Only through sacrifice on the part of the more fortunate would these poor be set free to follow the vanguard into the West.

Now on the plains of Iowa another link was added to the developing chain of cooperation. Crops were planted by the advance companies not for their own reaping but for the benefit of those who would follow to harvest. Only a people who had already developed a high degree of social solidarity could have conceived and put into practice such a plan of cooperative effort.

The agricultural encampment on Grand River was named Garden Grove, and a similar station farther west was called Mt. Pisgah. These would serve not only the refugees from Nauvoo, but increasing thousands who were expected to come from the East, from England, and later from Continental Europe.

Brigham's "marching industrial columns" as they have been described, lost no time in making preparations. At Garden Grove a hundred men were detailed to make fence rails, forty-eight to build houses, twelve to dig wells, ten to build a bridge and the balance of the 350 men to plow and plant grain. Very shortly an orderly town composed of well arranged block houses stood on the open prairie, surrounded by over seven hundred planted acres; a herd of cattle and sheep were allocated permanently to the camp. An eye witness aptly compared the bustling scene to the swarming of bees.

A "presidency" of three was assigned to remain at the station. They were to supervise the harvesting and storing of crops and distribute them to impoverished emigrants. Where members chose to remain, tilling the soil until more adequately equipped to resume the journey, they were allotted individual pieces of land. This on the basis of Joseph Smith's policy that none should acquire more than he could profitably use. Indeed Brigham went further to warn that a man failing to use his property should have it taken from him.

The same procedure enclosed several thousand acres of grain at Mt. Pisgah and the main camp moved on arriving at Council Bluffs on the Missouri, June 14, 1846.

Plowing and building was soon under way. But here the Mormons considered and accepted the U. S. Government's call for men to fight in the war against Mexico. They had invited an opportunity for cooperation with the government in their western migration but organization of the "Mormon Battalion" cost them a change in plans. With effective forces depleted by the military enlistment of five hundred able bodied men, the exiles were forced to delay their march to the West. Most of them moved across the river to establish "Winter Quarters" on the west bank of the Missouri. To this place and vicinity gathered "15,000 saints, 3,000 wagons, 30,000 head of cattle, a great number of mules and horses and immense flocks of sheep[4]."

Before snows fell the Mormon settlement consisted of five hundred and thirty-eight log and eighty-three sod houses capable of housing three thousand people. Scythes flashed in the prairie grasses to cut thousands of tons of hay which were cured before winter. Meat from abundant game was salted down and hundreds of bushels of wild berries added to their winter stores. Supplies not available in the wilderness were brought from St. Louis by freighters. Most of these teamsters were trail-breaking Mormons who had returned to Nauvoo and vicinity to bring up their wives and families. This traffic served also to solve the problem of mail service between the western outpost and the residue of their brethren at Nauvoo.

Winter Quarters was divided into a number of "Wards" for purposes of joint civil and ecclesiastical government.

Improvised schools flourished. The destitute who crowded in, refusing to be excluded from "apostolic presence," were made as comfortable as possible. Even so, more than three hundred graves marked the camp site before Spring. The principle of tithing, introduced to the Church when the Law of Consecration collapsed in Missouri, was urged upon the people. The "tithe" of the more fortunate eased the hardships of those in need.

Tithe paying was a modification of the earlier Law of Consecration. Instead of requiring that all "surplus" be turned to the common treasury, the new plan provided that all members "shall pay one tenth of all their interest annually[5]." Parley P. Pratt defined the law as follows:

> "The law of tithing is not peculiar to this Church or people. It is as old as the Bible. We see it illustrated in Abraham's day. To fulfill the law of tithing a man should make out and lay before the Bishop a schedule of all his property and pay him the one tenth of it; when he has tithed his principal once, he has no occasion to tithe again, but the next year he must pay the one tenth of his increase, and the tenth of his time, of his cattle, money, goods, and trade; and whatever use we put it to, it is still our own for the Lord does not carry it away with Him to Heaven. We have to establish the government of God on earth, and that requires means, and a knowledge how to use it, and to have everything written on 'Holiness to the Lord[6].' "

Another factor in the strength of Mormon migrations — both immediate and future — was the peculiar organization for travel. Months before the expulsion from Nauvoo Brigham Young had planned an organization designed to effect an orderly withdrawal into the wilderness. But in the emergency of forced retreat it had failed to function altogether according to schedule. Instead of an organized unit the exodus presented a straggly column governed by expediency, and with companies scattered widely over the Iowa plains.

Among numerous problems confronting Young was that

of assembling these scattered units into some sort of working whole. His diary for March 21, fretted over the insubordination of "Bishop Miller" who "seeks to go ahead and separate himself from his brethren, but he cannot prosper in so doing, he will yet run against a snag and call upon me and the camp for help[7]."

On March 27, Brigham assembled as many units as possible on the Chariton River. There he sought to recover some of the essentials of the organization which had been planned at Nauvoo and lost in the confusion of exodus. Young was unanimously elected president over the whole "Camp of Israel." Three men were elected captains of one hundred families each, another six were chosen captains of fifties, acting under those first named. This preliminary organization served fairly well in conducting the refugees to the encampments at Council Bluffs and Winter Quarters.

In spite of hardships involved and indeed to mitigate them, the Mormon camps often presented strange scenes to the Iowans. When the strenuous demands of a day's journey were over snow was scraped from the wagon enclosure and a huge fire kindled. Then to the accompaniment of "Captain Pitt's Band" the exiles danced and sang their troubles away. More than once the Mormon band gave of that spirit in frontier communities where their concerts were enthusiastically received. It gave wholesome promise of early recovery from experiences which might have embittered a less hardy and spiritually buoyant people.

During the winter of 1846-47, Brigham had ample opportunity to study ways and means of successfully transferring fifteen thousand unseasoned exiles to the far west. On January 14, he offered a far-reaching formula. Presented as a revelation, it later won a place in the Book of Doctrine and Covenants as Section one hundred and thirty-six:

"The word and will of the Lord concerning the Camp of Israel in their journeyings to the West: Let all the people of the Church of Jesus Christ of the Latter-day Saints, and those who journey with them be organized into companies with a covenant and a promise to keep all the commandments and statutes of the Lord our God. Let the companies be organized with captains of hundred, captains of fifties, and captains of tens, with a president and his two counsellors at their head under the direction of the Twelve Apostles. And this shall be our covenant that they will walk in all the ordinances of the Lord.

"Let each company provide themselves with all the teams, wagons, provisions, clothing and other necessities for the journey that they can. When the companies are organized let them go to with their might to prepare for those who are to tarry.

"When the companies with their captains and presidents decide how many can go next spring, then choose out a sufficient number of able bodied and expert men to take teams, seeds, farming utensils, to go as pioneers to prepare for putting in spring crops.

"Let each company bear an equal proportion, according to the dividend of their property, in taking the poor and widows and fatherless and the families of those who have gone into the army, that the cries of the widows and the fatherless come not up into the ears of the Lord against this people.

"Let each company prepare houses, and fields for raising grain, for those who are to remain behind this season. . . .

"Let every man use all his influence and property to remove this people to the place where the Lord shall locate a Stake of Zion.

"And if ye do this with a pure heart, in all faiithfulness, ye shall be blessed; you shall be blessed in your flocks, and in your herds, and in your fields, and in your houses, and in your families[9]."

It was after this plan laid down by the Utah Colonizer, that future Mormon migrations were patterned. In detail the methods necessarily varied, but in general, the organization remained peculiar to the Mormons. Orson Hyde, who was left to preside over the temporary encampment in Iowa, was charged with the responsibility of expediting the western movement with all possible speed. To this end he established the Frontier Guardian as a medium of communication. His announcements through its pages reflect the compact organization and disciplined procedure required in all Mormon companies.

"Whenever a company of fifty wagons have assembled on the camping grounds . . . they will forthwith be organized and started on their journey. This number can travel with much more ease, comfort, and speed than any greater number. Our experience has proven this to us. The men and boys that will naturally go with the fifty wagons will be quite sufficient to protect themselves on the journey against the Indians. Every man and boy capable of using a rifle, or musket, should, by all means, have one and a good one. If any are deficient in this respect, we will furnish every company with what they may lack, provided the captains and principal men of each company will become responsible for the arms, and deliver them safely to the High Council in the valley, as there are quite a lot of arms here that belong there and we wish to forward them on.

"The organization of companies will be strictly military and every one should be amply provided with arms and ammunition adequate to any and every exigency. Our experience last year on the Elk Horn River with the Omaha Indians, abundantly shows the importance of a rigid observance of the above. The bill of particulars embracing provisions and other articles to be taken will appear in the Guardian in due time.

"Every wagon before starting will be examined to see if it contains the requisite amount of provisions, utensils, and means of defense. If they are delinquent in these they will not be allowed to cross the river to proceed with our companies[10]."

Early expérience in conducting the first caravans across the plains gave valuable leadership to the later annual migrations. Each company was so organized as to become a disciplined travelling community. No sooner was an approved "fifty" or "hundred" launched on its way than it paused long enough to perfect its internal government. A typical company leaving the Missouri, illustrates the general procedure: It consisted of 105 wagons, 476 persons, 743 cattle, 19 horses and 273 sheep. Warren Foote had been appointed captain of the hundred by Hyde, and Otis L. Terry captain of the first, and William Wall of the second fifty. On the 17th of June the one hundred wagons made a brief halt while the appointed leaders met to draft the following by-laws for the regulation and good order of the camp:

"Resolved, first — the horn shall be blown at four o'clock in the morning, when the people shall rise, and after necessary preparations for starting, the horn will be blown again for the people to come together for prayers and at half past eight at night the horn will be blown again for evening prayers, which each family will attend in their wagon.

"Resolved, second — that if any person, while on guard at night, shall neglect his duty by sleep or otherwise, for the first offense he shall be reported publicly, and if afterward found guilty of neglect he shall again be reported and be subjected to extra duty in the day time herding cattle.

"Resolved, third — that any member of this camp who shall indulge in profane language shall be reported to his captain of ten, and if he shall afterwards persist in profanity he shall be published publicly.

"Resolved, fourth — that if any person practice unnecessary cruelty to their animals, and after being reproved by their captain of ten shall still persist in such cruelty, he shall be brought before the captains of the camp, who shall levy such fine or punishment as they may deem just[11]."

The resolutions did not represent arbitrary imposition of discipline upon the emigrants. Rather they became the accepted will of the company as a whole by which they were heard and approved.

The positive results from such effective organization did not escape attention on the plains and won favorable comment from Mormon and Gentiles alike. Said Samuel M. Smucker in his History of the Mormons, "The character of their every day life, its routine and conduct, alone marked an exclusive peculiarity. The romantic devotional services, and their admirable concert of purpose, and action, met the eye at once. After these the stranger was most struck perhaps by the strict order of march, the unconfused closing up to meet attack, the skillful securing of cattle upon the halt, the system with which the watches were set at night to guard them and the lines or corral — with other circumstances indicative of the maintenance of a high state of discipline. Every ten of their wagons was under the care of a captain. This captain of ten as they termed him, obeyed a captain of fifty; who in turn obeyed his captain of hundred, or directly a member of what they call the High Council of the Church[12]."

The Frontier Guardian made the following observation: "An endless train of vehicles and its hundreds of sheep, horses, mules, formed a picturesque and motley spectacle. Among the members were to be found the New England man with his stock of trading goods, the Southerner with his colored attendant, the Englishman with his box of mechanics tools, the Dane, the Swiss, the Scandinavian with his implements of agriculture. The great variety of types and professions among the emigrants did not seem to breed discord among them. There was no evidence of breaking up of companies into small groups as was so common among the general westward migration[13]."

William Chandless, who had an opportunity to observe the Mormons closely during his own crossing of the plains, adds a touch of romance in his description: "It was a pretty sight to watch them starting off for the day's march; great numbers of women and children walking in advance gaily, the little ones picking flowers, the boys looking for grapes or plums if there were trees near, and the mothers knitting as they went; all seemed willing to endure hardship, looking upon the journey as a pilgrimage to the promised land where they should have rest[14]."

In the Spring of 1847, the vanguard of these legions moved up the Platte River, on the opposite side from the Oregon

Trail. They continued up the Sweetwater, over the Divide, and down the Sandy to the Green River country, so familiar to the trapping fraternity. Near Fort Bridger they left the Oregon Trail to pick their course through canyons of the Wasatch Range and come at last upon the valley of the Great Salt Lake. Here on shores familiar to the trapper and explorer and dimly outlined in the consciousness of the Mormon leaders as a refuge for their people, Brigham Young announced, "This is the Place."

Joseph Smith had launched the latter-day Kingdom and defined its objectives. To Brigham Young and his associates fell the task of "lengthening the cords of Zion to the west" and gathering its members into organized "stakes." The two factors mentioned above — cooperation and organization — were vital to successful consummation of the project.

1   Roberts, B. H., Comprehensive History of the Church, Volume III, p. 45.
2   Roberts, B. H., Comprehensive History of the Church, Volume III, p. 49.
3   History of the L.D.S. Church, Period I, Volume VII: 608.
4   Roberts, B. H., Comprehensive History of the Church, Volume III, p. 52.
5   Doctrine & Covenants, Section 119:4.
6   Neff, Andrew L., History of Utah, p. 531.
    During the first four uncertain years after arriving in the Great Basin, the Mormons paid $353,755.69 as tithing to the Church treasury. (Cowley, Mathias, Life of Wilford Woodruff, p. 352.)
7   Pratt, P. P., Autobiography, 379-380. Bp. Miller affair.
8   Bancroft, H. H., History of Utah, p. 232. "A few months before, Nauvoo, with the neighboring Mormon settlements, had contained some 20,000 Saints, of whom in July about 15,000 were encamped on the Missouri River, or were scattered through the western states in search of employment."
9   Doctrine & Covenants, Section CXXXVI: This is the only section accredited to Brigham Young. The preceding 135 sections are accredited to Joseph Smith as revealed instructions in affairs pertaining to the Church.
10 Frontier Guardian, February 21, 1849.
11 Little, James A., From Kirtland to Salt Lake City, p. 240.
12 Smucker, Samuel M., History of the Mormons, p. 24.
13 Frontier Guardian, July 25, 1849.
14 Quoted in Coman's Economic Beginnings of the Far West, p. 199.

8

Deseret

"Resolved, that should we locate within the territory of the United States, as we anticipate, we would esteem a territorial government of our own as one of the richest boons of earth, and while we appreciate the constitution of the United States as the most precious among the nations, we feel that we had rather retreat to the deserts, island or mountain caves than consent to be ruled by governors and judges whose hands are drenched in the blood of innocence and virtue, who delight in injustice and oppression. . . .

"Resolved, that as soon as we settle in the Great Basin we design to petition for a territorial government, bounded on the north by the British and on the south by Mexican domains, and east and west by the summits of the Rocky and Cascade ranges[1]."

SO wrote Brigham Young to President James K. Polk in August of 1846. And as the Mormon columns stretched westward there rose from the wagons and around their camp fires the familiar strains of "The Upper California, oh, That's the land for me."

"The Upper California, Oh that's the land for me!
It lies between the mountains and the great Pacific Sea;
 The Saints can be supported there,
 And taste the sweets of liberty
In Upper California — Oh, that's the land for me.

"We'll go and lift our standard, we'll go there and be free;
We'll go to California and have our jubilee —
 A land that blooms with beauty rare,
 A land of life and liberty,
With flocks and herds abounding — Oh, that's the land for me!

* * * *

"Then join with me, my brethren, and let us hasten there;
We'll lift our glorious standard and raise our house of prayer
   We'll call on all the nations round
   To join our standard and be free
In Upper California — Oh, that's the land for me."

The Latter-day saints were moving in to hold the territory to which the trappers had already laid claim for the United States. Joseph Smith's prediction of a Rocky Mountain empire was about to be realized.

Twice the Mormons had issued the call for gathering on the American frontier and twice they had been uprooted. Zion in Jackson County, Missouri, had been ravaged by her enemies while her children fled to set up stakes in other places. But these in turn proved disappointing because the New Order came in conflict with the Old. The Mormons were not free from interference by those who came among them but who had no part in their enterprise.

But now in the far west, separated from the borders of civilization by a thousand miles, they were to find, for the first time, full range for their colonizing ambitions. Here nature had reserved for them alone unlimited resources with which to build; not to lavish upon them, but to yield in return for hard labor. Here also, far removed from the center of Zion, but still in a land "choice above all others" Brigham Young fell heir to the prophet's role as builder of the "latter-day Kingdom of God." The "stakes" would now be driven in the valleys of the mountains.

The advance company of the Mormon pioneers filed through the canyon which opened upon the Salt Lake Valley on July 22, 1847, followed by Brigham Young on the 24th. The historic pronouncement "This is the Place" served as a benediction upon the mountain circled wilderness. Just as Jackson County, Missouri had been transformed into a Mormon "Zion" under the very feet of the unseeing Missouri frontiersmen, so now the Salt Lake Valley became a hallowed place. The river, winding its course between the fresh and the salt water lakes, became the Jordan and the entire region became a new Holy Land. After all, no land is more sacred than the vision of its occupants and the most barren desert may become Bethel to the heart set on its consecration.

In this spirit Wilford Woodruff wrote:

"We came in full view of the valley or Basin (of the) Salt Lake and the land of promise held in reserve by the hand of God for a resting place for the Saints upon which a portion of the Zion of God will be built. . . . Thoughts of pleasing meditation ran in rapid succession through our minds while we contemplated that not many years hence — the house of God would stand upon the top of the mountain; while the valleys would be covered with orchards, vineyards, gardens, and fields by the inhabitants of Zion, the standard be unfurled for the nations to gather thereto[2]."

Plowing and planting commenced at once. Oxen strained at plows eager to break ground for seeds of the Kingdom. The ancient art of irrigation, all but lost in the Basin region, was reborn when mountain streams were lifted from their beds to flood the thirsty lands with life and reproductive power. Thomas Bulloch, secretary to Brigham Young, recorded:

"On this spot . . . the pioneers arrived on Thursday 23rd of July last, at five P.M.; the next morning removed to the spot where the city will be built; at noon consecrated and dedicated the place to the Lord; the same afternoon four plows were tearing up the ground; next day the brethren had planted five acres of potatoes and irrigated all the land at night. . . . During the short space between the 23rd of July and 28th August we ploughed and planted about eighty-four acres with corn, potatoes, beans, buckwheat, turnips, and a variety of garden sause. We irrigated all the land. . . ."[3]

As the water reached ever farther and farther to revive additional sleeping acres, Brigham Young laid down the law of land husbandry which was to govern the building of Zion in the tops of the mountains:

"No man should buy any land who came here — that he had none to sell; but every man should have his land measured out to him for city and farming purposes. He might till it as he pleased but he must be industrious and take care of it."

In these principles Joseph Smith's law of consecration lived again. Sounded originally in the Mormon social experiments in Ohio and Missouri, they were echoed at the "stations" on the plains of the middle west and now re-echoed through the valleys of the mountains. There was to be no "land grabbing." Land which was in the nature of a gift from God was not to be bought and sold. It belonged to the community and late comers were to have equal chance in receiving an inheritance in Zion with those who came early. Furthermore the original distribution of land was to be done by lot so that every man had equal opportunity. Wrote the President in the First General Epistle:

"A field of eight thousand acres has been surveyed south of and bordering on the city. The five and ten acre lots are distributed to the brethren by casting lots and every man is to build a pole, ditch, or stone fence as shall be most convenient around the whole piece in proportion to the land he draws; also a canal on the east side for irrigation."

Water shared the importance of land in the building of the Kingdom. For in the arid west land productivity depended largely upon irrigation. Water determined the location and extent of future settlements. Every stream which gushed from the Wasatch Canyons was the life blood of communities soon to be born. Under the average "every man for himself and the devil take the hindmost" system of frontier conquest these streams would have promptly become the prizes of the few. The principles of riparian rights would have defeated the widespread use of water as it developed under the Mormon practice of appropriation. The same rule which applied to land was applied to water. It must be distributed according to profitable use. Individual appropriations must be restricted within the limits of the common good. Lacking experience or written laws to guide them the Mormons developed their own system in harmony with a basic principle in the law of consecration[4].

Thus wisely the Mormons built their "Kingdom" upon agriculture. It was an act of self preservation as well as long range vision. Tribute has been paid them as follows:

"The leaders of these pioneers, with wisdom if not inspiration, made agriculture the foundation industry of the people. In this respect, the beginnings of Utah were different from those of every other arid state. Here, agriculture was from the first the principal industry; in many of the others it was, at the outset, a mere incident[5]."

Immediately upon locating in the Great Basin its possible resources challenged attention of the pioneers. Their position of isolation demanded a high degree of economic independence. So, while the majority tilled the soil of Salt Lake Valley, frequent excursions were made into the country round about. The nearby canyons must yield the secrets of their timber and water power, and distant peaks vied with each other in offering favorable observation points. Early in August the Bear River and Cache Valleys to the north were explored. This trapper's paradise was about to pass to the agriculturist in all but name. In December a company proceeded south to Utah Lake, source of the Jordan River, and returned through Cedar, Rush and Tooele Valleys. Also, late in the year, Davis and Weber counties were settled.

These were but preliminaries to persistent and ever lengthening thrusts into new areas. Assuredly these men of vision, refugees from unfortunate moods of civilization, must have repeated often, as they rode across their new domain, the words of one of their leaders, "It is in the mind and will of God that we should improve the opportunity which a kind

Providence has now offered for us to secure a permanent home. . . . where we shall be the first settlers and a vast majority of the people, and thus be independent of mobs; and be able to maintain our rights and freedom, and to assist in the redemption of our country and the emancipation of the world from bondage[6]." Also they must have sensed with John Taylor that "Our presence alone gives it value."

Colonial expansion into wide spread areas required men — an ever increasing supply of men. Scarcely had a base for operations been laid in and about the Salt Lake Valley when the "presiding brethren" repeated the call for a general "gathering." From Winter Quarters, on the Missouri River, whither they had returned in the fall of 1847 to organize the following season's emigration, they wrote their instructions:

"To all Saints in England, Scotland, Ireland, Wales and adjacent islands and countries, we say emigrate as speedily as possible to this vicinity, looking to, and following the counsel of the Presidency at Liverpool: shipping to New Orleans and from thence direct to Council Bluffs which will save much expense. Those who have but little means and little or no labor, will soon exhaust the means if they remain where they are therefore it is wisdom that they remove without delay; for here is land on which, by their labor they can speedily better their condition for their further journey. And to all Saints in any country bordering upon the Atlantic we would say, pursue the same course, come immediately and prepare to go west — bringing with you all kinds of choice seeds, of grain, vegetables, fruit, shrubbery, trees and vines, everything that will please the eye, gladden the heart, or cheer the soul of man, that grows upon the face of the whole earth; also the best stock of beast, bird and fowl of every kind; also the best tools of every description, and machinery for spinning, or weaving, and dressing cotton, wool, flax, and silk, etc., etc., or models and descriptions of the same by which they can construct them; the same in relation to all kinds of farming utensils and husbandry, such as corn-shellers, grain threshers and cleaners, smut machines, mills and every implement and article within their knowledge that shall tend to promote the comfort, health, happiness, and prosperity of any people. So far as it can be consistently done, bring models and drafts, and let the machinery be built where it is used, which will save great expense in transportation, particularly in heavy machinery, and tools and implements generally[7]."

The missionaries abroad were instructed, "Teach them the principles of righteousness and uprightness between man and man . . . tell them to flee to Zion . . . should any ask 'where is Zion' tell them in America, and if any ask 'what is Zion' tell them the pure in heart. . . . The Kingdom of God which we are establishing is not of this world but the Kingdom of the Great God. It is the fruit of righteousness, of peace, of salvation to every soul that will receive it. . . . The Kingdom of God consists in correct principles . . . come then ye Saints of Latter-days, and all ye great and small, wise and foolish, rich and poor, noble and ignoble, exalted and persecuted, rulers and ruled of the earth, who love virtue and hate vice, and help us to do this work which the Lord hath required at our hands; and inasmuch as the glory of the latter house shall excel that of the former, your reward shall be an hundred fold, and your rest shall be glorious[8]."

A second communication issued the following year reflects an almost feverish enthusiasm: "We shall have a comfortable supply for ourselves and our brethren on the way, who may be in need until another harvest; but we feel the need of more laborers, for more efficient help, and multiplied means of farming and building at this place. We want men; brethren come from the states, from the nations, come! and help us build and grow, until we can say enough, the valleys of Ephraim are full[9]."

Another matter demanded attention — the boundaries of the proposed commonwealth and a form of government. The activities of 1847 were upon Mexican soil and while the war with Mexico continued the future title to the Basin was in question. Following the treaty of Guadalupe Hidalgo (February 2, 1848,) Brigham Young moved in the direction of a convention for the purpose of organizing a provisional government. Accordingly, a call was issued, "To all citizens of upper California, lying east of the Sierra Nevada Mountains," which meant the territory bounded on the east by the Rocky Mountains, on the west by the Sierra Nevadas, on the north by the Territory of Oregon, and on the south by the Mexican Republic.

Such a call, issued to the four corners of an empty wilderness as large as the Ohio River Valley, could only echo back to its Mormon source in the region of the Great Salt Lake.

The convention began its proceedings on March 4th, and adopted a constitution which established the Provisional State of Deseret:

" . . . Whereas, Civil government and laws are necessary for security, peace, and prosperity of society; and whereas, it is a fundamental principle in all republican governments that all political power is inherent in the people; and governments instituted for their protection, security and benefit, should emanate from the same —

"Therefore, your committee beg leave to recommend the adoption of the following constitution, until the Congress of the United States shall otherwise provide for the government of the territory hereinafter named and described.

"We, the people, grateful to the Supreme Being for the blessings hitherto enjoyed, and feeling our dependence on Him for a continuation of those blessings, do ordain and establish a free and independent government, by the name of the State of Deseret; including all the territory of the United States within the following boundaries:" . . .

These boundaries included all of present Utah and Nevada, parts of Wyoming, Colorado, New Mexico, and Arizona, together with a strip to the seacoast in Southern California. Young was elected Governor together with his two ecclesiastical counsellors as Secretary of State and Chief Justice. Other high Church officials were also given civil authority and many of the bishops of local wards were elected as magistrates to serve in a civil capacity. Thus social and religious unity led to the establishment of a theo democracy in which Church and State fused in common administration[10].

Section Three of the new constitution however protected the traditional rights of religious worship: "All men have the natural and inalienable right to worship god according to the dictates of their own conscience; and the general assembly shall make no law respecting the establishment of religion, or prohibiting the free exercise thereof, or disturb any person in his religious worship or sentiments; provided he does not disturb the public peace, nor obstruct others in their religious worship; and all persons demeaning themselves peaceably, as good members of the state shall be equally under the protection of the laws; and no subordination to another shall ever be established by law; nor shall any religious test be ever required for any office of trust under this state."

The convention petitioned Congress for admission of "Deseret" into the Union as a free state. In face of delay and final substitution of a territorial form of government by Congress for desired statehood the Mormons protested consistently but to no avail: "We admit the boundary asked for is large when we consider the area, but if land susceptible to cultivation that will admit of a dense population, is taken into consideration, it is not so large; and we are not advised of a single dissenting voice within our proposed boundaries that objects to be included therein. What propriety or consistency is there in granting us a territorial and California a state government? When our actual settlers outnumber them as five to three; and moreover those who have been expected to locate there, are at this moment flocking back upon us by hundreds and thousands? We admit the potency of gold, but should not a nation be willing, nay, seek to cherish those who are endeavoring to render her most sterile and barren domain productive; who are extending settlements, making improvements, and developing the national

resources of hitherto unexplored regions, thereby adding to
the national wealth?[11]"

The provisional government continued in operation for
more than two years. Its enactments during that period reflected the political ideals of the Mormon faith and left its
impress indelibly upon the future of the commonwealth.
Then the State of Deseret gave way in legal form to the
Territory of Utah but the name which signifies the honey
bee[12] survived to symbolize the spirit of the Mormon hive.

1 History of Brigham Young, MS II, pp. 136-140.
2 Roberts, B. H., Comprehensive History of the Church, Vol. III, p. 231.
3 Neff, Dr. Andrew L., History of Utah, p. 104.
4 For further reading on this subject, turn to:
   George Thomas — the Development of Institutions Under Irrigation.
   Herbert Bolton — Mormons in the Opening of the Great West.
   John A. Widtsoe — Principles of Irrigation Practice.
5 Mead, Elwood, Irrigation Institutions, p. 220.
6 Pratt, Parley P., Letter, July 9, 1846.
7 Linforth, James, Route from Liverpool to Great Salt Lake Valley, p. 15.
   Also Millennial Star, Vol. 10: pp. 81-88.
8 Millennial Star, Volume 10: pp. 81-83, General Epistle, written from
   Winter Quarters, December 23, 1947.
9 Little, James A., From Kirtland to Salt Lake City, p. 20.
10 Gunnison, J. W. Lt., The Mormons, p. 23.
   "We found them in 1849, organized into a state with all the order of
   legislature, judicial and executive offices regularly filled, under a
   constitution eminently republican in sentiment and tolerant in religion; and though the authority of Congress has not sanctioned this
   form of government, presented and petitioned for, they proceed
   quietly with all the routine of an organized self-governing people,
   under the title of a territory . . . while professing a complete divorce of
   Church and State, their political character and administration is made
   subservient to the theocratical or religious element. They delight to
   call their system of government a "Theo-Democracy," and that in a
   civil capacity, they stand as the Israelites of old under Moses."
   Also Stansbury, Howard, Report to the Government of the Survey of
   the Great Salt Lake, Executive Document, No. 3. Special Session,
   March, 1851, pp. 131-132.
   "While however there are all the external evidences of a government
   strictly temporal, it cannot be concealed that it is so intimately blended
   with the spiritual administration of the Church, that it would be impossible to separate the one from the other. The first civil governor
   under the constitution of the new state, elected by the people, was the
   president of the Church, Brigham Young; the lieutenant governor
   was his first ecclesiastical counsellor, and the secretary of state his
   second counsellor; these three individuals forming the "Presidency" of

the Church. The bishops of the several wards, who by virtue of their office in the Church had exercised not only a spiritual but a temporal authority over the several districts assigned to their charge, were appointed under the civil organization, to be justices of the peace, and were supported in the discharge of their duties, not only by the civil power, but by the whole spiritual authority of the Church also. This intimate connection of Church and State seems to pervade everything that is done. The supreme power in both being lodged in the hands of the same individuals, it is difficult to separate their two official characters, and to determine whether in any one instance they act as spiritual or merely temporal officers. "The establishment of a civil government at all, seems to me to have been altogether the result of a foreseen necessity, which it was impossible to avoid. As the community grew in numbers and importance, it was not to be expected, as has been before remarked, that the whole population would always consist solely of members of the Church, looking up to the Presidency, not only as its spiritual head, but as the divinely commissioned and inspired source of law in temporal matters and policy also. It became necessary, therefore, to provide for the government of the whole, by establishing some authority which could not be disputed by any, and would exercise a control over them as citizens, whether they were members of the Church or not; and which, being acknowledged and recognized by the government of the United States, would be supported by its laws and upheld by its authority."

Also Creer, Leland H., Utah and the Nation, pp. 59-62.

11   Deseret News, September 21, 1850.
12   Book of Mormon, Ether 2:3.

9

Lengthening the Cords

ONE of the first official acts of the State of Deseret was to commission an exploration party. It was to follow the mountain ranges southward to the rim of the Basin and "to become acquainted with the character of the country beyond and ascertain its availability as a place for settlement." A company of fifty men under command of Parley P. Pratt started the latter part of November 1849. It consisted of twelve wagons, one carriage, twenty-four yoke of cattle, thirty-eight horses and mules, an odometer to measure distances, one brass field piece, small arms, seven beeves, and about one hundred and fifty pounds of flour for each man besides crackers, bread and meat.

The exploring party familiarized itself with the natives and resorces of San Pete and Sevier Valleys east of the Wasatch Range. Then it crossed to the west side to follow the foothills leading to the Little Salt Lake some two hundred and fifty miles south of the greater saline body. Here the company divided. Nineteen men, with horses and mules continued with Pratt southward beyond the Basin and thirty men remained to explore the vicinity of the miniature lake.

The smaller group descended rapidly from the southern rim of the Basin to reach the Virgin River which empties into the Colorado. They passed through "a wide expanse of chaotic matter, high hills, high sandy deserts, grassless, waterless plains, perpendicular rocks, loose barren clay, dissolving beds of sandstone, in short through a country of ruins, dissolved by pelting storms of ages, or turned in-side-out, or up-side down by terrible convulsions." But they continued down the Virgin River "whose bottoms expanded to a mile in width, the soil being loose, sandy, fertile and easily irrigated, to the mouth of the Santa Clara. At this point, though January, the climate was like spring, buds swelling, grass springing into new life, and occasional showers[2]."

The observation relative to irrigation and climate on the Virgin, together with the equally important discovery of iron ore by the party exploring the region of the Little Salt Lake, was especially important in the official report delivered to Governor Young. The extended survey proved to be the forerunner of a string of settlements nestled in practically every valley skirting the Wasatch range. Wherever the melting snows issued forth from the canyons in streams of water, there was an invitation to home building.

The magnitude of the Mormon colonizing program with its insatiable demands upon manpower is reflected in some of the major thrusts into new areas included in the following catalogue of activities. These pages do not propose to take into account every exploring and colonizing venture nor make deserved acknowledgment of leadership involved. Rather they seek to reflect typical methods employed and the spirit involved in the expansion of the Kingdom.

Thirty miles north of the initial Mormon encampment the Weber River pours its waters into the Great Salt Lake. The spacious valley at the river's mouth had long served as a favorite trappers retreat. Here in 1841, on a tributary named after Peter Skeen Ogden came Miles Goodyear to establish himself on a Mexican land grant. The ranch at once attracted the Mormons and a party, exploring as far north as Bear and Cache Valleys, stopped to enjoy its isolated hospitality. Wrote John Brown, a member of the party, as of August 9:

"At Weber we found the fort of Mr. Goodyear which consisted of some log buildings and corrals stockaded in with pickets. This man had a herd of cattle, horses, and goats. He had a small garden of vegetables, also a few stalks of corn, and although it had been neglected it looked well which proved to us that with proper cultivation it would do well[3]."

The following January Brigham sent Captain James Brown of the Mormon Battalion to purchase the ranch for $1,950.00. Brown's residence at the Fort became the nucleus for a growing settlement and in September, 1849, Brigham Young arrived to officially locate the site of the city of Ogden.

Forty miles in the opposite direction lay Utah Lake, source of the Jordan River and another trapper's rendezvous. It too was soon explored and the secrets of its beauty and utility recorded. Early in the spring of 1849 it was settled by a little colony led by John S. Higbee. "It was decided to build a city (Provo)[4] a mile square, in blocks of four acres each, reserving the central block of four acres for the site of a chapel and for school houses, the streets to be five rods wide[5]." Joseph Smith's plan for the city of Zion had come to the far west.

In the presence of Indian danger, Young wrote to the settlers, "advising them to speedily complete their fort, to keep near the settlement, to place their cannon on top of the fort, to gather a sufficient quantity of round stones for grape shot, to secure and guard their horses and cattle, to keep a vigilant guard at night, to look out for the Indians, not to make presents to them, but if they would be friendly, to teach them to raise grain and order them to quit stealing[6]."

Again, on October 18th, he wrote: "Stockade your fort and tend to your own affairs, and let the Indians take care of theirs. Let your women and children stay in the fort, and the Indians stay out; but, while you mix with them promiscuously you must continue to receive such treatment from them which they please to give. This is what we have told you continually and you will find it true.

"Let any man or company of men be familiar with Indians and they will be more familiar, and the more familiar you will find the less influence you will have with them. If you would have dominion over them, for their good, which is the duty of the elders, you must not treat them as your equals. You cannot exalt them by this process. If they are your equals you cannot raise them up to you.

"You have been too familiar with them, your children have mixed promiscuously with them, they have been free in your houses, and some of the brethren have spent too much time in smoking and chatting with them, and instead of teaching them to labor, such a course has encouraged them in idleness and ignorance, the effects of which you begin to feel.

"A steady and upright and persevering course may yet restore or gain the confidence of the Indians, and you be safe[7]."

Notorious Chief Walker with a party of twelve Utes came from the valleys southward, inviting settlement on their lands. Brigham discussed seriously with the wily redskin the advantages of changing from the uncertainty of the chase to raising of sheep and cattle, weaving of blankets by the women, schooling of the children, fixing terms of barter. "It is not good for Indians to fight," said Young. "Tell your Indians not to steal. We want to be friendly with you. We are poor now but in a few years we shall be rich. We will trade cattle with you."

"That's good," replied Walker, "It is not good to fight. It makes women and children cry. But let the women and children play together. I told the Pieds (a sub tribe) a great while ago to stop fighting and stealing, but they have no ears[8]."

In keeping with the governor's promise that a colony would be established "within six moons," scouts made a preliminary survey of San Pete Valley early in the fall of 1849 and reported that they had found in addition to timber and forage, a plentiful supply of mountain salt. At the

General Conference of the Church, held on October 6th, Isaac Morely and others were appointed to assume leadership of a proposed party of fifty to one hundred families moving into the valley. At a public meeting held in Salt Lake on October 28, Brigham urged the enlistment of young men for the enterprise. The party which left Salt Lake with thirty men was augmented by others as it proceeded southward until it numbered 124 men and 100 women when they reached the proposed site. The immediate fortunes are recounted in the Third General Epistle of the First Presidency, written the following April:

"They have suffered many inconveniences through the deep snows and severe frosts, for want of houses and other necessaries common in old settlements and have lost many of their cattle. But they have laid the foundation of a great and glorious work, and those who persevere to the end in following the council of heaven will find themselves a thousand times richer than those who have made gold their councilor and worshipped it as their God. Their cattle, now living, have been sustained by their shovelling snow from the grass, and feeding them with their provisions and seed grain, and we have sent them loaded teams to supply their necessities until after seed time. They have been surrounded by a tribe of Indians who appear friendly and who have suffered much from the measles, since they have been among them and many have died as have most of all of the tribes in the mountains; and those who live urged the brethren to remain among them and teach them how to raise grain and make bread; for having tasted a little during their afflictions, they want a full supply. There is plenty of firewood easy of access; some of the best of pine, bituminous coal, salt and plaster of paris at this settlement or its immediate vicinity[9]."

Thus another village was on its way as the Mormons pushed colonial shoots into every habitable valley adjacent to, and far removed from the Great Salt Lake. Typical of the latter, the Iron and Cotton "missions" on the southern rim and beyond the Basin will receive special attention in later chapters.

The early settlements were quite uniform in pattern presenting a frontier adaptation of the Mormon founder's City of Zion. They always began as forts — the houses being enclosed within heavy ramparts which formed the rear wall of the individual houses. These outer walls, built variously of mud, stone, or timber, usually formed an enclosure a half mile or a mile square affording, in addition to living quarters, barns, corrals, etc. The city was laid off in squares with wide streets intersecting at right angles. The meeting house which, in most cases, was also the school house, was located in the central square. Above it rose the "liberty pole" for flag raising ceremonies or just to mark the center for outdoor gatherings. Farming was generally done in one large enclosure nearby the fort with fences encircling a thousand acre field, more or less, according to circumstances. Cattle were grazed in cooperative herds under careful supervision.

Distribution of property in new locations was often effected by the simple device of drawing lots. Typical again of the spirit of Zion building was this fusion of individual with community good.

"On their arrival in Utah the English speaking immigrants were as naturally attracted toward Cache Valley as Scandinavians were toward San Pete. On the 21st day of June, 1859 the first settlers of Logan drew lots for their land. On July 3rd, a public meeting was called by Bishop Peter Maughan at which time Elder John P. Wright, John Nelson, and Israel J. Clark were appointed a committee to give out land to new settlers. On July 27, fort lots were laid out and drawn for by the new settlers and the work of building thereafter quickly commenced[10].

This compact village — the Zion pattern applied to the West — continued to characterize new settlements far into the future. Some of Brigham Young's successors present a clear statement of its advantages:

"In all cases in making new settlements the Saints should be advised to gather in Villages, as has been our custom from the time of our earliest settlements in these mountain valleys. The advantages of this plan instead of carelessly scattering out over a wide extent of country, are many and obvious to all those who have a desire to serve the Lord. By this means the people can retain ecclesiastical organization. . . . They can also cooperate for the good of all in financial and secular necessary improvements. Further than this they are a mutual protection and source of strength against horse and cattle thieves, land jumpers, and against hostile Indians should there be any, while their compact organization gives them many advantages of a social and civil character which might be lost, misapplied or frittered away by spreading out so thinly that inter-communication is difficult, dangerous, inconvenient, or expensive[11]."

The "meeting house" long remained the center of all public transactions as well as of worship in the community. The Bishop of the ward served in the capacity of local magistrate. The needs of the community were brought before the people either in one of the routine religious services or in a special meeting called for the purpose. Committee appointments usually followed public discussion and the project was under way, whether it related to fencing, cutting timber, quarrying, digging irrigation canals, or simply arranging for a public festival.

The Bishop was always, and indeed still is, in close touch with his flock through a system of "block teaching." The ward was divided into districts containing from eight to twelve families. Two "teachers" were called to visit each of the families in each district, monthly. In a brief family meeting the visiting teachers delivered their message and made inquiry as to the economic and spiritual welfare of the group. At a subsequent monthly "ward teachers meeting" all these emissaries of the Bishop reported directly to him the status of his entire flock. Thus informed he was in a position to care for their needs. In this personal service he depended heavily upon the "sisters" of the Relief Society organization.

The Fourth General Epistle of the Presidency reflects the growing consolidation of colonies:

"On the last of July (1850) Brothers Young and Kimball left home on a visit to Utah and San Pete and returned on the 12th of August, having found a place for a good settlement, located a city at San Pete, and noticed several intermediary sites, worthy the attention of smaller colonies, which we anticipate will be settled this fall, making a pleasant and safe communication from this to our most southern habitation. The San Pete settlement will also be strengthened, and others will spread on the north to and beyond Ogden, so that when the emigration of this season shall close there will be a continued line of villages at short distances for more than 200 miles in extent, and a company is already chartered by the general assembly of Deseret for the purpose of running a regular line of coaches between Ogden and San Pete, to commence as early next spring as the travelling will permit, and to be extended as fast as the settlements extend[12]."

The Presiding Bishop's Report read at the Conference of the Church in October, 1853, announced the distribution of population as follows: Salt Lake City with 19 wards, 5,979 people; Salt Lake County, 2,273; Utah County, 4,064; Juab County, 229; San Pete County, 765; Millard County, 304; Iron County, 847; Tooele County, 215; Davis County, 1,598; Weber County, 1,932; Total, 18,206.

Some corners of the Basin were colonized only after repeated attempts and more than one flourishing infant settlement had to be abandoned in the face of Indian troubles. A letter from Erastus Snow, who presided in Southern Utah, affords a glimpse of adjustment problems involved when established communities were broken up:

"I wish to offer a few suggestions that may prove beneficial in aiding you in your future operations.

"I deeply sympathize with you in your present embarrassing circumstances, being obliged, as you have been to vacate

Long Valley, leaving your growing crops as well as other improvements, in obedience to orders from my superior officers.

"I reenforced Long Valley in the Spring and now have ordered its entire evacuation, in accordance with instructions from the highest authorities recognized in our Territory. And hard as it may seem to you, I am fully convinced that it is a wise movement and will eventuate in the greatest good to yourselves; and to our people in the south generally. I submit for your consideration whether you will undertake to mature and gather your wheat and haul it away or whether you will include that with your other crops in a free will offering to the friendly Indians along the River.

" . . .In relation to your future locations; I would say that St. George and Washington have plenty of good land under their ditch which you will be welcome to use without charge the present season for corn, etc. if any of you choose to do so; You may perhaps find like facilities in Kane County. A few more men might be located at Virgin City. Perhaps a few might choose to locate at Toquerville and Harrisburg. We would like to add ten or fifteen men to the strength of Kanarra; these should be enterprising men with a moderate amount of stock.

"We propose moving Kanarra and building a fort on the southern slope of the divide a mile or so south of the present location. The brethren there are willing to divide their lands and water rights on liberal terms, so as to accommodate increased population. Brother L. H. Roundy is at liberty to make a selection of men for that place and report in person to me when I will give further instructions. . . .

"You had better abandon the idea of reoccupying Long Valley.

"May the spirit of our calling and Holy Religion rest upon you dear Brethren, wherever you may go, is the desire of your brother in the Gospel, signed, Erastus Snow.

As a sequel to this abandonment came the breakup of the Mormon colonies on the Muddy River. These, in 1870, found themselves on the Nevada side of the newly drawn Utah-Nevada boundary and oppressed by the gold tax. George A. Smith, writing under date of January 10, 1871, revealed that "Letters have been sent by Erastus Snow to former owners of land in Long Valley who left there because of Indian depredations and have since settled at Kanarra and Harmony, asking them if they would like to re-locate in Long Valley, and if not, if they would relinquish their claims in favor of the brethren from the Muddy or if not willing to relinquish but wish to sell their claims to state on what terms they would do so." President Snow suggested that the terms ought to be liberal giving those who had to break up their homes on the Muddy an opportunity to recover from their losses. The following blank was enclosed with the letters:

"Know all men by these presents: that we the undersigned do for and in consideration of the good will which we have for our brethren who are broken up on the Muddy and are seeking homes elsewhere, relinquish all our claims to land, houses, and other improvements formerly owned by us in Long Valley or Berry Valley, and we do hereby give our full free unqualified consent for the brethren from the Muddy to take and occupy our claims in said Long or Berry Valley; the same to be set off to individuals as their bishops may deem best.

"And we do further covenant and agree that we will never demand pay of these brethren for our claims and improvements in the aforesaid Valley."

Newly established colonies always clamored for more settlers. Here is how such requests might be received:

"Friday, September 6, (1850) at the General Conference held in Salt Lake City, President Brigham Young spoke of the propriety of strengthening the San Pete settlements and called for volunteers to return with Father Isaac Morley. Brother Morley then expressed his feelings and said he wanted a company of good men and women to go to San Pete Valley and he desired that no man should dwell in that Valley who was in the habit of taking the name of the Lord in vain. Pres. Young said, 'I have in my heart to ask the congregation if Father Morley shall have the right and privilege to select such men as he wishes to go to San Pete.' The conference voted that he be given the privilege and it was then decided by vote that Brother Morley should select 100 men — with or without families. President Young then said, 'It is as good a valley as you ever saw; the goodness of the soil cannot be beaten, there is only one practicable road into the valley and that is up Salt Creek; the inhabitants in San Pete settlement are number 1 and when I was there in that valley I prayed to God that he would never suffer an unrighteous man to live there[13].' "

Beyond the inner circle of Mormon colonies far-flung outposts hung upon the edges of the empire. San Bernardino, in California, anchored the southern end of a chain of colonies intended to facilitate immigration from the western coast. Las Vegas formed its first connecting link. On the western fringe of the Basin appeared a Mormon trading post in Carson Valley and beyond its northern rim the Salmon River Mission established Fort Limhi. Eastward, to ease the burden of the Mormon trek between the Missouri and Salt Lake Valley the Church bought Bridger's station near Green River and established "Fort Supply" nearby.

Then scarcely a decade after the pioneers of '47 passed that way an army of the United States government appeared on the Oregon Trail with orders to crush a "Mormon rebellion." Certain federal appointees to the Territory, finding their political plums unsavory, had carried reports to Washington that government records had been burned.

As the military caravan, with its camp following, moved menacingly toward the South Pass, news of its approach awakened memories of bloodthirsty mobs masquerading in soldiers' uniforms. The Mormon community which had fled before the monster of mobocracy in Missouri and again in Illinois stiffened in its mountain retreat, drew in all its exposed members to conserve its strength, and defied military approach. Too many times it had appealed in vain for legal justice and now, nourished for a decade on the freedom of the open west, it poised in self defense.

The approaching columns halted and this time before

the stranger was admitted within the gates of Mormondom the forces of law and order had triumphed over blinded prejudice. The nightmare of "Buchanan's million dollar blunder" as it was called, came and went, but it permanently affected the expansion of the Kingdom. The extended outposts, hastily withdrawn before the threat of conflict, were not revived. The Mormon commonwealth retreated to less pretentious boundaries but what it lost in area in gained in solidarity.

So the "cords of Zion's tent" were lengthened into the far west and stakes were driven firmly in the valleys of the Great Basin. The gold rush, sweeping over the Basin toward California before the Saints were firmly established, had tugged heavily upon the spiritual cords — but they held. Before a decade had passed the stakes were fixed too firmly to be uprooted. Zion, at last, had found her anchorage against outside forces and Brigham Young determined that nothing from within should sabotage the Kingdom.

The Kingdom must rise on its own economic foundations. Labor was its chief virtue, and the development of home industry its only salvation. The building of Zion must be sustained by unceasing industry and Brigham Young meant to see that it was so. A group of idlers about the court house in the capital city may have forgotten this. If so they were soon reminded, after Brigham passed that way. He was quick to diagnose the symptoms and apply the remedy. A clerk appeared among them to take their names and soon each one of them received a call to take a "mission" for the Kingdom; some were to raise cotton in Southern Utah, some to make new settlements elsewhere in the Territory, and some to convert the heathen in the South Sea Islands. The drone had no place in Deseret.

1   History of Brigham Young, M. S., November 1849, pp. 160-161.
2
3   Autobiography of John Brown, p. 81.
4   Named for trapper Etienne Provost.
5   History of Brigham Young, M. S., September 14, 1849, p. 133.
6   History of Brigham Young, M. S., April 1849, pp. 67-68.
7   History of Brigham Young, M. S., 1849, p. 155.
8   History of Brigham Young, M. S., pp. 89-92.
9   Roberts, B. H., Comprehensive History of the Church, Vol. I, p. 311.
10 Jensen, Andrew, History of Cache Valley.
11 Fremont Stake, M. S. History, December 26, 1862. As quoted in Hunter,
        Milton C., Brigham Young, the Colonizer.
12 Journal History, September 27, 1850.
13 Journal History.

10

Ripe for Harvest

THE spread of Mormon settlements across the Basin depended upon a constant influx of population. The original colonization in 1847 had drawn upon a reserve of approximately 25,000 Latter-day Saints in the United States and Canada. Already by 1849, more than eight thousand of these had reached Salt Lake Valley. Most of the remainder was concentrated on the Pottawattamie lands in Iowa while smaller groups were located in numerous "branches" of the Church in eastern cities. British converts arriving in the United States only to find Nauvoo crumbling in the hands of lawless mobs had been advised to locate in these branches pending selection of a new gathering center. Active proselyting continued to swell this colonizing potential in America.

Also in England the missionaries were recruiting large numbers of prospective colonists. There were already 6,614 adherents to the faith in Britain in 1840 when Joseph Smith had issued a call for gathering to Nauvoo. Five thousand of these emigrated to Illinois. Although a total of 10,319 emigrated to America during the succeeding decade (1840-1850), the remaining aggregate rose to 28,894. This favorable response to Mormon proselyting is better understood in relation to the following:

The *Millennial Star,* published in Liverpool by the Mormon missionaries, announced in February, 1842:

> "In the midst of the general distress which prevails in this country on account of want of employment, the high price of provisions, the oppression, priestcraft and iniquity of the land it is pleasing to the household of faith to con-

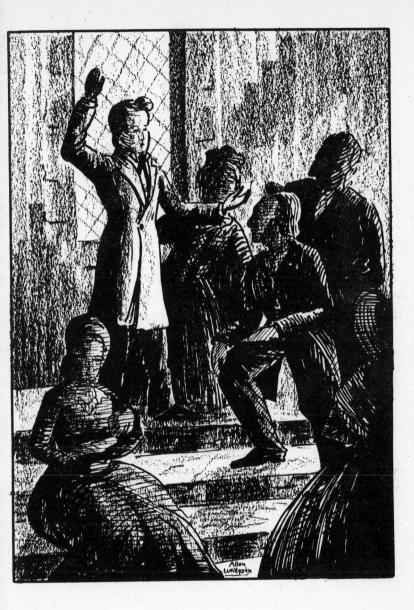

template a country reserved by the Almighty as a sure asylum for the poor and the oppressed — a country every way adapted to their wants and conditions — and still more pleasing to think that thousands of the Saints have already made their escape from this country, and all its abuses and distress, and that they have found a home, where, by preserving industry they may enjoy all the blessings of liberty, peace and plenty[3]. . . .

"Several large ships have been chartered by the Saints during the present fall and winter, and have been filled with emigrants, who have gone forth with songs of joy; and some of them have already arrived safely in the promised land, while others are, doubtless, still tossing upon the ocean.

"Who that has a heart to feel or soul to rejoice, will not be glad at so glorious a plan of deliverance? Who will not hail the messengers of the Latter-day Saints as the friends of humanity — the benefactors of mankind.

"We do not wish to confine the benefit of our emigration plan to the Saints, but are willing to grant all industrious, honest, and well-disposed persons who may apply to us, the same information and assistance as emigrants to the western states, there being abundant room for more than a hundred million of inhabitants."

Such a message fell upon willing ears. Prospects for a favorable hearing were never better than when the Mormon cry of deliverance came to the working classes of Great Britain during the middle 19th century.

A glance at conditions among the working classes of England at the time reveals considerable dissatisfaction and want. The first Chartist petition to Parliament in 1838, is representative of a general feeling among those classes. It complains, in part:

"Yet with all the elements of national prosperity, and with every disposition and capacity to take advantage of them we find ourselves overwhelmed with public and private suffering, we are bowed down under a load of taxes, which, not-with-standing, fall greatly short of the wants of our ruler. Our trades are trembling on the verge of bankruptcy; our workmen are starving. Capital brings no profit, and labor no remuneration. The home of the artificer is desolate, and the warehouse of the pawnbroker is full. The workhouse is crowded and the manufactory is deserted. We have looked on every side; we have searched diligently in order to find out the causes of distress so sore and so long continued. We can discover none in nature or in providence[4]."

Such conditions favored a missionary cause in which temporal welfare was so inseparably connected with the spiritual. A program such as the Mormons offered, with its promise of economic relief, could not fail to attract attention and many were influenced in their acceptance of it through worldly channels.

The ready response to the Mormon message directed the attention of numerous writers to both the missionary and the nature of his appeal. Their interpretations varied with their predispositions. Some, eyeing the whole Mormon program with suspicion, charged the missionaries with deliberately misrepresenting facts about opportunities in "Zion," while others limited their accusations to literary exaggeration and undue optimism[5]. Of the literature thus censored, the following which appeared in the Millenial Star was perhaps the most extreme:

"Beautiful for situation and ultimate joy of the whole earth is the State of Zion established in the mountains. In the elevated valley of the Salt and Euta (Utah) lakes with the beautiful river Jordan running through it from south to north is the newly established State of Zion. There vegetation flourishes with magic rapidity; and the food of man, or the staff of life, leaps into maturity from the bowels of mother earth with astonishing celerity. Within one month from planting, potatoes grew from 'six to eight inches' and corn from two to four feet. There the pregnant clouds introduce their fertilizing contents at a modest distance from the fat valley and send their humid influences from the mountain tops. . . . as if nature's lenses had obtained a focal point of nutritive power just in the valley of the Great Salt Lake. This valley is in the north and east corner of the Great Basin in dimensions nearly 300 by 500 miles. The streams and rivers are enriched by valuable water falls suited to the purpose of erecting mills and factories and all descriptions of machinery. This Great Basin is adequate to sustain many millions of people. It is generally cleared of all hindrance to settlement by the long and sharp scythe of time. The various timber of lofty mountains wait in proud readiness to bow at the signal of the axe and to go forth to beautify the temple of our God. The box, the fir, the pine, and maple have sprung up at the dictation of prophecy just where they are needed. Mills, factories, hamlets, mansions, houses, and cities can be supplied with building materials from the unculled forests of the ages[6]."

Truly such extravaganza might challenge the best efforts of the modern chamber of commerce. It is, however, illustrative of the extreme and reflects a run-away enthusiasm in the fascinating task of building Zion. Opportunity, as related to the building of the Kingdom, was generally presented as conditioned upon sacrifice and hard work. This would suggest that the missionaries were not disposed to lure converts into the net by false representations of personal ease or hopes of sudden acquisition of wealth[7].

The converts themselves came under suspicion. It was held that many were simply actuated by hope of material reward[8]. Further, it was maintained that the Church winked at this materialism in its desire to win large numbers to its standard.

It may be assumed that among the thousands who accepted the message of the missionary there were those who were not sincere and some who were prompted by worldly motives. The sifting process that soon discarded large numbers whose enthusiasm waned, left no doubt of that. Thousands were stricken from the Church records during that early period. In the five years from 1850 to 1854 inclusive, the records of the L.D.S. "European Mission" show 15,197 excommunications[9]. This action incidentally supports the position of the Church in relation to its strict requirements of genuine conversion[10]. Wrote Brigham Young to Franklin D. Richards, who presided over the British Mission in 1855:

> "I will here repeat my wish and council to you, that in your election of the Saints who shall be aided by the Fund, those who have proven themselves by long continuence in the Church shall be helped first, whether they can raise any means of their own or not; let those be brought so long as you can act within the means of the company, if they have not a sixpence in the world, but be wary of assisting any of those who come into the Church now, during these troubless times for Britain, whose chief aim and intention may be to get to America."

Industrial conditions did not improve and the desire to find relief in America spread feverishly among the working classes. The British "Saints" received no invitation from the Mormon leaders to join them in their exodus of 1846. Their destination was hardly definite enough for instruction at that time. However, permission was granted them to sail for Vancouver Island and settle there if they desired. In February, 1847, upon the advice of Orson Hyde, Orson Pratt, and John Taylor, the Mormons in England prepared a memorial to the Queen asking for aid in emigrating to America. Therein are revealed the feelings of the signatories toward prevailing conditions and their ambition for removal to a land of greater opportunity. The following excerpts from the petition tell their own story:

> "Your memorialists are moved to address your Majesty by the unexampled amount of abject, helpless, and unmerited misery which at present prevails among the laboring classes of this country. By all your memorialists this wretchedness has, to some extent, been witnessed; by all it has been deplored; and by many among them it has been bitterly felt. The sufferings and destitution of these portions of your Majesty's subjects have, in the judgment of your memorialists, reached a point at which it has become the duty of both sexes, and of all ranks to use every constitutional means for their relief and remedy.
>
> "Your memorialists are daily the witnesses of a frightful

increase of poverty and pauperism; while those who are at present in circumstances above the reach of absolute want, are constantly becoming less able to sustain the burden of supporting the poor.

"Your memorialists, without attempting to enumerate the many alleged causes of the present national distress and suffering, feel convinced that Emigration to some portion of your Majesty's vacant territories is the only permanent means of relief left to a rapidly increasing population, which, if retained here, must swell the aggregate amount of misery, wretchedness and want.

"Your memorialists believe that your Majesty cherishes the wish, and they pray your Majesty to exert all that constitutional influence and power which will effectually accomplish their removal to the distant shores of a country, the natural resources of which are waiting to be developed, to reward the hand of industry, and to fill with plenty thousands that wander here at present without employment, and consequently without bread.

" . . . And again your memorialists ask your Majesty to favorably consider the propriety of allowing to each male emigrant, who is more than twenty-one years old, who may become an actual settler, a grant of land corresponding in extent to grants proposed by the United States Government to its subjects, who become actual settlers in its extreme western territories, namely, from three hundred and twenty to six hundred and forty acres[11]."

The petition measured one hundred and sixty-eight feet in length and contained nearly 13,000 names. Attached to the memorial was a diagram suggesting a plan for land grants and concluding with the following: "In most schemes for emigration hitherto approved and aided by the government, great difficulty has been found to induce the people of this country to leave their native Isle; but we are prepared, and shall guarantee, to send twenty thousand people of all trades, and from most districts in Scotland, England and Wales at once, or as soon as vessels can be found to convey them[12]."

A copy of the petition was sent to each member of Parliament and other influential citizens. However, after some unimportant correspondence relative to the feasibility of the requests made, the memorial disappeared. The Prime Minister, Lord John Russel, speaking in the House of Commons, just previous to the circulation of the memorial, had opposed the removal of the poor as was then advocated and seems to have expressed the prevailing view of English statesmen in the matter of emigration.

At last came the long awaited word from America. The Great Basin was announced as Zion's new home. The "Saints abroad" were urged to come at once bringing tools, implements, seeds and all such articles as would contribute to its progress. They were assured that Mormon leaders would soon be among them after a period of unavoidable absence: "Since the murder of President Joseph Smith, false prophets and false teachers have arisen and tried to deceive many, during which time we have mostly tarried with the body of the Church, or have been seeking a new location . . . and now having it in contemplation soon to re-organize the Church according to the original pattern, with a First Presidency and Patriarch, feel that it will be the privilege of the Twelve ere long to spread abroad among the nations, not to hinder the gathering, but to preach the gospel, and push the people, the honest in heart, together from the four quarters of the earth."

Continuing, the communication urged upon the scattered members the necessity for the same unselfish cooperation which had characterized the main body of the Church in its repeated crises. "It is the duty of the Rich Saints everywhere to assist the poor, according to their ability, to gather; and if they choose with a covenant and promise that the poor thus helped, shall repay as soon as they are able. It is also the duty of the rich, those who have the intelligence and the means to come home forthwith, and establish factories, and all kinds of machinery, that will tend to give employ-

ment to the poor, and produce those articles which are necessary for the comfort, convenience, health, and happiness of
the people; and no one need be at a loss concerning his duty
in these matters, if he will walk so humbly before God as
to keep the small still whisperings of the Holy Ghost within
continually[13]."

Orson Spencer, in charge of Mormon activities in England,
immediately relayed the call to the waiting brethren under
date of February 1, 1848. Triumphantly he wrote: "The
channel of Saints Emigration to the land of Zion is now
opened. The long wished for time of gathering has come.
Good tidings from Mt. Zion! The resting place of Israel
for the last day has been discovered. . . . Now rejoice and
lift up your heads, O ye pure in heart and let the labouring
and the heavy laden, that have been bowed down under the
weight of accumulated oppressions in every nation, prepare
themselves to come to their inheritance in the land of promise. The day of release dawns and the notes of Millennial
Jubilee reverberate from the mountain heights of Zion. Let
all that can gather up their effects, and set their faces as a
flint to go Zionward in due time and order. All things are
now ready. The word of the Lord comes forth from Zion
to the upright of all the earth. Gather yourselves to the
place of your rest, for there is no time to be lost. Let your
preparations, however, be in wisdom and not in heedless
precipitancy. Hearken implicitly to council, lest a devious
step should make the way too rugged to be endured. . . .
The presidents of conferences (districts) are requested to
forward to us the number of those who are prepared to emigrate by the 9th of February and also the number that will
be ready by the 22nd of February. . . . The whole expense
from Liverpool to the Bluffs, for one person may be 10
pounds[14]."

In August of the same year Orson Pratt urged, through the
columns of the Millennial Star, that the rich dispose more
generously of their property to assist the poor to emigrate

and warned: "Oh ye Saints of the Most High, linger not, make good your retreat before the avenues are closed up[15]."

From that time forward "the Gathering" became the rallying cry of the Mormon leaders to their following scattered abroad. As the results of their toil demonstrated the practicability of their colonizing designs, in Utah, their enthusiasm increased. A circular from the Presidency, issued in 1850, reveals their growing confidence: "The crops have been abundant in all the settlements of Deseret this season, and we are confident if all will be prudent, there will be seed and grain and bread sufficient to sustain the whole till another harvest. The estimated population of 15,000 inhabitants in Deseret this past year, having raised grain sufficient to sustain the 30,000 the coming year inspires us confidently to believe that the 30,000 the coming year can raise sufficient for 60,000 the succeeding year, and to this object and end our energies will be exerted, to double our population annually[16]. . . ."

Zion had now unfurled her standard in the tops of the mountains and the call went forth for the "heirs of the Kingdom" to gather in from the four corners of the earth. The "field was white to harvest" and already hundreds of missionaries were "thrusting in the sickle to reap." The spirit of the Gathering rested upon thousands who had accepted the message of the restoration. Their clamor for ways and means of escaping to the promised land was soon to be answered. The Perpetual Emigrating Fund Company had already appeared in the offing.

1   Smith, Joseph, History of the Church IV: 269.
2   Smith, Joseph, History of the Church IV: 119, 133.
3   Smith, Joseph, History of the Church IV: 510-513.
4   Cheyney, Edward P., Readings in English History.
5   Linn, W. A., The Story of the Mormons, pp. 412-413.
        Also Brocket, L. P., Our Western Empire, pp. 1185-1186.
6   Millennial Star X:40.
7   Remy & Brenchley, A Journey to the Great Salt Lake, p. 222. These European observers concluded, "It is not the expectation of a lazy life that lures them out to Utah."

8 Bowles, Samuel, Our New West, p. 211. "The appeals to their desire for greater physical comfort, for a home of independence and plenty, brought abundant followers."

9 This figure has been compiled from the semi-annual reports of the European Latter-day Saints Mission as they appeared in the Millennial Star, Volumes VII to XVII.

10 Millennial Star, XIV: p. 275. "Thousands of those who have been cut off from the Church in these islands because of their slothfulness and indifference to the work, have seen the day when they might have gathered with the Saints."

11 Linforth, James, Route from Liverpool to Great Salt Lake Valley, p. 2-5.

12 Linforth, James, Route from Liverpool to Great Salt Lake Valley, p. 5.

13 Roberts, B. H., Comprehensive History of the Church, Vol. III, pp. 311-312.

14 Millennial Star, IX: 40.

15 Linn, W. A., Story of the Mormons, p. 414. Also Millennial Star, August, 1848.

16 Little, James A., From Kirtland to Salt Lake City, p. 227-230.

11

Launching The Perpetual Fund

DESPITE the Nauvoo pledge "that we take the Saints with us to the extent of our ability," many thousands were left behind on the banks of the Missouri. The unexpected retreat across Iowa in mid-winter found most of them unprepared. Equipment was woefully lacking for the entire journey to the Salt Lake Valley. Many continued to arrive from the east and even after the more resourceful of them evacuated during the summers of 1848-49, nearly eight thousand exiles remained on the "Pottawattamie lands[1]." But these members were not forgotten, and in the spirit of the "Nauvoo Covenant," Brigham Young wrote them as follows in the summer of 1849: "When the small matter of journeying more than a thousand miles over sage plains and settling and preparing to live are overcome, then the poor shall feel our helping hand to assist them to remove to this valley[2]."

In September of that year he proposed the creation of a revolving fund for the purpose of helping the poor to reach Salt Lake. This was to be done, "Agreeably to our covenant in the Temple that we would never cease our exertions by all the means and influence within our reach, till all the Saints who were obliged to leave Nauvoo shall be located at some gathering place of the Saints[3]." The Council of the Twelve approved the suggestion and the following were named as a committee to raise a fund as soon as possible: Willard Snow, John S. Fullmer, Lorenzo Snow, John D. Lee, and Franklin D. Richards.

During the Church Conference in October following, Heber C. Kimball introduced the subject to the members at large, urging approval of, and support to, the project. He reminded them of the pledge made before leaving Nauvoo and urged their united action in redeeming it[4]. The question was put directly "shall we fulfil the Covenant or shall we not[5]?" A motion to raise a helping fund was unanimously carried and Bishop Edward Hunter was appointed to "carry the funds back to the states, buy cattle, take the oversight of the property, and bring the poor to this place." Cash contributions began to pour in at once and at a meeting of the Bishops held on October 7th, thirteen yoke of Oxen were pledged[6]. About $5,000. were raised that season to lessen the pressure at Pottawattamie[7].

Bishop Hunter carried with him a letter of instructions from the First Presidency to Orson Hyde who was in charge of the exiles in Iowa. It explained the purpose and operating plan of the Perpetual Emigrating Fund. Because the movement which it initiated later came to national and even international, attention the letter is quoted in detail.

"The Lord has been devising, or rather making manifest, ways and means to facilitate the gathering of His Saints in these last days, and we lose no time in cheering your heart with the intelligence, and offering such suggestions as may be wisdom for you to follow in helping to roll on this glorious work of gathering Israel.

"We write you more particularly at this time concerning the gathering and the mission of our general agent for the Perpetual Emigrating Fund for the coming year, Bishop Edward Hunter who will soon be with you, bearing the funds already raised in this place, and we will here state our instructions to Bishop Hunter so that you may the more fully comprehend our designs.

"In the first place this fund has been raised by voluntary donations, and is to be continued by the same process and by so managing as to preserve the same and then to multiply.

"Bishop Hunter is instructed to go direct for Kanesville and confer with the general authorities at that place and, by all means within his reach, procure every information so as to make the most judicious application of the funds in the purchase of young oxen and cows that can be worked effectually to the Valley, and that will be capable of improving and selling after their arrival so as to continue the fund the following year.

"He will give early information to those whom we have directed to be helped, and such others as we shall deem wisdom, being aided in his judgment by the authorities among you, so that they may be preparing their wagons, etc. for the journey.

"Wagons are so plentiful here that it is very desirable not to purchase with the Perpetual Fund; but let those be assisted who will make wagons of wood, when they cannot get iron, such as will be strong and safe to bring them here, so that all the funds may be appropriated to the purchase of such things as will improve in value by being transferred to this place.

. . .

"The poor can live without the luxuries of life on the road and in the valley as well as in Pottawattamie and other places, and those who have means to purchase luxuries, have monies to procure an outfit of their own and need no help. Therefore, let such as are helped receive as little in food, clothing, wagons, etc., as can possibly make them comfortable to this place, and when they arrive they can go to work and get their outfit of all things necessary for comfort and convenience better than where they are, and even luxuries.

"As early in the spring as it will possibly do, on account of feed for cattle, Brother Hunter, will gather all his company, organize them in the usual order, and preside over the camp, traveling with the same to this place; having previously procured the best teamsters possible, such as are accustomed to driving, and be gentle, kind, and attentive to their teams. When the Saints thus helped arrive here they will give their obligations to the Church to refund to the amount of what they received, as soon as circumstances will permit, and labor will be furnished to such as wish on the public works, and good pay; and as fast as they can procure the necessaries of life, and a surplus, that surplus will be applied to liquidating their debt and thereby increasing the Perpetual Fund.

"By this it will readily be discovered that the funds are to be appropriated in the form of a loan rather than a gift;

and this will make the honest in heart rejoice, for they love to labor and be independent by their labor, and not live on the charity of friends, while the lazy idlers, if such there be, will find fault and want every luxury furnished them on their journey and in the end pay nothing.

"The Perpetual Fund will help no such idlers; we have no use for them in the valley; they had better stay where they are, and if they think they can devise a better way of appropriating the emigrating funds, then we propose to let them go to work, get the funds, make the appropriation, set us a better pattern and we will follow it; and by that time we are confident they will have means of their own and will need no help.

"Brother Hunter will return all the funds to this place next season, when the most judicious course will be pursued to convert all the cattle and means into cash, that the same may be sent abroad as speedily as possible on another mission, together with all that we can raise in the states will increase the funds by all possible means the coming winter so that our agents may return with a large company.

"The few thousands we send out by our agent at this time is like a grain of mustard seed in the earth; we send it forth into the world and among the Saints, a good soil, and we expect it will grow and flourish, and spread abroad in a few years so that it will cover England, cast its shadow in Europe and in the process of time compass the whole earth.   That is to say these funds are designed to increase until Israel is gathered from all Nations, and the poor can sit under their own vines, and inhabit their own house, and worship God in Zion.

"If for any cause, there should be a surplus of funds in the hands of our agent; when he leaves the states with a company, he will deposit the same with some good house, subject to our order, or bring it with him as wisdom dictates."

The Frontier Guardian, organ of the stranded Mormons in Iowa, soon communicated news of the forthcoming assistance from Zion. "The friends abroad throughout the states will do well to gather to this point as early in the spring as they can. . . . Come early to this place and if you are unable to go on you will be in time to put in crops; and if you are able to go on you will be in time to start with the first companies. . . . The first company will probably leave here for the mountains about the first of May, one about the middle of May, one about the first of June, and one about the fifteenth of June — none later. Each company of emigrants will have experienced guides, who know the route, who know the Indians, and who well understand the mode and manner of travelling on the plains[8]."

The Oregon-California trail was heavily travelled in 1850 and the south side of the Platte River presented a daily scene of moving caravans. The government agent at Laramie reported that by June 10th, four thousand, six hundred and seventy-two wagons had passed that way, with 16,915 men, 235 women, 242 children, 14,954 horses, 4,641 mules, 7,425 oxen and 1,653 cows[9].

Into this stream the Mormons poured an estimated 700 wagons that year. The wagons were generally drawn by two yoke of oxen and were accompanied by two to six cows. The companies included 4,000 sheep and 5,000 head of cattle, horses and mules. Each wagon carried an average of 1,850 pounds of freight. Included were two new carding machines in addition to other valuable machinery. The Guardian, observing the departing Mormon companies, was led to exclaim, "To see a people who, three or four years ago, had to sell their all to get bread to last them until they could raise it, and now see them with from one to four wagons each, with plenty of good teams, thousands of sheep and loose cattle, horses, mules, and machinery of every kind; wagons all new and stock all young and thrifty, is gratifying in the extreme[10]."

The Mormons usually followed the north side of the Platte, thus avoiding most of the California-bound traffic. How the problems of providing feed for their animals and taking precautions against the cholera scourge contributed to their choice of the northern bank may be gathered from the following: Orson Hyde wrote to the Guardian,

Upper Crossing of the Platte,
July 30, 1850.

"We crossed the Platte yesterday. Ferried over wagons and swam our horses, leaving Captain Milo Andrus and company on the banks crossing.

All well. . . .

Grass is scarce though the rains through the Black Hills have been constant and powerful. But how the vast multitudes of cattle and horses are to get through, God only knows. There will be no lack of water, but grass is eaten up root and branch; and in many cases the animals have eaten out the wild sage.

"August 1, at Independence Rock on the Sweetwater.

"All well.

"We have just passed through the 'valley and shadow of death' a country of about fifty miles in extent, where the waters are deeply impregnated with nitre, saleratus, sulphur, etc. There is little or no grass at all through this region, but is mostly a sandy desert. The carcasses of cattle and horses lying along the roadside are very numerous, having perished through fatigue, hunger, and through drinking poisonous waters.

"This country lies between the upper crossing of the Platte and the Sweetwater River on the banks of which we are now comfortably encamped. . . . We are now beginning to overtake the California and Oregon emigration. They have suffered much in the loss of teams and animals; and oh! the sacrifice of wagons, clothing, fire arms, beds, bedding, buffalo skins, trunks, chests, wretchedness and woe, and yet thousands and tens of thousands follow on the way with the hope of securing the wealth of the world. . . .

"There are about five hundred new graves on the south side of the Platte and but three deaths are reported at Laramie as having occurred on the North side. . . . If wood were as plentiful as tools, wagon tire, and iron in general, on the road, we could have our hot dodger, coffee, and fried or boiled bacon whenever we pleased."

Removal of the Mormons from the Pottawattamie lands of Iowa did not proceed as rapidly as the Presidency desired. In their communication of 1850, it announced that the gathering must take temporary precedence over missionary service. "Viewing the gathering of Israel, which produces our increased population in the valleys of the mountains, an important part of the Gospel of Jesus Christ, and one of the most important at the present time, we shall send few or no Elders abroad to preach the Gospel this fall; instruct them to raise grain and build houses, and prepare for the Saints, that they may come in flocks like doves to their windows; and we say, arise! to your wagons and your tents, O scattered Israel! Ye Saints of the Most High! rich and poor, and gather to the state of Deseret. Bringing your plows and drills, your reapers and gleaners, your threshers and cleaners of the most approved patterns so that one man can do the labor of twenty in the wheat field, and we will soon send the Elders abroad by hundreds and thousands to a harvest of souls among the nations, and the inhabitants of the earth shall speedily hear of the salvation prepared by Israel's God for His people[11]."

In the fall of 1851, attention was centered on final evacuation of these lands which, though intended as a temporary resting place in the flight to Zion had assumed too much of an aspect of permanency. Addressing those who lingered through the Guardian, the Presidency announced the appointment of Ezra T. Banson and Jedediah M. Grant to assist them in removing to "the valley" the following spring. "They are sent expressly to push the Saints to the valley" ... "we desire you to give heed to their counsel in all things, and come to this place with them next season, and fail not. ... What are you waiting for? Have you any good excuse for not coming? No! ... arise and come home. ... We wish you to evacuate Pottawattamie and the states and next fall be with us[12]."

These efforts to gather in the hesitating members of the flock resulted in unusually heavy Mormon migration to the west in 1852. At least twenty-one companies, averaging sixty or more wagons to the company brought approximately

10,000 settlers to the Salt Lake Valley[13]. The agents sent to effect the evacuation of Pottawattamie had done a good job. The obligations of the Nauvoo pledge of 1846 had been faithfully discharged. All the exiles from Nauvoo who wished to come had been removed to Zion.

While the Church was thus engaged, the Perpetual Emigrating Fund itself was assuming corporate form. The fund increased in Utah to about twenty thousand dollars in 1850[14]. It was also introduced into the British Mission and considerable sums were accumulating there[15].

Successful application of these funds to the expanding needs of the Kingdom demanded improved organization. Shipping agencies had already been established abroad as well as supervised control of overland travel in America, but there was need of greater coordination all along the line. A corporation was needed which could handle the whole gathering movement on a legal basis and in a business-like way[16]. Collecting and disbursing funds (involving in their details such activities as converting chattels and farm produce into cash and the care of the property during the process), chartering ships and collecting for transportation involved, establishing buying agencies for equipment necessary to cross the plains, directing the activities of hundreds of agents in its service, and keeping of proper accounts, called for careful administration. An emigrating enterprise of whatever nature, would have to deal with business corporations in its buying and selling and even in issuing paper of credit if conditions should demand.

With reference to this latter, President Young wrote shortly after a company had been incorporated, " . . . should a proper proportion of cash be wanting the company will issue paper for the purpose of fitting out the emigrants abroad, which paper will always be good, as a sufficiency of the stock will be retained, in deposit by the company, to redeem that paper at any moment: and any person coming to this place, can with more convenience, bring the paper than flour, stock or even gold; which will make it an object for the brethren who have the means, and travellers bound for Deseret, to secure the Company's paper, wherever they can find it; for with that paper they can get such articles as travellers most need when money will not purchase them in this market[17]."

On September 7, 1850, at a Conference of the Church, a committee of three was appointed to have direction of the Perpetual Fund operations. This committee included Willard Snow, Edward Hunter and Daniel Spencer. It was furthermore agreed to organize the Perpetual Fund with its officers into a company and to have it chartered by the Provisional State Assembly. A week later, September 14th, the Assembly passed an act incorporating the Perpetual Emigrating Company. It began:[18]

"Whereas, in the fall of 1849, the Church of Jesus Christ of Latter-day Saints in this state did, by voluntary donation, create a fund for the laudable and benevolent purpose of facilitating the emigration of the poor to this state, — and —

"Whereas, labor, industry, and economy is wealth, and all kinds of mechanics and laborers are requisite for building up and extending the benefits of civilized society, subduing the soil and otherwise developing the resources of a new country, — and —

"Whereas, there are many good and worthy people who would gladly emigrate to this state if they were provided with the means, — and —

"Whereas, we consider it a subject worthy of consideration and encouragement, fraught as it is, with the best interest of society; . . . Therefore, to encourage and perpetuate this enterprise we, the General Assembly of the State of Deseret do ordain and establish the following ordinance, to-wit:"

The act of incorporation[19] was made legal by the Territorial Legislature on October 4, 1851, and amended and confirmed by the same body, January 12, 1856[20].

On September 15th in keeping with the provisions of the act, a public meeting at the Bowery[21] resolved itself into a special conference of the Church and officers of the new company were elected. Brigham Young was chosen President, with the following assistants, Heber C. Kimball, Willard Richards, Newel K. Whitney, Orson Hyde, George A. Smith, Ezra T. Benson, Jedediah M. Grant, Daniel H. Wells, John Brown, William Crosby, Amasa Lyman, Charles C. Rich, Lorenzo D. Young, Parley P. Pratt. At a subsequent meeting the company completed its organization as follows: Willard Richards, Secretary; Newel K. Whitney, Treasurer; Thomas Bullock, Recorder. Upon the death of Whitney soon thereafter, Daniel Spencer succeeded him as Treasurer. Orson Hyde, Orson Pratt, Franklin D. Richards and John Brown were appointed travelling agents for the company[22].

In later years enemies of the Mormon Church, seeking to block operations of its emigration agency, charged union of Church and State in Utah. True, the Territory of Utah served the bidding of the Church when it gave legal sanction to the Perpetual Emigrating Fund and thereby placed in the hands of the ecclesiastical body an agent for expediting its immigration program. But it should not be overlooked that at that time the population of Utah was practically all of one faith and largely of one mind as far as the development of the territory was concerned. While there was no legal union of Church and State, it was nevertheless not surprising that in such a community of one faith, its legislative enactments should be representative of Mormon will.

1 Smith, Joseph, History of Reorganized Church, p. 11.
2 Little, James A., From Kirtland to Salt Lake City, p. 196.
3 Ibid.
4 Linforth, James, Route from Liverpool to Great Salt Lake Valley, p. 7.
5 Journal History, Minutes of General Conference held at Great Sale Lake City, October 6, 1849. See date given.
6 Ibid.
7 Deseret News I:110.
8 Frontier Guardian, January 23, 1859.
9 Little, James A., From Kirtland to Salt Lake City, p. 221.
10 Frontier Guardian, Juna 25, 1950.
11 Little, James A., From Kirtland to Salt Lake City, pp. 227-228.
12 Frontier Guardian, November 14, 1851.

13　Millennial Star, November 13, 1852. Also Little, James A., From Kirtland to Salt Lake City, p. 237.

14　Jensen, Andrew, Contributor XIII, 83.

15　Deseret News, Volume I:110-112. Some spectacular stories have been told with reference to the supposed wealth of the Company. In "The Latter-day Saints" by Kaufman and Kaufman, p. 60, appears the following, "The Perpetual Emigrating Fund mentioned by the Examiner was indeed a fact. It was established in 1849 ostensibly to enable only' indigent converts to emigrate to the promised land. At its start three and a half tons of gold were laid aside for the fund's beginning, gold gathered in the mining camps of the Rocky Mountains and the Sierras, and equal to about 376,320 pounds. That done, donations and taxations kept up the amount."

16　Deseret News I:114. Brigham Young commented after the organization had been given legal form: "It is now in a shape that makes it comprehensible; we have the legal right from the authorities of the State to pursue lawfully, a system to gather the poor."

17　Deseret News, I:129.

18　Deseret News, I:112. On September 11th, "Daniel H. Wells presented a bill for an ordinance to incorporate the Perpetual Emigrating Poor Fund Company, which was read and accepted and referred to a select committee of five, namely:　D. H. Wells, G. A. Smith, P. P. Pratt, W. Snow, and E. T. Benson." The act of incorporation was confirmed by the Territory of Utah on October 4, 1851, when the Territory replaced the Provisional State.

19　Deseret News, I:119. An Ordinance Incorporating the Perpetual Emigrating Company.

"SECTION 1.　Be it ordained by the General Assembly of the State of Deseret, that the General, or Special Conference of the Church of Jesus Christ of Latter-day Saints, to be called at such time and place as the First Presidency of said Church shall appoint — is hereby authorized to elect by a majority, a company of not less than thirteen men, one of whom shall be designated as their President, and the others Assistants.

SECTION 2.　This Company is hereby made and constituted a body corporate, under the name and style of the Perpetual Emigrating Company; and shall have perpetual succession, and may have and use a common seal, which they may alter at pleasure.

SECTION 3.　This Company, under the name and style aforesaid, shall have power to sue, and be sued, plead, and be impleaded, defend, and be defended, in all Courts of law or equity, and in all actions whatsoever; to purchase, receive, and hold property, real and personal; to receive, either by donation, on deposit, or otherwise, money, gold dust, grain, horses, mules, cows, oxen, sheep, young stock of all kinds, as well as any and every kind of valuables, or property, whatsoever; to emit bills of credit and exchange; to sell, lease, convey, or dispose of property, real or personal, and finally to do and perform any and all such acts as shall be necessary and proper for the interest, protection, convenience, or benefit of said Company.

SECTION 4.　A majority of said Company at Head Quarters shall form a quorum, to do business, and shall elect from their number a

Secretary, Treasurer, and Recorder; and shall have power to elect and appoint all other officers and agents necessary to transact the business of said Company.

SECTION 5. It shall be the duty of the President of the Company to superintend all the business of the Company; He shall also sign all certificates, bills, vouchers, as well as all other papers and documents pertaining to the general business of the Company, which shall be countersigned by the Secretary.

SECTION 6. It shall be the duty of the Recorder, to record in a fair and legible hand, all the general business transactions of the Company, in good and sufficient books suitable for the purpose, which he shall procure at the expense of the Company, and safely keep and preserve the same.

He shall also make a faithful and accurate record of all donations to the Fund, of the names of persons donating, the amount, kind of property, etc., in books separate and apart from any other entries, and safely keep and preserve all the books and papers of the Company, the said books being free to the inspection and examination of all persons interested.

SECTION 7. The President and Assistants shall individually give bond and security in a sum of not less than ten thousand dollars, to be approved by the First Presidency of said Church, and filed in the General Church Recorder's office.

SECTION 8. The Secretary, Treasurer, and Recorder, and all other officers or agents appointed by the Company, shall give bond and security to be approved by the President of the Company, and filed in the Company Recorder's office; and all the Company shall be responsible for the acts of all officers and agents so appointed.

SECTION 9. There shall be a general settlement of all business transactions of the Company, so far as returns are received from abroad, as often as once in each year; and it shall be the duty of all the officers and agents, to make out correct returns of all their transactions, and deliver or transmit the same to the Secretary of said Company, on or before the first day of December in each year; and it shall be the duty of the President of the Company to produce or exhibit a manifest of the same, and file it in the Recorder's office; as also a copy of the same in the General Church Recorder's office, as soon as practicable thereafter.

SECTION 10. It shall be the duty of the Treasurer to keep an accurate account of all money or property received and disbursed by him and make returns as herein before directed.

SECTION 11. The Company being collectively responsible for their own officers and agents, shall have the power of substituting others in their places or dismissing them or any of them from office, and it shall be the duty of all persons so superseded or dismissed to pay over and to pass into the hands of their respective successors, or the Company, all money, property, books, papers, accounts, of every name and nature, belonging, or in any way pertaining to the business of said Company.

SECTION 12. It shall be the duty of the Company to procure wagons, cattle, mules, horses etc. as shall be necessary for the purpose of the emigration of the Poor; who shall also have the general direction of all matters and things pertaining to said emigration, while abroad; and he or they shall also make their annual returns as herein before directed.

SECTION 13. The entire proceeds of the business of this Company shall inure to the Perpetual Emigrating Fund for the Poor, whether arising from donations, insurance, deposits, exchange, increased value of property, or in any other way or manner whatsoever. And the general business of the Company shall be devoted, under the direction and supervision of the First Presidency of the Church, to promote, facilitate, and accomplish the Emigration of the Poor.

SECTION 14. The members of this Company shall hold their offices at the pleasure of the conference herein before mentioned; but the First Presidency of said Church shall have power to fill all vacancies that may occur by death, removal, or otherwise; and all such persons so appointed, shall qualify as hereinbefore directed, and hold their offices until superseded by an election.

SECTION 15. No officer, agent or member of the Company shall be permitted to retain in his hands any portion of the funds of the Company, as compensation, but shall receive such remuneration as shall be awarded him or them upon settlement with the Board of President and Assistants.

SECTION 16. All persons receiving assistance from the Perpetual Emigrating Fund for the Poor, shall reimburse the same in labor or otherwise, as soon as their circumstances will admit.

SECTION 17. The Islands of the Great Salt Lake, known as Stansbury's Island, and Antelope Island, are hereby reserved and appropriated for the exclusive use and benefit of said Company, for the keeping of stock, etc."

20 Compiled Laws of Utah, (1876) 233-237, Sections 556-568. Bancroft, H. H. History of Utah, 415.

21 The Bowery was an open air structure covered with branches which served as a forerunner to the now well-known Mormon Tabernacle.

22 Deseret News I:114, 127. Young's selection for the presidency was not done as a matter of course, for five other names were presented in nomination, all of them outstanding leaders, namely: George A. Smith, Daniel H. Wells, Willard Richards, John Smith, and Newel K. Whitney.

12

Fishers of Men

THE abandonment of Nauvoo in 1846 had brought disruption generally to the organized forces of "the gathering." Proselyting had come to a temporary halt while the Church conserved its energies for survival in the wilderness. But scarcely had it found a resting place in the Great Basin before it sprang back with all its former vigor to rally its bewildered forces scattered through America and England.

In the spring of 1848, before Brigham Young returned with his second company to the Salt Lake Valley, the broken missionary organization was repaired. Wilford Woodruff was sent to preside over the Mormon following in Canada, Jesse C. Little to the Eastern States, and John Brown to the Southern States. Ezra T. Benson, Amasa M. Lyman and others were sent as roving missionaries to urge the gathering to the west. Orson Pratt was sent to preside in England and Orson Hyde was appointed to take charge of the exiles in Iowa until they could be removed to Salt Lake Valley.

The Mormons held annual "General Conferences" on April 6th, the anniversary of their organization. These yearly events, when the faithful gathered from far and near to sit at the feet of their prophets, were supplemented with semi-annual conferences in October. Such gatherings served as convenient contacts between the hierarchy and those who sustained them. They were made occasions for launching important undertakings by the Church.

The fall conference, held in Salt Lake City in 1849, not only brought the Perpetual Emigrating Fund into being to redeem the pledge of the Nauvoo Covenant, but was also productive of other measures which were to have far reaching effects on "the gathering." Heretofore, overseas missionary activity had been confined to the British Isles and immigration had been limited to English speaking peoples. But the message of "the Restoration" which was for "every nation, kindred, tongue and people" could not longer be restrained. It was now ready to move into continental Europe and henceforth the membership of "Zion" would assume an international pattern.

Men, carefully chosen for the new advance, were appointed at the conference and charged to hasten their journey to the waiting nations[1]. Less than two weeks later thirty-five missionaries started eastward with twelve wagons, one carriage, forty-two horses and mules. This expedition of 1849, as well as similar companies of succeeding years, presented a strange contrast to the general migrations of the mid-century. Their point of departure was on the very edge of the gold fields which Mormons had helped to discover[2]. A substantial amount of the yellow metal had found its way to the Salt Lake Valley with members of the Mormon Battalion. But it did not greatly disturb the Kingdom. There were some who yielded to its lure and joined the swelling hordes who fought their frenzied way across the continent to worship the golden calf. But "Zion," as a whole, had larger vision. Its modern prophet joined with those of the past in proclaiming that only human values count and the Kingdom had been entrusted into their hands for the purpose of saving men.

So these "latter day" missionaries turned their backs upon California and pushed their way into the dust clouds raised by gold seekers and emerged at the eastern end of the trail. They differed from the west-bound caravans no less in purpose than in direction. Instead of material wealth they sought the promotion of a great spiritual enterprise — the building of the Kingdom of God on earth. In that spirit they spread abroad as fishers of men to declare His word and to gather His children.

From the middle of the century until the death of Brigham Young in 1877, two thousand, six hundred and fifty-six men, married and single, responded to the call of "the Presiding Brethren" and set out to share with the world the message of deliverance which had already brought them out of "Babylon." Their far-flung activities carried them to thirty nations and to every continent.

Erastus Snow and his friends who had been sent to Scandinavia, were not long in Copenhagen before the message of the restoration began to spread — first among the working classes in the larger centers and then through the countryside. By September 15, 1850, a "branch" of the Church was organized in Copenhagen with fifty members, and the following month another was effected in Aalborg. However, John E. Forsgren, who had been assigned to Sweden had already rounded the Scandinavian peninsula and sailed up the Baltic to convert his brother, along with nineteen others in the town of Gefle. These baptisms were a modest beginning to hundreds which were soon to follow. A year later missionaries landed in Norway to baptize their first converts and organize the first Norwegian Branch. A conference of the Scandinavian mission was held in Copenhagen on August 16, 1851. During his stay of twenty-two months in Denmark, Erastus Snow baptized six hundred converts.

In the southern countries there was less favorable response to the message of the Mormons. Nevertheless, branches began to appear in widely scattered areas, including Paris, Geneva, Hamburg, Northern Italy, Gibraltar and the Island of Malta. Four years after the arrival of the missionaries on the Continent, the "European Mission" embraced sixty-seven districts, seven hundred and thirty-eight branches, with a total of 32,627 members. Of these 29,441 were in England, 2,447 in Scandinavia, two hundred ninety-nine in Switzerland and Italy, three hundred and twenty-six in the French Mission, fifty-six in Germany, forty on Malta and eighteen at Gibraltar[3].

The Scandinavian response to the message of "the Restoration" was divided between prejudice against the new religion and a warm feeling for the land of its origin. In the end the sentiment in favor of America tempered religious prejudice sufficiently to afford a hearing, and soon the "land of promise" assumed a double significance. America, as a land of opportunity, now became, in a spiritual sense, a "land favored above all others." As converts increased the spirit of the gathering soon manifested itself and the Mormon stream became increasingly important in the Scandinavian emigration to America.

On January 31, 1852, nine Mormon converts sailed from Copenhagen bound for America via England. Erastus Snow followed on March 4th together with nineteen additional members who had yielded to the urge to flee to Zion. These twenty-eight Scandinavian Mormons embarked on the ship Italy, which sailed from Liverpool on March 11th. Two months later they arrived in New Orleans. An additional five months brought them to the Valley of the Great Salt Lake on October 16th.

In January of the following year a sufficiently large number of Scandinavian emigrants assembled in England to justify a separate ship for their transportation and two hundred and ninety-seven of them sailed from Liverpool on January 16th under leadership of John E. Forsgren. This was the first of eight shiploads of Mormon converts sailing from Liverpool that season. The balance included a total of 2,289 Englishmen. In 1854 when two shiploads of Scandinavians, totaling 678, sailed for America, other nations began a modest contribution to the "Zion" movement. That year's immigration included thirty-three German, fifty-eight Swiss and forty French[4].

The press was quickly called into Mormon proselyting service. The *Millenial Star* was launched in 1849 in Manchester by Parley P. Pratt. It was the first foreign publication of the Church. The prospectus announced:

"Its columns will be devoted to the spread of the fullness of the gospel — the restoration of the ancient principles of Christianity — the gathering of Israel — the rolling forth of the Kingdom of God among the nations — the signs of the times — the fulfillment of prophecy, recording the judgments of God as they befall the nations, . . . in short, whatever is shown forth indicative of the coming of the 'Son of Man' and ushering in of His universal reign upon the earth."

On the front cover the poet missionary inscribed the spirit of "the Restoration":

"The morning breaks the shadows flee: Lo! Zion's standard is unfurled!
The dawning of a brighter day majestic rises on the world.
The clouds of error disappear before the rays of truth divine;
The glory, bursting from afar, wide o'er the nations soon will shine.
The Gentile fulness now comes in, and Israel's blessings are at hand;
Lo! Judah's remnant, cleans'd from sin shall in their promised Canaan stand.
Jehovah speaks! Let earth give ear, and Gentile nations turn and live!
His mighty arm is making bare, His covenant people to receive.
Angels from Heaven and truth from earth have met and both have record borne:
That Zion's light is bursting forth, to cheer the children's glad return."

Subscriptions to the *Millennial Star,* which continues to the present as a weekly publication, rose with increasing membership of the Church. Orson Pratt, presiding over the British Mission, wrote in March of 1850: "It is now over six years and a half since our arrival in this country; during this period the Kingdom of God has rolled forth with unparalleled success; its numbers have increased in Great Britain alone, from eighteen thousand to nearly twenty-nine thousand souls (increase of 11,000). Two thousand of this number have emigrated to America. The circulation of the Star, during the same period has increased from thirty-seven hundred to fifty-seven hundred. The great reduction proposed in the price of the Star will, no doubt, have a tendency to soon quadruple its circulation[5]." Before he turned Mission affairs over to his successor Franklin D. Richards in 1851, the Star subscriptions had risen to twenty-two thousand.

Similar missionary publications appeared in America. Also, "Stars" were printed in the tongue of each foreign country invaded. Added to this was the task of translating the Book of Mormon and other literature into the various languages. But the linguistic barrier was successfully hurdled as printed copies of this strange book appeared in Danish in 1851; Welsh, German, French and Italian in 1852; Hawaiian, 1855; Swedish, 1878; Spanish, 1886, Maori, 1889; Dutch, 1890; Samoan, 1903; Tahitian, 1904; Turkish, 1905; and Japanese in 1909.

The nations of Europe responded to the message of the gathering as they had ears to hear. Latin peoples of Catholic faith were not responsive, but the Protestant nations in the north heard and contributed liberally to the "building of the Kingdom." Of course there was resistance to the Mormon invasion and missionaries, as well as converts, suffered indignities and persecution, including mobbings, imprisonment and banishment. But the message of "the restoration" continued to spread and with it the spirit of "the gathering." Thousands heard, believed, and joined the emigration companies that trickled out of the various fatherlands to converge into an international stream at Liverpool. Thenceforth in the long and arduous journey to Zion, they learned to submerge nationality in the larger meaning of the Kingdom. Thus the missionaries of the Restoration sought out "one of a city and two of a family" to "gather scattered Israel into the Kingdom of the Latter Days[6]."

Of interest among the "Mormon ships" which sailed from

Liverpool in 1852 was the "Rockaway" which carried, in addition to thirty Mormons, a cargo of machinery purchased by John Taylor for the manufacture of sugar in Utah. The missionaries of 1849 who went as "fishers of men" had been instructed by Brigham Young to keep an eye open for every enterprise which might add to the social and economic welfare of the Kingdom. Taylor became interested in the sugar beet industry of northern France. Returning to England he organized the "Deseret Manufacturing Company" and arranged with Faucett, Preston and Company for manufacture of machinery at a cost of $12,500. This, together with five hundred bushels of beet seed, made up the Rockaway cargo. The freight arrived in New Orleans in April and thence re-shipped up the Mississippi to Fort Leavenworth. Here it was loaded on fifty-two wagons for transportation across the plains, by means of two hundred oxen. The wagons proved to be too light and, breaking down, were replaced by forty others of the heavy Santa Fe type. Many of the original wagons were given to the poor immigrants who could not provide their own transportation across the plains.

The ships of the North Atlantic did not carry all of the "latter-day" couriers. Hundreds of Mormon missionaries headed westward across the Pacific and southward to the lands down under. Already they were in the Hawaiian Islands. In June of 1851, George Q. Cannon, with a number of associates began baptizing converts on a large scale and a branch was organized. The natives' response was so hearty that three years later the Hawaiian members began to concentrate on the single island of Lanai which had been designated as a gathering place for them.

John Murdock and Charles Wendell commenced operations in New South Wales, Australia, 1851, and another outpost of Zion was established. William Wallis was sent from England to Calcutta, where, assisted by Joseph Richards, he succeeded in assembling a branch of forty Europeans and three hundred natives. On November 8, 1851, Parley P.

Pratt and Rufus Allen arrived in Valparaiso, Chile, to introduce the Gospel of the Restoration to that land, but soon
returned without success. Finally, on August 28, 1852, one
hundred and six missionaries were called at a special conference in Salt Lake to bolster the several far flung missions
of the Church. Their assignments included: six to the
United States; four to Nova Scotia and other North American British provinces; two to British Guiana; four to the
West Indies; thirty-nine to Great Britain; one to France;
four to Germany; three to Prussia; four to Gibraltar; one
to Denmark; two to Norway; nine to Calcutta and Hindu-
tan; four to China; three to Siam; nine to the Hawaiian
Islands; three to the Cape of Good Hope in South Africa
and ten to Australia.

The latter field responded by sending back to Zion small
companies of Australian saints during the next two successive
years. The islands of the Pacific, Australia and South Africa
were added to North America and Europe as promising
fields for harvest. But Continental Asia remained unrespon-
sive. Proselyting there was discontinued in 1855.

The Church of the Latter-day Saints took its responsibilty
to preach the message of the Restoration so seriously that its
efforts in proportion to numbers and circumstances were
singular in Christian history. In July 1851, while penetration of Asia was just beginning the First Presidency wrote:
"During the twenty-one years since the organization of the
Church, the Gospel has been preached in Europe, Asia,
Africa, America, the East and West Indies, and many islands
and clusters of islands in the Atlantic and Pacific; many
thousands of saints have gathered from various parts of the
earth unto Zion; to America; the land which God has pointed
out as a place of safety for His people, in these last days; and
which will prove a place of refuge for kings, and princes,
and nobles, and honorable men of the earth of all nations,
whether rich or poor, who are disposed to seek refuge therein, when the overflowing scourges of God's wrath shall

destroy the nations, and depopulate the earth on account of the multiplied infidelity and abominations of the inhabitants thereof. The unparalleled spread of the Gospel in so short a space and time, and the rapid gathering of the Saints, is another token of Messiah's near approach[7]."

1 John Taylor, together with Curtis C. Bolton and John Peck, was assigned to open a mission in France and Germany; Lorenzo Snow, assisted by Joseph Toronto, T. B. H. Stenhouse, and Jobez Woodward, to begin operations in Switzerland and Italy; Erastus Snow with Peter A. Hansen and John Forsgren to invade Scandinavia; and Addison Pratt, James Brown, and Hiram H. Blackwell to extend operations already begun in the Society Islands. In addition to these, Franklin D. Richards was appointed to introduce the Perpetual Emigrating Fund to England and succeed Orson Pratt as President of that mission.

2 Members of the Mormon Battalion returning from California at the close of the Mexican war participated in the discovery of gold at Sutter's Mill.

3 Jensen, Andrew, Church Chronology, p. 52.

4 Jensen, Andrew, Church Chronology — as per dates given.

5 Millennial Star XII:89.

6 Jeremiah III:4.

7 Fifth General Epistle, Brigham Young Journal History, July, 1851.

13

By Sea

THE Perpetual Emigrating Fund Company was introduced into a program already well under way. Thousands of Mormon converts would have continued to find their way to Zion had no emigrating fund been created at all. The special mission of the Fund, was to assist the poor. It added greatly to the total number of those who came out of "Babylon" to participate in the building of the Kingdom. In addition to this direct contribution the company aided the migrating movement generally as those who paid for their own transportation shared in the benefits of its routine work. As its agents went about chartering ships, buying supplies and equipment, and exercising general supervision over routes of travel and the safety of the emigrants, the company became the core of the whole gathering movement for nearly four decades[1].

The general plan of migration to Zion included two major divisions. First there was the shipping agency in England, charged with the task of assembling the emigrants and providing for their safe passage overseas. The President of the British Mission usually served as shipping agent. Second, there was the receiving agency on the American frontier whose responsibility was to account for the newly arrived immigrants and provide for their continued journey overland to Utah. This agency included a representative at the port of entry and another at the outfitting place on the frontier. Operations in America varied with changing ports of entry, changing modes of transportation, and shifting frontier stations. In general the procedure was the same for the "P. E. F." emigrants as for the "independents."

Without special reference to the fund the following reviews the salient features of the emigration system as it transported thousands of foreign converts from Liverpool to deliver them, eight to ten months later, in the Salt Lake Valley.

Subscribers to the Millennial Star which had wide circulation among the British Saints, read the following in a winter issue:

"The John Cummins is chartered for us, and is to sail on the twentieth of February, 1842. Immediate application should be made by those who wish a passage. Passage costs from L3 15 s to L4 including provisions. Passengers bring their own bedding and cooking utensils; and all luggage goes free. On arriving at New Orleans, a passage can be obtained up the Mississippi River, fifteen hundred miles by steamer, for fifteen shillings and freight free, as we have learned by letter from Elder Joseph Fielding who sailed with 200 passengers in the Tyrean last September."

Applicants responding to *this* notice in 1842 were thinking of emigration to Nauvoo and expecting there to meet Joseph Smith. However, those who read the following, a decade later, were looking forward to meeting Brigham Young in the Salt Lake Valley:

"Notice of first ship of season will sail early in January 1853. Applications to be accompanied by name, age, occupation, and nativity of applicant and deposit of one pound. Parties will provide own bedding, cooking utensils, etc[2]."

Such announcements appeared with increasing frequency in the Star as the gathering increased in momentum. The British agent chartered ships as applications for passage justified. Sometimes these were for exclusive Mormon use. Transportation rates depended upon what ships could be chartered for, but generally Mormon credit was good and the agent was in a position to deal favorably with shipping companies. Occasionally large numbers from a single district in England made application for passage. Under such circumstances, arrangements were also made with railways for reduced rates to Liverpool.

The conduct of these Mormon emigrations from Europe was as patriarchal as the early church itself. Always missionaries escorted the departing members to Liverpool and once in the port of embarkation the passengers were ushered immediately on board ship. Not for a moment were they left to the mercy of "runners" or professional shipping agents[3]. Watchmen were appointed to stand guard while the vessel lay in harbor to prevent any who did not belong from passing among them.

Mormon Companies became known for their heavy luggage. Mechanics and other craftsmen, who made up a large percentage of the emigrants, brought all available tools with them much to the dismay of the ships' captains. Some complained that the ship lay at least an inch lower in the water on account of this excess baggage.

When all were on board the Mormon Agent arrived to organize them for their overseas journey. First he appointed a president to preside over the entire company which varied in size from occasional small groups to four and five hundred. The president, together with two counsellors were usually selected from returning missionaries and were presented to the company for a sustaining vote. The presidency of the company now proceeded to divide the ship into "wards" or "branches" with bishops or presiding elders and assigning to each a particular part of the ship.

The presiding elders soon acquainted the members of their respective wards with customary procedure on such journeys. After rising at an appointed early hour the first duty was to thoroughly clean their portion of the ship and dispose of all refuse overboard. Then, they would assemble for prayer before breakfast. This latter, the emigrants prepared themselves with cooking apparatus provided by the ship. Beyond the barest necessities for preparation of meals, the passengers provided their own utensils, as they also did their bedding. Breakfast over, and necessary clearing away of dishes, etc. accomplished, the day belonged to each passenger to divide between minor duties and amusements as he chose. At eight or nine at night prayer was again conducted in each ward and all retired. Except in cases of married couples and children, the sexes were berthed apart in strict compliance with provisions of emigration laws[4].

The routine of the Mormon emigrants on board ship was regarded as superior to that of passengers generally. So unusual was their conduct in contrast with that of current emigration practice that no less a writer than Charles Dickens was led to visit one of their ships to make first hand observations. He came away with the following comment:

> "Two or three Mormon agents stood ready to hand them (the emigrants) on to the inspector, and to hand them forward when they had passed. By what successful means, a special aptitude for organization had been infused into these people, I am, of course, unable to report. But I know that, even now, there was no disorder, hurry or difficulty . . . I afterwards learned that a dispatch was sent home by the captain before he struck out into the wide Atlantic, highly extolling the behavior of these emigrants, and the perfect order and propriety of all their social arrangements . . . I went on board their ship to bear testimony against them, if they deserved it, as I fully believed they would; to my great astonishment they did not deserve it, and my predispositions and tendencies must not affect me as an honest witness. I went over the Amazon's side, feeling it impossible to deny that, so far, some remarkable influence has produced a remarkable result which better known influences have often missed[5]."

Standards of health and morals, as well as of ordinary comforts, maintained by the Latter-day Saints exceeded those of legal enactments regulating emigration between Great Britain and America. The Passenger Act of 1852 required a minimum of food provisions for seventy or eighty days depending on the time of sailing: The weekly ration for each adult, with one half the amount for minors, was as follows: Two and one half pounds of bread or biscuit, not inferior in quality to navy biscuit, one pound of wheat flour, five pounds oatmeal, two pounds rice, half pound sugar, two ounces tea, two ounces salt, also three quarts of water daily for each passenger." Substitutes were permitted, including potatoes, beef or pork, preserved meat, dried fish, split peas and rice.

In addition to the above, the Mormon companies were furnished for the voyage with two and a half pounds of sago, three pounds of butter, two pounds of cheese and one pint of vinegar for each adult and half the amount for those under fourteen. Such provisions, in many cases exceeded the living standards to which the emigrants were accustomed at home.

Another advantage in favor of the Mormon system was the provision that all food not consumed upon arrival at New Orleans belonged to the passengers and was not returned to England as in general practice. Often favorable sailing winds provided them with considerable food supplies upon arrival. For instance, the John M. Wood, sailing in the spring of 1854, left the Perpetual Emigrating Fund passengers with 150 pounds of tea, nineteen barrels of biscuits, five barrels of oatmeal, four bags of rice, and three barrels of pork[6].

Two passenger acts — British and American — passed in 1855, raised the standards of the earlier law. They provided for more room per passenger, better dietary scale, and improved health requirements. These last provided for supplies and a doctor and two cooks when the number of adults exceeded three hundred. Since the British act more than covered all of the provisions of the American, the Mormon Agents generally complied with the former.

The Mormon shipping operations attracted the attention of State departments, as well as journalists. While the United States and Great Britain were engaged in revising their immigration laws, the latter had occasion to call upon the Mormon Agent for assistance. A committee of the House of Commons sent for Samuel W. Richards, presiding in Britain in 1854, asking that he appear before it to be questioned relative to Latter-day Saint emigration activities. A

London correspondent of the Cambridge Independent Press
gave the following picture of the hearings:

> "On Tuesday I heard a rather remarkable examination
> before the committee of the House of Commons. The
> witness was none other than the supreme authority in Eng-
> land of the Mormonites, and the subject upon which he was
> giving information was the mode in which the emigration
> to Utah, Great Salt Lake, is conducted. The curious per-
> sonage is named Richards; he is an American by birth; is
> a dark rather good looking man: I should judge of fair
> education, and certainly of more than average intelligence.
> He gave himself no airs, but was so respectful in his de-
> meanor and ready in his answers, that, at the close of the
> examination, he received the thanks of the committee in
> rather a marked manner. According to his statements, about
> 2,600 Mormonite emigrants leave Liverpool during the
> first three months of every year. They have ships of
> their own, and are under the care of a president. The
> average cost of a journey to Utah is about 30 pounds —
> that is, to steerage passengers. On arriving at New Orleans,
> they are received by another president, who returns to
> Mr. Richards an account of the state in which he found
> the ship, etc. They have then 3,000 miles to go, and after
> leaving the Mississippi, 1,000 miles are traversed overland
> in wagons. . . . There is one thing which, in the emigration
> committee of the House of Commons, they can do — viz.,
> teach christian ship owners how to send poor people decent-
> ly, cheaply, and healthfully across the Atlantic[7]."

The Edinburgh Review for January 1862, made this report: "The select committee of the House of Commons on
emigrant ships for 1854 summoned the Mormon agent and
passenger broker before it and came to the conclusion that
no ships under the provisions of the "Passenger's Act" could
be depended upon for comfort and security in the same
degree as those under his administration. The Mormon ship
is a family under strong and accepted discipline, with every
provision for comfort, decorum and internal peace[8]."

The regular emigration season extended over January
and February with New Orleans as the earlier port of dis-

embarkation. Early departures were urged in order to escape the unhealthy seasons on the Mississippi and Missouri rivers. It was also desirable for those who contemplated a "through journey" to arrive in the states in time to allow for the overland journey before winter set in.

Close confinement on a sailing vessel tossing upon the broad Atlantic for eight or ten weeks demanded every precaution against all that such a situation might breed. Ordinarily the ship's captain found it necessary to rule with an iron hand as all the changing moods of the sea were reflected in his human cargo. But somehow these Latter-day Saint companies seemed different. It was not unusual that he relaxed his vigilance and before the journey's end had granted privileges and concessions quite beyond the regular practice. The following excerpts, from eye witnesses, present a composite picture — reflecting the general spirit of the "Zion bound" emigrants.

"The splendid ship Metoka, Captain M'Laren, sailed from Liverpool, September 5, 1843 under favorable circumstances. The Saints on board gave expression to their feelings in various hymns which they sang as the vessel was towed into the river. The ship which was admirably adapted for passengers, together with the respectable appearance of the emigrants appeared very much to surprise the bystanders, who were compelled to acknowledge that they had not often witnessed the departure of such a people[9]."

Wrote William Kay on March 9th, 1843: ... "The Captain and the crew declared they never experienced such a passage before; but such a captain and crew for kindness I believe could scarcely be met with; his liberality exceeds all that ever came under our notice. ... The cabin and its provisions have been at the service of all who stood in need of them, and the captain has with his own hand ministered unto the necessities of all who required it. ... We have had two deaths on board. ... We have had regular meetings or prayer morning and evening, and three times each Lord's day, administering the sacrament in the afternoon. The Saints generally have shown a willingness to give heed to the counsel from myself and Brothers Hall and Cuerden[10]."

However, there was not always unbroken peace in the Mormon emigrant ranks as Parley P. Pratt reflects in an earlier report. "We had a tedious passage of ten weeks and some difficulties, murmurings and rebellions; but the Saints on board were called together, and chastened and reproved sharply, which brought them to repentance. We then humbled ourselves and called on the Lord and he sent a fair wind and brought us into port in time to save us from starvation[11]."

Charles R. Savage wrote, following a crossing a few years later: "We left Liverpool on Wednesday, December 12, at seven A. M. and had a fine run down the channel, sighted Cape Clear on the Friday morning following and had mild weather with a fair wind for three days after. During this time we had leisure to devise plans for the maintenance of order and cleanliness during the voyage. Notwithstanding that our company consisted of Danes, Norwegians, Swedes, Icelanders, Italians, English, Irish, and Scotch, the rules adopted proved efficacious in maintaining a strict entente cordiale among us all. The Saints were by the sound of the trumpet called to prayer morning and evening. Meetings were also frequently held in the Danish, English and Italian languages during the voyage. On the whole we enjoyed ourselves first rate, notwithstanding the gales and hurricanes we experienced. . . . We had much sickness on board from the breaking out of measles, which caused many deaths among the Danish, chiefly among the children. In the English and Italian companies we lost three children. The weather got worse after crossing the Banks, so much so, that we were driven into the Gulf Stream three times and many of our sailors were frost bitten. Our captain got superstitious on account of the long voyage and ordered that there should be no singing on board. The mate said that all ships that had preachers on board were *always* sure of a bad passage[12]."

James Linforth wrote in 1853, "After looking around the good ship and taking a peep at the passengers who were to be my companions during the voyage to New Orleans, I selected a berth quite to my taste in the second cabin. A small house on deck fitted up with single berths for eight persons. . . . The steerage passengers, of whom there were three hundred, were composed one half of English and the other half of Welsh causing a confusion of tongues quite amusing until one was personally interested in what was said. They however managed very well and most heartily and lustily helped each other . . . Soon the land grew less distinct and as it became more and more grey there rose above all other sounds voices mingling in the song "Yes my native land I love thee." Then the deck became deserted, as the motion of the ship began to affect the heads and stomachs of men and women hitherto used only to steady terra firma. . . . The next day the necessary instructions were given to the emigrants relative to the regulations deemed necessary for their comfort, health, and safety. The married men and women had already been placed in the center of the ship, and the unmarried portion at the two extremities — the males at the bow and the females at the stern. The whole of the passengers were divided into districts of equal numbers with a president . . . etc. The presidents of districts also had to see that no principle of morality was violated; to meet their districts at 8 P. M.; to pray with them and give any general instruction thought necessary; and to daily meet in council with the president of the whole company. . . [13]."

William Howell, who presided over the Mormons sailing on the Olympus in March 1851, reported in part as follows: " . . . dancing billows pleasing to sight extending around us for miles the ship steadily running her course Zionward, the helmsman keeping her bows in a direct line with the setting sun. On the poop I observed a number of our young brothers and sisters listening with attention to an instructive

lecture on the science of grammar, delivered by old Father
Waddington, who Diogenes life, sat in the midst of his
pupils asking them various questions. . . . The whole length
of the deck was crowded with interesting groups worthy of
an artist's pencil; in one place I observed one of the young
sisters teaching others the art of knitting lace in various patterns; opposite on the larboard side of the vessel, a number
of mothers amusing their little ones, at the same time con-
versing with one another with grateful hearts, about the
goodness of God, in delivering them with their families from
the confusion and poverty of Babylon, that often caused
their hearts to fail within them, but now going to their homes
in Zion, containing peaceful habitations, sure dwellings and
quiet resting places. . . . The brethren sat in various groups
here and there, some singing, some reading the Bible, Book
of Mormon, Doctrine and Covenants, Millennial Star, Voice
of Warning, Spencer's Letters, with Brother Orson Pratt's
profound philosophical works, a library more valuable in
the estimation of the Saints than all the gold of California.
. . . Some females in groups were partaking out of various
dishes . . . for the sea appetite is sharp, the little children . . .
looking up to the faces of their parents with lamb-like innocence just as if they said, 'We are happy indeed[14].' "

Schools were conducted particularly for the children in
the day time in which English and French were taught. The
curriculum was widened and varied with the hobbies and
interests of the teachers. In the evening lectures were given
at which the adult company gathered around the speakers
on the deck floor. Among the subjects which received
consideration were astronomy, geography, agriculture and
experiences of the missionaries, some of whom had travelled
considerably.

But the scenes were not always as peaceful as here por-
trayed. Wilson G. Nowers, passenger on the same ship
Olympus added to the Howell narrative: "The cloud increased rapidly . . . By this time the outrigger sails were

all hauled down, and the men were engaged in close reefing the main topsail, when the squall struck the ship, causing her to tremble and reel like a drunkard. This proved to be as the captain had expected, a regular white squall, the fury of which was such that it carried the foremast overboard, and seriously sprung the mainmast at the decks. . . . Shortly before midnight the captain called Mr. Rogers . . . then the second mate, ' . . . You go to the captain of the Mormons and tell him from Captain Wilson that if the God of the Mormons can do anything to save the ship and the people, they had better be calling on him to do so for we are now sinking at the rate of a foot every hour, and if the storm continues we shall all be at the bottom of the ocean before daylight!' The order was given in such a tone that I heard distinctly what was said. . . . President Howell arose, dressed himself and called a few of the brethren (about twelve, myself included) to his side all of whom engaged in prayer . . . we continued our toils at the pumps, and at length the dawn of the Sabbath broke upon us clear bright and calm. Capt. Wilson acknowledged the miraculous hand of God in our preservation."

Then followed an unprecedented event on the open seas. Although baptisms were not uncommon with succeeding companies, only once did they approach the following in numbers involved. " . . . The sailors were busy righting up the tacking of the ship, and making preparations to rig a jury mast in place of the fore topmast that had been carried away, while the faces of all who came on deck beamed with joy and gratitude for their marvellous escape from a watery grave. The Saints attired themselves in clean clothing and newly shaved faces were seen for the first time since leaving Liverpool. There was talk of holding religious services for which purposes a delegation of the Saints waited on Captain Wilson in order to obtain his consent, which was readily granted. It was also proposed that an opportunity should be offered for those who desired it to have

the holy ordinance of baptism attended to, for several of
the non-Mormon emigrants had been converted to the faith
of the Saints and now expressed their conversion by presenting themselves as candidates for baptism, if only an opportunity could be obtained. Accordingly, one of the largest
barrels, in which fresh water had been stored for the use
of the passengers, was brought out and placed on deck, the
head of the same was removed, a short ladder of the ship's
gangway was placed by the side of the barrel and another
on the inside which gave easy access in and out for the candidates. The barrel was then filled with sea water to the
depth of a man's waist, and twenty-one persons of both sexes
were initiated by baptism into the Church. . . . Sometime
afterward about twenty others, all males, were baptized in
the ocean by means of a platform improvised by the side of
the ship. . . . In this manner the candidate was placed beneath the briny wave and brought forth therefrom, and
thus was the ordinance of baptism performed in the Atlantic
ocean where soundings were then unknown."

"During the voyage fifty persons were baptized, including
one baptism just prior to embarking and one after the arrival
of the company at New Orleans[15]."

Births, deaths, marriages and conversions to the faith were
common on the high seas as the "Mormon ships" continued
to speed the "gathering." During the voyage of the International in 1853, seven deaths, seven births and five marriages took place. This company of 425 Saints under presidency of Christopher Arthur rivaled that of the Olympus
two years previous in wholesale conversions. Arthur's report to Samuel W. Richards in England recounts in addition
to conversions, further incidents quite typical of these Mormon migrations. "Never," he begin, "since the days of
Old Captain Noah until the present emigration, has a more
respectful company of Saints crossed the wide deluge of
waters, to be freed from Babylon's corruption than has sailed
on the International. . . . I also appointed meetings to be

held every evening for worship, testimony bearing, teaching, etc., under prescribed order, which was carried fully into effect. . . . The Saints without exception have enjoyed a great amount of the spirit of God. . . . These things and the good conduct of the Saints, have had a happy result in bringing many to a knowledge of the truth. And I am now glad to inform you that we have baptized all on board, except three persons. We can number the Captain, first and second mates, with eighteen of the crew most of whom intend going right through to the Valley. The carpenter and eight of the seamen are Swedish, German and Dutch. There are two negroes and others from Otaheite, etc. Many of them have already testified to the truth of this work, and are rejoicing in anticipation in building up Zion. The others baptized were friends of the brethren. The number baptized in all is forty-eight since we left our native shores. . . .

"On the sixth of April we held the twenty third anniversary of the organization of the Church, which was in our circumstances a splendid affair. Early in the morning a goodly number of brethren assembled on the forecastle and fired rounds of musketry to usher in our festivities. At half past ten we marched in regular procession to the poop deck in following order: . . . Presidents and counsellors with sashes and white rosettes on their breasts, who took their seats with their backs to the main-mast. After them followed twelve young men appropriately robed, each with a white rod in his hand, with sashes, rosettes, etc. Then followed twelve young women in light dresses, each holding in her hand a scroll of white paper bearing the significant motto 'Utahs rights,' adorned with ribbon and white rosettes. The young men took their seats on the right hand of the Presidency, and the young women on the left. Then followed twelve old venerable men, dressed similar to the young men each carrying a Bible and a Book of Mormon in his hand, led by Father Waugh, who read portions out of each book, illustrative of this Latter-day work.

"We then took the Sacrament, and attended to the celebration of four marriages, which finished our forenoon service.

"At two o'clock we met and took our seats as formerly,
and after an address from the President, songs, speeches and
recitations commemorative of the occasion followed in due
order for three hours. Henry Maiben, from Brighton, composed and sang a song graphically and wittily portraying our
happy company and our progress from Liverpool.

"In the evening we met on the quarter deck, and skipped
the light fantastic toe until a late hour. During the whole
day everything was done with the highest decorum and I
can say, to the credit of the company, that a more harmonious
festival was never before held on the high seas. . . . "

So this composite company of Mormons, crossing the
Atlantic annually for a half century following 1840, arrived
at the mouth of the Mississippi River. James Linforth, already quoted on the high seas, now gives a final picture of
the arrival at New Orleans. "When we got up the last
morning before arriving at the anchorage at the mouth of
the Mississippi River, we found that the water had changed
from its deep ocean blue and was already contaminated by
the light muddy water of the Mississippi, and then when the
pilot boat came along side and the pilot got on board there
came in with him a feeling of security and satisfaction. He
was an assurance of safety, and seemed a sort of amphibious
animal to convey us from the dangers of the deep to the
security of terra firma.

"At the bar we found a ship (the Golconda) which had
started from England two weeks before us, detained at the
mouth of the river on account of the shallowness of the
water. We should have remained there too had not our
crafty old captain represented his ship as drawing less water
than she really did. The consequence was that in two or
three hours a huge Mississippi steamboat came alongside,
and having bound herself to us, very soon carried us safely

inside the bar. Then another boat of similar appearance took hold of us and we began to ascend the far famed and mighty Mississippi. . . . The distance from the bar to New Orleans is between ninety and one hundred miles, and the *Jersey* was four days in being towed up. For thirty miles from the entrance of the channel nothing is seen but muddy swamps and rushes, but above Fort Jackson the plantations commence. . . . The banks on the side of the river are very low, and as far up as New Orleans they present the same general appearance. We arrived at New Orleans on the twenty-first of March. (1853) . . .

"We had now entered the great Republic of the United States of North America, and had ascended from ninety to a hundred miles into the interior of the State of Louisiana, and our ship was moored along side the levee of the thriving city of New Orleans.

"Here the emigrants were met by Elder John Brown, the agent appointed by the Church authorities to receive and forward them to St. Louis. The gentleman rendered every assistance to the passengers in disembarking, etc., and acted in concert with George H. Halliday, who had led the company over the sea, in giving advice to the emigrants, and protecting them from depredations. . . . The advice given to the emigrants was so well observed that as a general thing they escaped the numerous evils with which all foreigners arriving at this place are beset.

"Owing to the promptness of Elder Brown, the steamboat John Simonds was soon engaged for the passengers. The passage for adults was two dollars and twenty-five cents, for children between fourteen and three years, half price, and those under three went free[16]."

When agent Brown had assisted the Mormon passengers in clearing the customs at New Orleans, helped them transfer their luggage to the Mississippi River steamer bound for St. Louis, and waved them farewell, he retired to his quarters to make the customary report of the company's arrival to the shipping agent in Liverpool. He felt fortunate indeed in this instance that none had been delayed in New Orleans due either to quarantine or the necessity of securing employment to provide funds for the river journey.

1 Millenial Star, XVIII: 713, "A prompt observance of these instructions, concerning deposits and remittance of funds, is as necessary on the part of those who intend to go through independent of the P. E. F. Company, but who wish our agent to have their outfit in readiness for them on their arrival on the frontiers, as it is for the P. E. Fund passengers."

2 Millennial Star, XV: 618.

3 Tullidge, Edward W., History of Salt Lake City, p. 100.

4 Bancroft, H. H., History of Utah, 418-319.

5 Dickens, Charles, Uncommercial Traveller, pp. 209, 213.

6 Jensen, Andrew, Contributor, XIII: 183.

7 Richards, Samuel W., Contributor, Vol. XI: 158-159.

8 Todd, Rev. John D. D., Sunset Land, p. 182, "A committee of the British Parliament has sat at the feet of the Mormons to learn their system of aiding emigration."
   Also Burton, R. F., City of the Saints, pp. 296-297.

9 Jensen, Andrew, Contributor, XII: 448.

10 Jensen, Andrew, Contributor, XII: 449.

11 Jensen, Andrew, Contributor, XII: 446.

12 Millennial Star, XVIII: 206.

13 Jensen, Andrew, Contributor: XIII, 460-461.

14 Jensen, Andrew, Contributor: XIII, 345.

15 Jensen, Andrew, Contributor: XIII, 345-349.

16 Linforth, James, Route from Liverpool to Great Salt Lake.

14

By Land

IF the "Zion" bound immigrant, arriving at New Orleans from Liverpool, entertained any impressions that he was nearing the end of his journey, he was doomed to disappointment. Ahead of him lay three more links in the wearisome journey all of which presented greater hazards than the sea voyage he had just completed. Immediately ahead lay the seven hundred mile journey up the Mississippi to St. Louis. This he usually negotiated by river steamer in a week. Then, assuming that conditions favored his immediate departure from that place, he took another river boat to the city nearest the designated "outfitting" rendezvous. Prior to 1852, the Mormons outfitted at Kanesville (later named Council Bluffs), a distance of nearly five hundred miles from St. Louis. This journey required about two weeks on the Missouri River[1]. Upon arriving at Kanesville the immigrant had come twelve hundred miles inland from New Orleans. Beyond that stretched the wagon trail of a thousand miles to the Salt Lake Valley.

The hazard of the inland journey, however, lay not in distance, but rather in the unhealthful climate surrounding the sluggish rivers. The annual death toll from cholera and other diseases on the river was appalling. It was to avoid this hazard, so far as possible, that Brigham Young ordered a change in the emigrant route. In 1854, he wrote to Franklin D. Richards, in charge of emigration in England:

> "You are aware of the sickness liable to assail our unacclimated brethren on the Mississippi River; hence I wish you to ship no more to New Orleans, but ship to Philadelphia, Boston, and New York, giving preference in the order named. Whenever you ship a company whether it be

small or large, be careful to forward to Elder John Taylor
at New York City, a correct list of the names of the persons
of each company with the occupation and approximate
amount of property or means and forward it in season for
Elder John Taylor to receive it before the company arrives
in port that he may be so advised as to be able to meet
them, or appoint some proper person to do so, and counsel
them immediately on landing as to the best course for each
and all in every company to pursue, whether to tarry for
a season or proceed to Cincinnati or its regions, etc.

"In case any should still choose to ship by New Orleans,
ship them from England no later than about the first of
December that they may be able to get off the rivers before
the sickly season sets in for many have died off with the
cholera and other diseases incident to the sickly season in
the rivers, and I do not wish the brethren to be so exposed as they have been. And counsel them to hurry up
the rivers and get off from them into Missouri and Iowa
to work, or onto the plains as the case may be before the
warm weather sets in[2]."

The report of the receiving agent at the port of debarka-
tion to the shipping agent in Liverpool might have appeared
to end all responsibility of the latter for the migrating companies. His charges were now off the high seas and safely
in the hands of the American outfitting agent. But the
British agent's duties went farther than this and his helping
hand was soon felt on the Mississippi frontier. Even before
the companies arrived in St. Louis his personal representative
sent from Liverpool, was cooperating with the frontier agent
in chartering boats and purchasing supplies and equipment
for the overland journey.

Then when the immigrants arrived at St. Louis they were
received by men of experience who catered to their immediate needs. Housing was provided in the city for those
who remained, either from choice to find temporary employment, or from necessity due to low water, or ice in the river.

Those who continued the journey without stopovers
found that the agent had already contracted for passage to
the outfitting place. Cost of transportation varied. For

example, William Empy, serving as agent in 1854, discovered to his embarrassment that freight charges, as well as passage on the steamer from St. Louis to Kansas City, had more than doubled in twelve months. The previous year such passage had been one dollar per capita: the transportation of luggage from twenty-five cents to fifty cents per hundred pounds. Freight on wagons, which were usually purchased in St. Louis or Cincinnati, ranged from four dollars to five dollars each. In 1854, passage had risen to three dollars and more; luggage up to two dollars per hundred pounds, and the cost of transporting wagons from ten to fifteen dollars each. The excessive rates were caused by low water in the Missouri River which made navigation difficult.

When the immigrant arrived at the frontier rendezvous he found his outfit waiting for him in accordance with his order, given in England. Perpetual Emigration Fund passengers also found arrangements made for their continued journey. They were assigned ten persons to a wagon. Each adult was allowed a hundred pounds of luggage, including beds and bedding. Half that amount was permitted passengers between ages ten and four. An outfit for crossing the plains consisted of one wagon, two yoke of oxen and at least two cows. Prices rose sharply as the demands of the California-Oregon migrations increased. In 1854, a yoke of oxen cost from seventy-five to one hundred dollars and cows cost twenty-five to forty dollars per head. These were purchased in great numbers by the Mormon agents from cattle dealers on the frontiers and driven in herds to the outfitting place. The price of wagons in St. Louis was sixty-seven dollars.

In view of such unexpected advance in costs many immigrants faced the choice of remaining over a season or borrowing from the Perpetual Emigrating Fund Company. Frequently independent immigrants with means, came to the rescue by making necessary loans to less fortunate brethren whose journey to Zion was threatened with delay.

Wagon covers and tents were indispensable for the journey. A good grade of twilled cotton was usually purchased in England and distributed to the emigrants before leaving Liverpool. When supplied with proper dimensions, the Mormons sewed their own tents during the sea voyage thereby making it possible to procure both tent and cover for about ten dollars. Minimum food provisions for the overland journey appear in the following allowances for the thirteen pound P. E. F. emigrants in 1854: 1,000 pounds flour, fifty pounds sugar, fifty pounds bacon, fifty pounds rice, thirty pounds beans, twenty pounds dried apples and peaches, five pounds tea, one gallon vinegar, ten bars soap, twenty-five pounds salt. Independent members added to these basic necessities as the purse permitted, such items as dried herrings, pickles, molasses, etc. In addition to these articles, cows were depended upon for milk and there was always a good chance of wild game in the wilderness.

All these activities of the Perpetual Emigrating Fund Company, beginning with chartering of ships in Liverpool and ending with safe delivery in "Zion" of thousands of migrating converts, required most careful planning and preparation. Its transactions engaged the services of hundreds of people in various capacities. Their guiding and protecting hands were in evidence everywhere as annual shiploads of immigrants were received, provided for, and launched, fully equipped, on their way to the Salt Lake Valley.

To continue inland and overland with some of the companies which disembarked at New Orleans in the preceding chapter:

In 1851 echoes of the wholesale conversions on the Olympus reached a thousand miles inland. That ship's company under the direction of Mr. William Howell moved up the Mississippi to St. Louis and thence into the long and winding Missouri. They arrived at Kanesville (Council Bluffs) a month after setting foot on American soil. Shortly after their arrival the following appeared in the Frontier Guardian:

"The Steamer Statesman, from St. Louis, thirteen days out, arrived at Kanesville's landing on Tuesday the 20th of May having on board a company of Saints . . . Among the passengers . . . our celebrated French missionary Wm. Howell and family who was so successful in making converts crossing the Atlantic on board the ship Olympus. We are informed that there were only fifty-two passengers on board the Olympus who did not belong to the Church . . . and out of that number fifty were baptized before they arrived at New Orleans; and no less singular is a circumstance that occurred on the Statesman. After her arrival here her cooks and deck hands left her, preferring rather to be teamsters across the plains for 'Mormons' and have their society in fair Utah, than remain any longer as cooks and deck hands on the muddy waters of the Missouri[3]."

The first company of P. E. F. immigrants, arriving in 1852, was not so favored. It was their misfortune to suffer the only serious accident to Mormon companies on the water routes. Eagerness for early arrival in Zion and the agent's concern to avoid delay in St. Louis led to chartering passage on a boat of questionable soundness. Wrote William C. Dunbar years later:

"When the Kennebec passengers arrived in St. Louis we were met by Elder David J. Ross, who had emigrated in a previous company. He told me personally that a boat called the Saluda, had been chartered to bring a company of Saints up the river, and that she was now waiting to complete her list of passengers. She was not represented as one of the best boats in the river by any means, but she had been secured on cheap terms, which was an important consideration for the Saints who were nearly all short of means. And as the first class boats would not start out for some time to come, because of the immense masses of drift ice in the river, and the Saluda would, a number of the new arrivals deemed it best to take advantage of this opportunity and go on for fear that the Saints by tarrying in St. Louis might be compelled to spend their last money here, and thus be unable to continue the journey to the Bluffs and Valley that season."

The Saluda braved the ice packed stream with 120 aboard of whom 90 were Mormon immigrants. On April 4th, it became necessary to lay over at Lexington which she did until the ninth. In attempting to get under way again three boilers burst with terrific explosion, killing and seriously injuring many. The writer quoted above, in referring to responsibility for hiring such a boat states significantly, " . . . It was perhaps nothing but an over anxiety to get the Saints away from St. Louis where so many of those who had previously stopped had apostatized, and never went to the valley[4]."

The inland migrations of 1853 followed closely the following course taken by a Scandinavian company which had arrived under leadership of John E. Forsgren. Five of their number died on arrival at New Orleans on March 8th. Before they left that city on the sixteenth two others passed away and one family apostatized.

They arrived at St. Louis on March 31, where tents and other equipment for the continued journey were acquired. A month's stop-over in that city brought six more deaths while two couples were married. Proceeding directly up the Mississippi for 200 miles they arrived at Keokuk, Iowa. Here they waited to receive their teams for the three hundred mile journey across Iowa. Other European companies joined them. In all fully a thousand Latter-day Saints assembled to receive equipment and be organized into travelling companies for the overland journey.

The Scandinavian company, numbering thirty-four wagons, left the camping grounds on May 21, and arrived at Council Bluffs three weeks later. After resting for several days at this place they crossed the river and followed the California trail into the west. The dreaded cholera still hounded them, taking more lives on the plains. Even more tragic, in the eyes of the faithful, was the loss of others through apostasy. The company arrived in Salt Lake Valley on the 30th of September.

While cholera raged generally in the migrations to the west, it appears that among the Mormons fleeing to Zion, the Scandinavian companies suffered most. In 1854, out of 700 Latter-day Saints sailing from Copenhagen only five hundred reached their destination. The balance succumbed to the plague of the river country and other diseases.

In 1854, in keeping with instructions from Salt Lake City, the New Orleans route was abandoned and the first company sailing the new route arrived in Philadelphia on April 20th. From here it was transported by rail to Pittsburgh and then down the Ohio River to St. Louis. The unusually large immigration of that year, numbering 3,626 imposed real problems on Erastus Snow, frontier agent. Before the season closed about fifteen hundred of the foreign immigrants had reached the Valley. The balance located temporarily on the frontier or sought employment in New York, Philadelphia and Cincinnati.

Snow had anticipated the season's rush of emigration with the following pertinent instructions published in the Luminary[5] on January 16th. "It is intended that the remainder of our European Emigration destined for Utah the present year will sail during the months of February and March, from Liverpool via Philadelphia, Cincinnati, and St. Louis to a point on the Missouri River, hereafter to be determined as a point of outfit for the plains. . . . All others from the Eastern States or British Provinces, who intend crossing the Plains this season, will do well to concentrate at St. Louis, and report themselves to this office during the month of April, or early in May, and embark hence under my personal arrangements.

"Those of Northern Illinois, Iowa, and Wisconsin, who choose to travel by land across the country should also rendezvous at the same place on the Missouri River. . . .

"My assent will not be given to any Saint to leave the Missouri River unless so organized in a company of at least fifty effectual well armed men, and that too under the command of a man appointed by me.

"I will furnish at this point of outfit, for such as desire it, wagons, oxen, cows, guns, flour, bacon, etc.

"Choice wagons made to order and delivered at the point of outfit with bows, projectors, etc. will be about $78, without projectors, $75. Oxen with yokes and chains from $70 to $85 per yoke; cows from $16 to $25 cash.

"My experience derived from six journeys over the plains, enables me to know what kind of teams and outfits are wanted for the plains.

"One wagon, two yoke oxen, and two cows will be sufficient (if that is the extent of their means) for a family of eight or ten persons, with the addition of a tent for every two or three families. Of course with that amount of teams, only the necessary baggage, provisions, and utensils can be taken, and then the persons ride but little[6]."

The frontier agent was ably assisted by Milo Andrus, who in company with thirty-five of the season's first arrivals at St. Louis, left that place on a purchasing tour. The task before him was to secure cattle, arrange for provisions necessary to the season's emigration and locate a suitable rendezvous which could serve as an outfitting place.

Andrus travelled up the Missouri for about five hundred and fifty miles to the village of Atchison. Here he employed a guide and travelling four miles west came upon the head of Deer Creek which seemed admirably suited to his purposes. It was situated in a high rolling prairie well supplied with springs. There was plenty of hickory wood, splendid range for cattle, and good farming lands. The place was immediately selected for the season's outfitting rendezvous and served so well that it continued as a Mormon emigrating center for a number of years.

Atchison was selected as the landing place on the River and from this point a good prairie road led to the camp grounds which were christened Mormon Grove. The sudden rush of Mormons into that vicinity boosted the frontier village to an important business center. Though located in Missouri and not far from scenes of earlier Mormon conflicts, the people of Atchison cooperated freely with the movements of the migrating "Saints."

Snow commenced shipping immigrants from St. Louis to Mormon Grove early in April and companies continued pouring in from Europe until July. Andrus conducted one of the first companies to the new landing at Atchison. He and his associates concluded to fence a farm of 160 acres on Deer Creek for the benefit of the P. E. Fund immigrants. Accordingly, upon arriving at Atchison, four or five families were sent out to Mormon Grove to put in early crops. The majority of the first arrivals, however, camped temporarily hard by the village of Atchison. This camp was described by the local newspaper, Squatter Sovereignty:

> "The camp of the emigrants just back of town, presents a citylike appearance, their tents leaving streets, alleys, etc. between them. The health of the emigrants is good, with but little or no sickness among them. Those who were indisposed when they first landed had regained their accustomed health, and were congratulating themselves on being landed on so healthy a point[7]."

Soon the first fruits of Andrus' purchasing trip appeared in the form of a herd of five hundred and fifty cattle. As other herds of cattle and sheep arrived during the early summer, together with horses and mules in lesser quantities, and hundreds of wagons rolled off the river steamers, Atchison and Mormon Grove presented a busy picture indeed. Snow, arriving at the Mormon camp on May 29th, wrote:

> " . . . We surveyed the town (Atchison) and the few tents and detachments of companies still remaining on the old camp ground just back of the town, and later in the day visited the general encampment at Mormon Grove — about four miles west — which presented the appearance of a city of tents and wagons, beautifully arranged in the open woodland, and covering several undulations. Our visit was emphatically one of business, but it proved equally one of

pleasure. The lowing of cattle — the din and bustle of
the camp — and the joyful greetings, were to us what
martial music is to the soldier. Although we had allotted
ourselves only three or four days in camp, the great amount
of business relating to the P. E. Fund emigration, as well
as the Danish and other independent companies, which required our personal attention, detained us until the tenth
inst (June) and then it was with reluctance that we bid them
adieu, to return to our duties in the city (St. Louis[8].")

Prior to Snow's departure from St. Louis a month earlier,
he had been unable to give the waiting immigrants much
hope of large scale migration to the "Valley" that season.
However, during his absence at Mormon Grove, Daniel
Spencer arrived in St. Louis as personal representative from
Franklin D. Richards, Mormon shipping agent in England.
He had been sent in the usual manner to cooperate with the
frontier agent in expediting the migration to the west. In
Snow's absence he cheered them greatly by his confidence
that all should receive assistance.

Finding Snow had gone to Atchison, Spencer followed
him thither and helped make good his promise to the immigrants that all who wished to start for the Valley should
have the opportunity. Spencer was deeply impressed with
Mormon Grove:

"While gradually ascending the long and smooth hill upon
which stands a beautiful grove, I beheld the land in all
directions spotted with white tents and wagon covers, the
active motion of the Saints, some ploughing, some planting,
some driving cattle, repairing wagons, tents, etc., and my
mind was called back to the scenes which occurred on our
exit from Nauvoo and the results thereof[9]."

Snow and Spencer, assisted by many others, labored zealously to secure the necessary outfits and provisions. Before
leaving Mormon Grove they had organized four companies,
numbering a thousand Latter-day Saints, for the journey
westward. Most of these were immigrants who had arrived
early in the season by way of New Orleans. Continuing

their labors after returning to St. Louis, they secured additional supplies, on easy terms and announced in church services that all who wished to migrate that season should board the river steamer Saramac on July 28th and that their passage would be paid to the Salt Lake Valley. The usual resourcefulness of the P. E. F. agents had triumphed in behalf of the waiting immigrants.

A total of eight fully organized companies of Mormon moved out of Mormon Grove in 1855 bound for "Zion." They included, in addition to immigrants, a large number of members gathered from the United States. In keeping with instructions each company was well stocked with provisions and thoroughly armed to meet any emergency. Averaging over forty wagons each, the companies began the season's exodus the first of June and departures continued until August 5th. Erastus Snow, with others, left on the third, carrying the United States mail for Utah. They overtook and passed all of the emigration trains enroute and entered Salt Lake Valley on August 31st. Three days later the first company which left Mormon Grove that season arrived. The last company appeared in the Valley on October 24th. The total emigration to Utah that year included 2,030 people, 337 wagons, 2,433 oxen, 319 cows, eighty-six horses and mules. In addition to these were a number of families and teamsters who travelled with the merchant trains.

1   In 1853 Keokuk on the West bank of the Mississippi in southeastern
    Iowa was selected as outfitting place.   In 1854, Kansas City on the lower
    Missouri was chosen.
2   Millennial Star, XVI:684.
3   Frontier Guardian, May 30, 1851.
4   Jensen, Andrew, Contributor, XIII:413.
5   The Luminary was a Mormon publication in St. Louis.
6   Millennial Star, XVII:218.
7   Jensen, Andrew, Contributor, XIII: 549.
8   Jensen, Andrew, Contributor, XIII: 550.
9   Jensen, Andrew, Contributor, XIII: 350.

15

The Emigrating Fund in Europe

THE immediate purpose of the Perpetual Emigrating Fund was to relieve the pressure of "poor Saints" gathered on the Pottawattamie Lands in Iowa. But clearly it was also intended to reach its helping hand overseas, and this it did, hardly waiting for the completion of its primary objective.

On October 14, 1854, the Presidency wrote to Orson Pratt, presiding in England, as follows;

> "Dear Brother, . . . We have thought proper to write you more particularly in relation to . . . the Perpetual Emigrating Fund for the poor Saints. This fund we wish all to understand, is perpetual, and in order to be kept good, will need constant accessions. To further this end we expect all who are benefitted by its operations, to reimburse the amount as soon as they are able, facilities for which will, very soon after their arrival here, present themselves in the shape of Public works. Donations will also continue to be taken from all parts of the world and expended for the gathering of the poor Saints. This is no joint Stock company arrangement, but free donations. Your office in Liverpool is the place of deposit for all funds received either for this or the tithing funds for all Europe and you will not pay out only upon our order, and to such persons as we shall direct[1]."

The Joint Stock Company referred to is of interest at this point as a reflection of earlier thought on the question of aid to foreign immigration. The company, known as the British and American Joint Stock Company, had been organized in England by Reuben Hedlock, Thomas Ward and others who had been left in charge of the Mission when the Apostles were called home during the Nauvoo crisis. Its expressed objective was to aid in building up Zion and promote emigration to it through development of a world wide commercial business. Initial capital was to be obtained through selling stock to church membership.

The company was organized under the laws of Great Britain with privileges of trading as merchants between England and America, or hiring or purchasing ships and constructing factories[2]. The members were urged to buy its stock so that they might be aided in future emigration to America through company earnings. The pages of the Millennial Star during 1845 carried frequent announcements and exhortations to support the enterprise. "The Glory of God, the Building up of Zion, the Gathering of the Saints," it said, "have been the grand motives that have led to its origin and establishment[3]." Without official sanction the organization was presented as a subsidiary of the Mormon Church.

As a result of mismanagement of funds the company suffered reverses[4] and dissatisfaction among stockholders spread. In July 1846, Orson Hyde, Parley P. Pratt, and John Taylor were appointed by the Church authorities at Council Bluffs, Iowa to make investigation of the whole affair. Their first action upon arriving in England was to declare the Joint Stock Company wholly independent of the Church and to advise the members to discontinue patronage to it. Upon Hyde's appointment to preside in England in October of 1846, the Company was dissolved. Examination of the books revealed that the people's means had been squandered, and settlement was made with a payment of one shilling, three pence on the pound[5]. Both Hedlock and Ward were dropped from fellowship in the Church.

Franklin D. Richards arrived in England on March 29, 1850, to commence operations of the Perpetual Emigrating Fund in that country. Until the end of that year he acted in concert with Orson Pratt, succeeding the latter as president of the Mission on January 1, 1851. Immediately upon introducing the subject of assisted emigration to the British "Saints" the Fund began to grow. Contributions, ranging from a few shillings to four hundred pounds, were made, reaching the sum of 1,440 pounds in 1852. This was approximately the amount raised in Utah[6].

Continued donations to the Fund in Britain brought the total amount subscribed to 6,832 pounds in July 1854. Missions on the Continent also responded, depositing 280 pounds with the British Agency, thus raising the European total to 7,113 pounds[7]. This sum was added to the increasing Fund in Utah to be administered jointly from Salt Lake City and Liverpool to assist the "poor Saints" to emigrate to Zion. The company agents served strictly in the capacity of missionaries without salary or remuneration[8].

The removal of the exiles from the Pottawattamie lands on the Missouri resulted in a temporary decrease in European immigration. Heretofore, the British members had been urged to migrate to America regardless of whether they had the means to continue the journey direct to "the Valley" or not. The Mormon settlements in Iowa had served as stopping places where they might accumulate the necessary equipment to complete the journey at a later season. But evacuation of the Pottawattamie lands contemplated cessation of such stop-over migration. Also it was hoped to discontinue immigration by way of the Mississippi and Missouri rivers altogether. The Fifth General Epistle of the Presidency, issued in April, 1851, expressed high hopes in the advantages of a proposed new route:

> "It is wisdom for the English Saints to cease emigration by the usual route through the States, and up the Missouri River, and remain where they are until they hear from us again, as it is our design to open up a way across the interior of the continent by Panama, Tehuantepec, or some of the interior routes, and land them at San Diego, and thus save three thousand miles of inland navigation through a most sickly climate and country[9]."

Anticipating the success of the new plan, a colony was established at San Bernardino, California, to receive the immigrants from the West Coast. Franklin D. Richards was directed by the Presidency to make investigation in Britain relative to transportation facilities between Liverpool and San Diego and check comparative costs. However, the British agency found no satisfactory connections available and that costs involved were prohibitive. This report, resulted in restoration of emigration over the old route. But, said the Sixth General Epistle of September 22, 1851, "Although emigration is again opened on the old route it is not opened on the old plan. Let those only leave England who can go through either on their own means or by means of the emigrating fund[10]."

These instructions came as a keen disappointment to the thousands of British "poor Saints" heavily charged with the spirit of gathering. The extent to which the new plan would limit emigration from England can be appreciated by reference to a letter written two years earlier when the "through journey" plan was first suggested. Wrote Orson Pratt at that time: "There has been much inquiry amongst the Saints of late whether it is their privilege to go from this country unless they have sufficient means to carry them through to Salt Lake Valley. We answer that if none were to go only such as have sufficient funds to perform the whole journey there would not be much gathering from this Island. We would hardly judge that there were a hundred families among the Saints in Great Britain who are able to go direct from this to the Salt Lake Basin. . . . We are in hopes that the time will soon come when there will be capital sufficient to enable the Saints to pass on to the place of their destination without any delay[11]."

That hoped for assistance had now arrived in form of the Perpetual Emigrating Fund. While the total Mormon emigration from England in 1852 dropped sharply to 760, it included 251 beneficiaries of the Emigrating Fund. These were the first to share its benefits in Europe. They sailed, together with the regular emigrants, in two chartered vessels (the Kennebec and Ellen Maria) on January 10th. John S. Higbee and Isaac C. Haight were in charge of the companies.

The Emigrating Fund in Europe in 1852 amounted to 1,410 pounds and the total cost of shipping two hundred and fifty-one emigrants under its provisions exceeded that amount by more than one thousand pounds. The shipping agent was able to make up the deficit temporarily and Abraham O. Smoot, a missionary of wide experience, was sent ahead to the American Frontier to purchase necessary outfits for crossing the plains. The immigrants arrived at New Orleans late in March and early April and proceeded by River steamers to St. Louis where Smoot awaited them with supplies. Here Isaac C. Haight, who had cooperated with Smoot in the purchase of equipment left his company and returned to England while the latter remained to assist the immigrants up the Missouri River to Council Bluffs. It was one of these groups which suffered in the Saluda explosion referred to previously.

At Council Bluffs the European P. E. F. emigrants found themselves in the midst of the evacuation process of 1852. Their own company, under the continued leadership of Abraham O. Smoot, was added to the great overland exodus of twenty-one companies averaging fifty wagons to the company and totaling not less than ten thousand people. This imposing procession of migrating Mormons left the Missouri River during the month of June and arrived in the Salt Lake Valley during August and September. The following excerpts from the Deseret News of September 18th, with reference to the P. E. F. immigrants reflects the spirit of the Gathering movement:

"Captain A. O. Smoot's Company of thirty-one wagons was escorted into the city by the First Presidency of the

Church, some of the Twelve Apostles, and many of the citizens on horseback and in carriages.

"Captain Pitt's band, in the President's spacious carriage, met the company at the mouth of Emigration Canyon, where the Saints of both sexes, . . . danced and sang for joy, and their hearts were made glad by a distribution of melons and cakes; after which the band came in the escort and cheered the hearts of the weary travellers with their enlivening strains.

"Next in the procession came a band of pilgrims — sisters and children, walking, sunburnt, and weather beaten, but not forlorn; their hearts were light and buoyant, which was plainly manifested by their happy and joyful countenances.

"Next followed the wagons. The good condition of the cattle, and the general appearance of the whole train, did credit to Bishop Smoot, as a wise and skilful manager — who was seen on horse, in all the various departments of his company during their egress from the Canyon to encampment.

"As the escort and the train passed the Temple Block, they were saluted with nine rounds of artillery, which made the everlasting hills to shake their sides with joy; while thousands of men, women, and children gathered from various parts of the city to unite in the glorious and joyful welcome.

"After corralling on Union Square, the emigrants were called together and President Brigham Young addressed them as follows:

" ' . . . First I will say, may the Lord God of Israel bless you, and comfort your hearts. (the company and bystanders responded Amen.)

" 'We have prayed for you continually; thousands of prayers have been offered up for you, day by day, to Him who has commanded us to gather Israel, save the children of men by the preaching of the Gospel and prepare them for the coming of the Messiah. You have had a long, hard, and fatiguing journey across the great waters and the scorched plains; but, by the distinguished favors of heaven, you are here in safety. . . .

" 'You are now in a land of plenty, where by a reasonable amount of labor, you may realize a comfortable subsistence.

" 'You have had trials and sufferings in your journey, but your sufferings have been few compared with thousands of your brethren and sisters in these valleys. We have, a great many of us, been under the harrow for the space of twenty-one years. I trust you have enjoyed a good measure of the Spirit of the Lord in the midst of your toils; and now, as you have arrived here, let your feelings be mild, peaceable, and easy, not framing to yourselves any particular course that you will pursue, but be patient until the way opens before you.

" 'Be very cautious that you do not watch the failings of others, and by this means expose yourselves to be caught in the snares of the devil; for the people here have the failings natural to man, the same as you have; look well to yourselves, that the enemy does not get the advantage over you; see that your own hearts are pure, and filled with the Spirit of the Lord, and you will be willing to overlook the faults of others, and endeavor to correct your own.

" ' . . . No person here is under the necessity of begging his bread, except the natives; and they beg more than they care for, or can use. By your labor you can obtain an abundance; the soil is rich and productive. We have the best of wheat, the finest of flour; as good as was ever produced in any other country in the world. We have beets, carrots, turnips, cabbage, peas, beans, melons, and I may say, all kinds of garden vegetables, of the best quality.

" 'The prospects are cheering for the fruits of different kinds.

" ' . . . With regard to your obtaining habitations to shelter you in the coming winter — all of you will be able to obtain work, and by your industry, you can make yourselves tolerably comfortable in this respect before the winter sets in. All the improvements that you see around you, have been made in the short space of four years. Four years ago this day, there was not a rod of fence to be seen, nor a house, except the Old Fort as we call it, though it was then new. All this that you see, has been accomplished by the industry of the people; and a great deal more that you do not see, for our settlements extend two hundred and fifty miles south, and almost one hundred miles north.

" 'We shall want some of the brethren to repair to some of the other settlements, such as mechanics and farmers; no doubt they can provide themselves with teams, etc., to bear them to their destinations. Those who have acquaintances here, will all be able to obtain dwellings, until they can make accommodations of their own.

" 'Again, with regard to labor — don't imagine unto yourselves that you are going to get rich, at once, by it. As for the poor, there are none here, neither are there any who may be called rich, but all obtain the essential comforts of life.

" 'Let not your eyes be greedy. When I met you this afternoon, I felt to say, this is the company that I belong to — the "poor company," as it is called, and I always expect to belong to it, until I am crowned with eternal riches in the celestial kingdom. In this world I possess nothing, only what the Lord has given to me, and it is devoted to the building up of His kingdom. . . .

" 'Don't any of you imagine to yourselves that you can go to the gold mines to get anything to help yourselves with; you must live here; this is the gathering place for the Saints. . . .

" 'I will say to this company, they have had the honour of being escorted into the city by some of the most distinguished individuals of our society, and a band of music, accompanied with a salutation from the cannon. Other companies have not had this mark of respect shown to them; they belong to the rich, and are able to help themselves. . . .

" 'No man or woman will be hurried away from the wagons; but you may have the privilege of living in them until you get homes.

" 'I hope the brethren who live near by, or those who live at a distance, will send our brethren and sisters some potatoes and melons, or anything else they have, that they may not go hungry; and let them have them free of charge, that they may be blessed with us, as I exhorted the people last Sabbath[12].' "

The first year's foreign operations of the Emigrating Company having proved successful, except for the financial deficit, interest in the gathering reached new heights for the coming year. The Church leaders fanned the enthusiasm of prospective emigrants into a clamor for action. "Let all who can procure a loaf of bread and one garment on their backs, be assured there is water plenty and pure by the way, and doubt no longer, but come next year to the place of gathering, even in flocks, as doves fly to their windows before the storm[13]."

Such urging found the spirit more than willing but the flesh bound by circumstances from which it could not escape. Many appeared before President Franklin D. Richards begging for the privilege of going in companies organized to walk the entire overland distance, if need be. It became necessary to lay a restraining hand upon their ambitions lest, in the extremities of the gathering spirit they pay too dearly for their coveted freedom. The fund could not begin to meet the demands upon it with the result that a new plan was evolved for the coming year to supplement it. This was known as the "ten pound plan." It was estimated that through judicious purchasing at the outfitting point in the States, the journey could be made to Utah for ten pounds each for adults and five pounds for those under one year. In other words this class would buy passage at reduced rates. Nine hundred and fifty-seven availed themselves of this plan but the cost of transportation had been greatly under estimated and a loan was necessary to help this group complete the journey[14].

Another important provision of the fund allowed members in Utah to send for friends and relatives in foreign lands wherever agencies of the company were established. This was done by making deposits with the P. E. Office in Salt Lake which in turn directed its agent abroad to forward the parties designated. This practice became increasingly popular in Utah as well as an annoyance to the President of the company. The desire on the part of many to extend "the blessings of the gathering" to friends and relatives too often led them to the company's office with only good intentions in their hearts. With no desire to dampen their interest in sending for friends, Brigham Young urged that they support their requests with something more substantial, "In the midst of war and distress of nations," he wrote, "it is the highly commendable duty of every lover of truth in the valleys of the mountains to extend all reasonable aid for gathering the oppressed Saints from every clime where they are to be found. But to do this requires cash, and indebtedness on the part of the Church, or available articles than can at any time be converted into money. This fact should be constantly borne in mind by those who are desirous of sending for their friends or relatives, and then they will not waste their time or ours by continually running to the President's office to know whether, this, that, or the other person can be sent for, until they have deposited, or have in hand the full amount necessary for the transportation of those desired to be sent for, and that, too, in money or its equivalent. The necessity of this course is obvious to all who feel disposed to assist in the great work of gathering and in relieving their brethren from a deep and untold distress which is constantly increasing. . . . With this plain statement to the people it is expected that no one will again present requests to send for their friends without being prepared with requisite means[15]."

There were now four classes of emigrants coming from Europe to Utah — the P. E. Emigrants sent for from Salt Lake, the P. E. Emigrants selected in the missions by presiding officers there, the ten pound Emigrants, and those who paid their own way. This latter class sent money through the company to its outfitting agent on the frontier for the purchase of teams and equipment. The total Mormon emigration for the year was 2,312 from the British Isles and 314 from the European mainland. Nine hundred and fifty-five of the British emigrants either arranged for their own outfit or sent money ahead with the P. E. Agents[16]. Of the Continental emigrants 297 were Scandinavian and 17 German. The entire expenditure of the P. E. Company in 1853 was thirty thousand pounds[17].

The next year (1854) brought further changes. The ten pound scheme having proved inadequate, the sum was raised to thirteen pounds. But the number who availed themselves of the plan was reduced to eighty-six. Another plan proved more attractive. Many who could neither pay their own way at thirteen pounds nor qualify as immediate beneficiaries of the P. E. Fund accepted a third alternative. They donated what funds they had to the Emigration Company in return for transportation to Utah. Then they signed a note to pay back the full cost of the journey. In other words their donations assured them a company loan. The amount thus contributed in 1854 was 1,800 pounds and eight shillings[18]. This sum was further swelled through urging the "Thirteen pound Emigrants" to accept a company note for all their surplus funds. This relieved in a measure the need for cash to purchase equipment.

The various districts in England contributed one thousand, two hundred[19] pounds to the fund in 1854. Three thousand one hundred and sixty-seven emigrated, of whom in addition to the eighty-six Thirteen Pound passengers, 1,075 came under the Fund and 875 paid the regular emigration rates[20]. The increase in price of teams to forty-five pounds was a major factor in the reduction of L. D. S. emigration from England in 1854. It is estimated that the total emigrating cost for the years 1853-1954 was seventy thousand pounds[21].

Emigration increased sharply in 1855 over that of any preceding year. This in spite of the fact that cost of teams had reached fifty-five pounds. Out of a total of 4,225 emigrants, 1,161 came under the fund and three hundred and seventy-three furnished their own teams. The sum of fifteen pounds for each adult and nine pounds for those under one year was paid for each P. E. F. passenger. The total operating cost for the year was approximately thirty thousand pounds[22].

The period from 1852 to 1856 marked the high point of the British L. D. S. Mission, both in membership increase and in numbers emigrated annually. At this time the mission also enjoyed its peak of financial credit when, during the seasons of emigration, its deposits in London and Liverpool amounted to some thirty thousand pounds ($150,000). Says Franklin D. Richards' biographer, "The credit of the mission was so sound and confidence in it so complete that the great shipping companies dealt with it very much as they would have done with the government of a nation with first class credit. This gave President Richards power to deal with the shipping companies on the most advantageous terms for the emigrating people. The vessels chartered by him were for the time being, in the service of the Church; and sea captains and their officers held the Saints in special charge. 'Upon the shoulders of the Philistines Israel was flying toward the west[23].' "

1 Linforth, Janes, Route from Liverpool to Great Salt Lake Valley, p. 8.
2 Ibid.
3 Millennial Star, VII:72.
4 Millennial Star, VII:88.
5 Millennial Star, VIII:36. "Hedlock, anticipating the arrival of the investigators, fled to London, but Ward continued to urge support for the enterprise and wrote on August 15, 1856: 'Again with regard to the objects of the company, we fear that some have not fully comprehended but have supposed that it was merely an emigration society, by which the Saints might be enabled to reach their destination in the West. This is altogether a mistake. The spirit of the company in the first place is to employ the capital thereof in trade and commerce for the mutual benefit of the shareholders, that they may receive interest for their money deposited in the same; but in the second place it is intended to provide a means of emigration for the Saints at the same time that we are seeking by commerce to promote the interests of the company. But the grand object of the same is to assist our brethren in their new location, by trading with them and others, and by taking out instruments of husbandry, machinery, manufactured goods and other articles which otherwise might cause them years of labor to produce, and thus to facilitate the building up and establishing a permanent home for the people of God.' "
6 Millennial Star XIV:27.
7 Linforth, James, Route From Liverpool to Great Salt Lake Valley, pp. 7-9.
8 Millennial Star, XL:57. "It is often enlarged by donation and in rare instances by bequest, and none of it is frittered on high toned officers by way of salaries or emolluments."
9 Millennial Star, XIII:209.
10 Millennial Star, XIV:27.
11 Millennial Star, XI:278.

12 Deseret News, August 21, September 18, 1852.
13 Millennial Star, XIV:325.
14 Jensen, Andrew, Contributor, XIII: 124, 125.
15 Deseret News, Volume V: 157.
16 Linforth, James, Route from Liverpool to Great Salt Lake Valley, p. 9.
17 Jensen, Andrew, Contributor, XIII: 124, 125.
18 Jensen, Andrew, Contributor, XIII: 136.
19 Millennial Star, XVII:322.
20 Linforth, James, Route from Liverpool to Great Salt Lake Valley, 120.
    Also Contributor XIII: 137. In 1854 Scandinavia sent 678 converts of
    whom two came under the fund. It is estimated that it cost no less
    than 10,000 pounds to remove these 678.
21 Jensen, Andrew, Contributor, XIII:137.
22 At the close of 1855, 21,911 European immigrants had responded to
    the call to gather to "Zion." Of these 5,000 had arrived at Nauvoo,
    Illinois before the exodus from that place in 1846. 16,911 of them
    sailed from Liverpool between 1848 and 1855, bound for Utah. Follow-
    ing the commencement of P. E. F. operations in 1852, the immigration
    was aided as follows: 2,887 came under the provisions of the fund;
    957 came under the ten pound arrangement; eighty-six under the thirteen
    pound plan. The balance, while paying for their own transportation,
    enjoyed the benefits of the Perpetual Emigrating Fund Company
    through its purchasing agencies and its supervisory functions. It is
    estimated that at least 125,000 pounds ($625,000) were expended by the
    Company during the four years from 1852 to 1855 in emigrating the
    "poor saints" from Europe to the Rocky Mountains.
23 West, Franklin L., Life of Franklin D. Richards, pp. 132-133.

16

The Iron Mission

THE choice between circling a hemisphere or traversing
a continent occupied the Mormons seriously in the middle
nineteenth century. Between the Zion bound converts at
Liverpool and the Salt Lake Valley, lay the Atlantic Ocean
and almost the entire breadth of North America. Increasing
momentum of the "gathering" emphasized the disadvantages
of a long overland route with its physical obstructions, and
conditions menacing the health of the immigrants. The
Mormon leaders looked westward. They compared the distance between Salt Lake and the Pacific Coast with the
eastern approach. The northern route from San Francisco
via the Humbolt River shared the disadvantage of the eastern
in being closed to travel during the winter months. The
southern route, however, from Los Angeles by way of the
Virgin River, afforded definite advantages of climate and
was open the year round. The old Spanish Trail between
Sante Fe and California passed through the Virgin country.

It was over this route that Jedediah Smith, two decades
before the coming of the Mormons, had passed on his way
to Los Angeles. The Pratt exploration of 1849 had also
pushed southward as far as the lower Virgin. As a logical
sequence, the boundaries of the State of Deseret were made
to include a southern approach to the sea. A line of colonies
began to reach southwest toward a seacoast terminal.

The Federal Government failed to include this "Mormon
corridor[1]" to the sea in the Territory of Utah. Brigham
Young, nevertheless, planned to maintain the Pacific contact through a chain of colonies. So when Amasa Lyman
and C. C. Rich, who had been in charge of missionary work

in "western California" recommended in 1851 the purchase of a hundred thousand acre ranch at San Bernardino, the President took advantage of the opportunity to thus establish a Mormon base within fifty miles of the coast. Two years later he sent a company to settle on the Las Vegas Springs as another link in the desired chain of communication.

It was while these efforts to establish a convenient immigrant route from the West Coast to the Basin were being made, that the Presidency in April, 1851, advised the Mormon agency in Britain to investigate the possibilities of cheaper shipping routes by way of Panama or around Cape Horn — instead of by river from New Orleans and overland from Missouri[2]. The British agency, as mentioned previously, made a negative report and immigration continued over the old route.

In 1857 came contraction of the Mormon colonial empire before the threat of invasion by the United States army and San Bernardino and Las Vegas were permanently abandoned. But, as the western outposts were sucked back in the interest of consolidation, the U. S. Government gave encouragement to another possible approach to Utah from the Pacific. The Department of War sent Lieutenant Joseph C. Ives in the fall of 1857, to investigate the possibility of bringing supplies for the "Utah Army" by way of the Colorado River. The officer's report, after pushing his way upstream for several days brought the venture to a close: "It appeared therefore that the foot of Black Canyon should be considered the practical head of navigation and I concluded to have a reconnaissance made to connect that point with the Mormon road and let that finish the exploration of the navigable portion of the Colorado[3]."

Having previously caused some investigation of that same route, Young now directed another party of twenty men under the leadership of George A. Smith to follow up the Ives explorations. They were also to look for suitable colony sites on the Virgin River near the Colorado. The report of this company on Colorado navigation was negative as former reports had been, but the succeeding years did bring a number of settlements into the vicinity of the Colorado. We shall revert to this development before noting the final outcome of the Colorado River enterprise.

Iron, for the manufacture of grist mills, saw mills, and other urgent necessities rolled across the western plains nearly a century ago in the form of wagon tires and hub bands. Having served the purpose of holding the wagons intact in their progress to Zion it now yielded to the greater urgencies of mills and other devices vital to survival.

A hundred and thirty miles west from Winter Quarters on the Missouri lay several plows, and large quantities of iron scrap which had been abandoned by "forty-niner" wagon trains. Iron, being more precious than gold in the building of the Kingdom, could not thus be left to waste, and was gathered up by the Mormons. And so each company which poured through the canyons east of Great Salt Lake brought its contribution of metal to be turned, after careful consideration, to the uses of first necessity.

But the humble tribute of Iron thus squeezed from the wagon trains could not keep pace with expansion of the Kingdom. Young expressed the need with emphasis. "Iron we need and iron we must have. We cannot well do without it and have it we must if we have to send to England for it." It was therefore with no small interest that he heard the report of the Pratt exploration company that iron ore had been found in Southern Utah, as well as outcroppings of coal. The Great Basin had yielded one more of its secrets to the pioneers with a challenge to make use of it if they could. Brigham accepted the challenge and an "Iron Mission" was organized to commence operations 250 miles south of Salt Lake City.

On July 27, 1850, the following announcement appeared in the Deseret News under title of "Little Salt Lake":

"Brethren of Great Salt Lake City and vicinity who are

full of faith and good works; who have been blessed with means; who want more means and are willing to labor and toil to obtain these means, are informed by the Presidency of the Church, that a colony is wanted at Little Salt Lake this fall; that fifty or more good effective men with teams and wagons, provisions and clothing are wanted for one year.

"Seed grain in abundance and tools in all their variety for a new colony are wanted to start from this place immediately after the fall conference, to repair to the valley of the Little Salt Lake, without delay. There to sow, build and fence; erect a saw and grist mill, establish an iron foundry as speedily as possible and do all other acts and things necessary for the preservation and safety of an infant settlement among the Indians; also for furnishing provisions and lumber the coming year for a large number of emigrants, with their own families . . . Farmers, blacksmiths, carpenters, joiners, millwrights, bloomers, moulders, smelters, stone-cutters, brick-layers, stone masons, one shoemaker, one tailor and others of various occupations who have the means and are willing to sacrifice the society of wives and children for one year, (believing that he who forsakes wife and children for the sake of the Kingdom of God shall receive an hundred fold) are requested to give in their names in writing, together with their occupation, residence, strength of team, wagons, amount of grain, tools, etc., for an outfit without delay, and without further notice to Brother Thomas Bullock, or leave same at the post office directed to Willard Richards, General Church Recorder[5]."

George A. Smith, who together with Ezra T. Benson, had been selected to head the expedition, urged the necessity of one hundred men. Following publication of a long list of accepted applicants the following announcement appeared in November:

"Wanted: one hundred men, ready to start on the first day of December, with five hundred bushels of wheat, thirty thousand pounds of bread stuff, or three hundred pounds to each person; 34 plows, 17 drag teeth, one ax, spade, shovel and hoe to each man; one millwright, five carpenters and joiners; two blacksmiths; two shoemakers, and one surveyor, each with tools; 4 top and pit sawyers, with saw, one stone-cutter, two masons, grain and grass scythes, sickles and pitch forks, fifty each, one gun and two hundred pounds of ammunition for each man; fifty horses, twenty-five pair of holster pistols, one gun-smith, one cow to two persons, fifty beef cattle, potatoes and seed of the ball; radish, beets, squash and garden seeds of all kinds; also Henry Miller with his threshing machine next year[6]."

Provo City was announced as the rendezvous where all members of the expedition would gather during the week of December 7th to 15th, prior to launching the expedition. Here the genial, giant figure of George A. Smith rose before them to assume command. "This is the first time we have seen each others faces. Those who have obeyed this call have done it by the voice of the Presidency. I have been appointed to gather and lead out this company to the place of our destination. I would like to know your minds regarding my being your leader."

Following proper motion and unanimous pledge of support, he continued, "I hope our ears will not be saluted with swearing or the taking of the name of the Lord in vain. We want no gambling. We are going to gather the Saints and build the Kingdom of God. We should act as though we are on a mission to preach the Gospel. The Sabbath should be observed in all cases; six days we should labor and we should rest on the Sabbath. We shall try to move every day, if we do not go but a few miles. It will be better to change camp. I will prophesy if we work with our heart and mind we shall perform our mission and return in safety. I hope that every person will remember to call upon the Lord at the close of the day and in the morning pray to the God of Heaven. The Bishops will act in their office and calling and take charge of all meetings and settle any difficulty that might come up. All cases will be settled by Bishop Elisha H. Groves. President Young required that before we left the settlements we should send back an account of the organization; take the census and leave it with Captain Pace[7]."

Officials of the organization were then duly elected, including John D. Lee as camp clerk, Henry Lunt, assistant, Bishop Anson Call, captain of the first fifty and Simon Baker of the second fifty. These companies were then divided into smaller units of tens. Joseph Horne who had been over the route the year previous with the Pratt party was chosen company pilot and Thomas S. Wheeler, Indian interpreter.

Taking cognizance of Indian danger, a military organization was also effected with Almon L. Fullmer, captain of horse and James A. Little, captain of foot. These were responsible to the military of the State of Deseret. "We are a military people and are bound to be as we are going into an Indian country," said the leader, "We should have about 120 men and it is necessary for every man to get his arms ready at a minute's warning. Be careful with your arms. . . . The protection of the settlement rests upon these companies. We are the citizens of Iron County and do not want a mean man in that country. I bless you in the name of the Lord[8]."

Thus was a new county set afoot to find its permanent home in Southern Utah. As the company of 120 men, 30 women and 18 children moved forward it was equipped as follows: 101 wagons, two carriages, 368 oxen, 100 horses, six mules, twelve cows, 146 beef cattle, 20 dogs, 14 cats, and 18 chickens. The total arms and ammunition included one six pounder brass cannon, 129 guns, 52 pistols, nine swords, 1,001 pounds ammunition and 44 saddles. The inventory revealed substantial supplies of flour, wheat, corn, oats, barley, potatoes and groceries. Tools and implements included nine and one fourth sets of carpenter's tools, three and one half sets blacksmith's tools, one set of mill irons for saw mill, three whip saws, 57 plows, 137 axes, 110 spades and shovels, 98 hoes, 72 scythes and cradles, 45 grass scythes, 45 sickles, 436 sights of glass, 190 pounds of nails, and 55 stoves[9].

Such a caravan was a new spectacle for the redskin to gaze upon and even Smith was moved to compare it to a line of steamboats, "judging from the smoke pipes[10]." Camp regulations were few and simple. Said the veteran leader, "Some want rigid camp rules, but it takes wise legislatures to make laws that will not fetter our feet. It is better to suffer wrong than to do wrong. . . . There is a company of eleven wagons behind. I have left word for them to keep together, that they might not be "tithed" by the Indians. I want the pilot to have two men with him having "the tools" in case of surprise. Be careful with your firearms that no accident may occur. The President wants Salt Creek bridged as he intends to visit us next June[11]."

From December 16th to January 11th they pressed southward. Christmas day was marked in the clerk's diary[12] with a temperature of twelve degrees below zero. On the 26th an Indian and a twelve year old boy were captured for killing oxen and the redskin agreed to give the boy in ransom. President Smith then warned the native that if any more cattle were killed the company would wipe out the whole tribe.

December 27: "We travelled nine miles today — crossed a range of mountains — the road was very sideling — had to hold the wagons to keep them from tipping over which caused much delay — camped in a beautiful valley at half past 4 P. M. — no water — had to melt snow — wood one half mile from camp. Snow here ten inches deep . . . January 1, 1851: By wish of the majority of the company we laid over today — procured some wood and in the evening made some large fires in the corral and enjoyed ourselves in the dance in which the ladies participated. . . . January 7: . . . The snow today was 12 inches deep and in some places drifted 3 feet deep which made it very hard work for the cattle — there are many cattle in camp with very tender feet — some of the brethren made some moccasins out of the hide of the ox which the wolves killed and put them on the

cattle. January 8: Snowstorm. Camp started at 11 o'clock
A. M. Travelled about 13 miles — camped on a branch
of the Beaver River — Plenty of grass and water and a little
wood . . . . this is a fine valley, rich soil." Finally on January
10th, they came in view of their objective. The camp recorder finds the company somewhat scattered at the time:

"Friday, January 10, 1851. We doubled teams for 60
rods; the road for a mile was steep and rocky and we had
to clear timber — we then commenced to go down a very
steep hill — locked our wheels for a half mile — winding
amongst the trees several of the wagons had the bows broke
and corners torn — we passed through a gap in the second
range of mountains, ascended a hill steep, sideling and
rocky — at the summit we could see the valley of the Little
Salt Lake. The descent was steep and rough — after a
journey of six miles we camped in the edge of the Valley.
Our camp now consisted of 23 wagons, most of the weak
teams out of five tens — our cattle are very much exhausted
with the journey over the mountain — no water or wood,
some bunch grass — supposed to be six miles to a spring.
George A. Smith called the camp together at 8 P. M. and
examined our fire arms, and, as some had been loaded a
long time, he wished to fire them off and reload. The
brethren wish to make a little on their arrival in Little Salt
Lake Valley. The cannon was fired and 24 stand of small
arms, followed by 3 cheers for Iron County and 3 for the
Governor of Deseret. The company that was camped six
miles ahead at the spring heard our firing and supposed that
we were attacked by Indians and sent 2 men on horse back to
see. They also sent messengers to the company camped at
Red Creek as some of the best teams in Captain Baker's
fifty had reached that point. When the Company at Red
Creek received the news they put out a strong guard and
sent quite a company of horsemen to the aid of the companies in the rear. And as the first and last companies were
some 15 or 16 miles apart it was about 3 o'clock on the
morning of the 11th before all were assured that peace pre-
vailed in our various camps[13]."

The entire company settled on Center Creek and there
followed the usual rapid exploration of surroundings, locat-

ing mill sites, and building of corrals and a suitable fort. In the center of the corral a stately "liberty pole," duly dedicated, rose into the blue. This was to become the agricultural base for the "Iron Mission" and preparations were made toward farming operations in the spring.

Camp routine was broken three times by welcome visitors. On January 16th, Captain Jefferson Hunt with five companies suddenly came upon the new camp as they were returning to Salt Lake from California. It was the occasion for a great feast and election of County officers. Captain Hunt was elected representative from Iron County and proceeded on his way. In April came Parley P. Pratt and C. C. Rich, both of the Quorum of Apostles, enroute to California. Special religious services were held and, to George A. Smith's disappointment, a few of his company could not resist joining the California bound party. On May 10th Brigham Young arrived with a company of high officials. This was the high point in the camp's social calendar. In addition to special religious services, it became the occasion for formal organization of the City of Parowan.

Such visits did much to strengthen the morale of the isolated settlement. But each individual was spiritually fortified for the task ahead. The assistant clerk confided to his diary on July 20, 1851. "This day I am 27 years old. I return thanks to my Heavenly Father for his protecting care over me on my perilous voyage from England and my journey to this land, and that I am a member of His Church. May my life still be preserved and prolonged that I may continue to throw in my mite toward building up the Church and the Kingdom of God[14]." The whole program of Zion building in the wilderness rested upon thousands of such individual testimonies which were demonstrated through a willingness to sacrifice and a spirit of unselfish cooperaton.

Summer came and went and the harvest season was soon over. Now it was time to give attention to the real purpose of their mission. On November 3rd, George A. Smith

journeyed with a small party to Coal Creek, twenty miles distant, for the purpose of locating a new fort. On November 11th a party of thirty-five men, largely miners and iron workers, followed under command of Henry Lunt to make a settlement to be called Cedar City. This was to be the nucleus of the iron manufacturing colony.

Given a few weeks for attention to necessary living accommodations, they soon began to ferret out the coal and iron resources about them. Roads were built into the accessible timber areas. A good grade of clay for brick manufacturing having been discovered the men alternated between road construction and hauling clay. Soon a blast furnace was rising in their midst. The nearby canyons yielded suitable timber for the blacksmith and machine shops. Wagon wheels were robbed of their tires to supply necessary iron in full confidence that soon these would be replaced by metal of local manufacture.

Brigham Young visited the colony in May when "The Iron Company" was officially organized with duly elected officers. The summer focused the community's attention toward the day when the first test of the furnace would reveal the results of their labors. It was a momentous occasion when the entire settlement gathered for the verdict. "On the 29th of September the blast was put on the furnace and charged with iron ore that had been calcined. The fuel used was stone coal coked, and dry pitch pine wood in the raw state. On the morning of the 30th the furnace was tapped and a small quantity of iron run out which caused the hearts of all to rejoice[15]." The rejoicing found expression in repeated shouts of "Hosannah, Hosannah to God and the Lamb!" as the molten stream poured from its reservoir. Before the day was done five horsemen were on their way with samples of the product for inspection by "the Brethren" in Salt Lake. It was the first iron manufactured west of the Mississippi.

In the meantime the Presidency was tapping the resources

of "the gathering" for material aid to the Iron Mission. Converts were always urged to enlist their talents and their means in the cause of the Kingdom, but the Sixth General Epistle issued in September of 1851 contained a more specific charge. Erastus Snow and Franklin D. Richards, then presiding in England, were directed to solicit funds for the organization of an iron manufacturing company. The response from British members included one 2,000 and two 500 pound sterling subscriptions together with a number of smaller contributions. These "iron capitalists" met in Liverpool on April 28, 1852, to organize "The Deseret Iron Company" with Erastus Snow, president, and Franklin D. Richards, secretary[16]. These two men, returning to America in the fall of that year, laid the infant corporation at the feet of the First Presidency.

Representatives of the Deseret Iron Company arrived in Cedar City, less than two months after the first eventful tapping of the blast furnace, to absorb the pioneer unit into its more pretentious organization. "On the 29th of November a meeting was held in the school house by the brethren of the Iron Company, when it was resolved that the company sell out to Snow and Richards. Also resolved that the Company agree to take whatever Snow and Richards say they will give and that it be left entirely with them[17]." The $2,865.65 offered was duly accepted. Some of the members of the original company bought shares in the Deseret Iron Company and together the stockholders read the eighteen articles of incorporation. This corporate instrument concluded its legal formalities with a clause which linked the enterprise firmly with the larger program of the Kingdom:

> "For as much as we invoke the blessings of our Heavenly Father upon our capital and business, therefore, Resolved that each member of the Deseret Iron Company shall hallow his stock vested in the company unto the Lord by paying tithes thereon and that the company regularly tithe its increase ever after[18]."

For a number of years the Deseret Iron Company struggled bravely to fulfill its mission and iron products of native manufacture became commonplace. The people of the territory followed "iron notes" in the Deseret News with interest:

"An excellent air furnace was nearly finished at the date given (February 26, 1853) built of adobes with a funnel 300 ft. long to convey the smoke to a chimney stack 40 feet high which was in course of erection. The stack was so constructed that it could answer for four furnaces when completed. An extensive frame building had been erected for a casting house."

"April 2, 1853: In the beginning of March, 1853, the blast furnace was run once a week, during which 2,500 lbs. of clear good iron was made and 600 bushels of charcoal was consumed."

"Oct. 15, 1853: We have six men with the herd of cattle daily, well armed, and a strong guard every night around the fort, and as soon as the fort is enclosed, we hope to commence the iron works anew. A tremendous flood came down Coal Creek on Saturday, September 3, carrying away bridges, dams and everything before it; brought an immense quantity of logs and rocks of great size. It did considerable damage to the Iron Works."

Nor was the Mission without its grim humor,

"Peter Shirts and Brother Jones built a smelting furnace, having found a kind of ore which could be worked. They built their furnace outside the fort wall. John D. Lee opposed this, saying that the Indians could hide behind it, and shoot into the fort. As the owners refused to pull down the furnace John D. Lee and his men made short work of the building and tore it down. It was stated that after this was accomplished, 50 Indians could have hidden in the ruins where ten could not have hidden before."

A final note of encouragement came in 1855:

"Isaac C. Haight started the large furnace in Cedar City in April 1855; it worked well and was kept running for some time turning out as high as 1,700 lbs. of good iron in 4 hours[19]."

The fruits of these modest beginnings were to be delayed for a century when capital beyond the wildest dreams of the pioneers would vindicate their faith[20].

But the Iron Mission itself was not destined to become a permanent factor in the early building of the Kingdom. Its decadence was already apparent in 1857, when the U. S. Army's approach to Utah temporarily paralyzed much pioneer activity. It never fully recovered before the approach of the transcontinental railroad stifled it completely. Iron County remained a promising agricultural and livestock center. With grim satisfaction the pioneers of the Iron Mission watched one of the last runs at the old blast furnace transform seven loads of cannon balls brought by the invading "Utah Army" into mill rollers and other articles more in harmony with the program of Zion building[21].

1   Hunter, Milton R., Brigham Young, Colonizer.
2   Millennial Star, XIII:309.
3   Hunter, Milton R., American Historical Review, XVIV: 549-555.
4   Young, Brigham, Journal Discourses, II:282.
5   Deseret News, I:50.
6   Deseret News, I:154.
7   Jensen, Andrew, History of Parowan Ward, p. 9.
8   Ibid.
9   Ibid, p. 15.
10 Deseret News, 1:81.
11 Jensen, Andrew, History of Parowan Ward, p. 15.
12 Lunt, Henry, Diary. Secretary of George A. Smith.
13 Ibid.
14 Ibid.
15 Palmer, Wm. P., History of Iron Manufacturing, MS.
16 Ibid.
17 Ibid.
18 From Original Iron Company Constitution, by courtesy of Wm. R. Palmer.
19 Deseret News, V:60.
20 Recent years have brought revival of Iron Mining near Cedar City. A steady stream of high grade ore moves over the Union Pacific lines to modern steel plants near Provo, Utah. Government surveys have located major ore bodies in Iron County to justify the post war purchase by United States Steel Corporation of the $200,000,000 Geneva Plant.
21 Palmer, Wm. R., Iron County Record, September 4, 1933.

17

The Cotton Mission

THE Iron Mission on the southern rim of the Great Basin served as a base for expansion beyond its borders. This expansion first took the form of missionary labor among the Indians, but soon developed into a "Cotton Mission." The Indians of the Virgin River country had first learned of white men through the Spanish Fathers and subsequent Spanish traders passing between New Mexico and California. With good reason they regarded the arrival of additional strangers with apprehension for it was the custom of both Mexicans and Ute Indians to make raids upon them to steal their children. However, the Mormon missionaries soon assured them of their intention to remain in their homelands as friends and brothers. They had come to teach them; to help them plant and harvest so that the earth might yield more abundantly. They also brought them a strange book.

The Book of Mormon, the natives were told, was the record of their forefathers who long ago were a favored people upon the land. Through wickedness they had forfeited their heritage, but now after many centuries through the mercy of God the way to the happy life was open to their descendants. Whether the natives understood fully the message of the white men, or not, they showed much interest. Not many days had passed before a number of them, at their own request, were baptized in the Santa Clara River.

The first white men to come upon the Virgin River Indians had reported signs of primitive agriculture among them. Now the Mormon Missionaries observed in greater detail, their patches of wheat, corn, squash and melons cultivated by sticks and watered by crude methods of irrigation. Having completed the construction of a log cabin for their own lodging, the missionaries soon joined forces with the red men to compel the river to lift its waters more generously into irrigation canals. The eight hundred natives in the little valley followed the building of this first dam in the reluctant river with child-like interest and signified hearty approval as they witnessed the water spread itself over ever widening garden areas.

For many years, first under direction of Rufus C. Allen and later Jacob Hamblin, a group of outstanding Mormon leaders labored among the natives. Well known among them were Thales Haskell, Ira Hatch, Samuel Knight, Augustus P. Hardy and others who first came to Santa Clara under instructions to make permanent settlement. They preached to the Indian, helped him to improve his living conditions and, perhaps with more practical results, kept him at peace with the white man who was crossing his lands on the way to California or pre-empting his domain. To the Mormons engaged in extending the boundaries of the Kingdom, cultivating friendship with Indians was a very important part of the program. The governing spirit of these men is reflected in Young's letter to Jacob Hamblin:

"Elder Jacob Hamblin:

You are hereby appointed to succeed Elder R. C. Allen as President of the Santa Clara Indian Mission. I wish you to enter upon the duties of your office immediately.

Continue the conciliatory policy towards the Indians which I have ever commended, and seek by works of righteousness to obtain their love and confidence. Omit promises where you are not sure you can fill them; and seek to unite the hearts of the brethren on that mission, and let all under your direction be united together in the holy bonds of love and unity. . . . do not permit the brethren to part with the guns and ammunitions, but save them against the hour of need. Seek the spirit of the Lord to direct you; and that he may qualify you for every duty, is the prayer of your fellow laborer in the Gospel of Salvation,

Brigham Young[2]."

Hamblin fell ill in 1855 and a messenger found it necessary to travel 85 miles to Parowan to secure medical aid.
In addition to the coveted medicine, he incidentally took
back with him to Santa Clara a quart of cotton seed which
was given him by a convert from the Southern States. A quart
of cotton seed can have far reaching consequences. Fem-
inine pioneer ingenuity converted the first harvest of lint
into thirty yards of cloth. There was no gin to separate the
lint from the seed, and the spinning wheel and treadle loom
were as primitive as their surroundings. But the thirty yards
of cloth were sufficient to excite interest in another possible
step toward economic independence.

The following year Brigham Young sent twenty-eight additional families to settle on the Virgin. Most of them came
originally from Texas and carried with them a meager
supply of cotton seed. Immediate results from the 1857
colony were disappointing. The desolation of their surroundings, the weird volcanic formations raised above them
had a depressing effect upon the Texans and they became
easily discouraged. Unfamiliar with irrigation, they labored
with difficulty to thread the river water through countless
furrows etched on the clearings. So they complained that
their mission was a hard one and many of the original group
which settled at "Washington" drifted elsewhere. The
remainder acclimated themselves along with their cottonseed
and the settlement survived. In the meantime, peach stones
and grape cuttings from California found their way into
the little valley and responded generously to the care given
them. The survivors also discovered that they were in the
midst of productive sheep and cattle ranges located above
the volcanic rims and edged between the crumbling ledges.

Succeeding years brought additional families and new
colonies to the Virgin country to step up cotton production[3].
But despite priming from the north, the enterprise languished. In May and June of 1861, Brigham toured the
southern colonies with a large entourage. The company in-

cluded 48 men, 14 women, 2 children, 23 carriages, 21 horses, and 42 mules. It was a high moment in the experience of the isolated communities when couriers brought news of the approaching party. Horsemen rode out to meet it. Usually an escort accompanied the visitors toward the next settlement until new hosts appeared to take them over. The tour extended to Santa Clara on the lower Virgin and then followed upstream to inspect and counsel each of the newly rooted communities extending to the very entrance of the now famous Zion Canyon. Returning to Salt Lake on June 8th, the President was more determined then ever that the Virgin valleys must become Utah's "Dixie."

Accordingly, in the general conference held in October, he appointed Erastus Snow and George A. Smith to lead 309 families on a cotton mission to the south. "It is expected," said the President, "that the brethren will become permanent settlers in the southern region, and that they will cherfully contribute their efforts to supply the Territory with cotton, sugar, grapes, tobacco, figs, almonds, olive oil, and such other articles as the Lord has given us the places for garden spots in the south to produce."

Those selected for the southern assignment were among the most enterprising citizens in the Salt Lake Region and included, by order of the president, "mechanics, coopers, blacksmiths, carpenters, masons, plasterers, and joiners." Also there were to be millwrights and "musicians and singers, and farmers to make the settlements thereby efficient." . . . "Brothers Pratt and Snow in partnership will take out a carding machine, threshing machine, and a sugar mill. Brother W. H. Branch and A. M. Harriman, it is expected, will put up a saw mill somewhere on the Rio Virgin[4]."

The sudden call to forfeit newly acquired advantages and comforts to face the problems of conquering the desert again on the southern borders of Zion may have tried the faith of some, but they were generally too discreet to make any inner rebellion known. One such at least found emotional release through an almost endless poem of which the following verses reflect the buoyant humor of the pioneer:

"Oh once I lived in 'Cottonwood' and owned a little farm
But I was called to "Dixie" which gave me much alarm;
To raise the cane and cotton — right away must go,
But the reason why they sent me, I'm sure I do not know.

"I yoked old Jim and Bally up, all for to make a start;
To leave my house and garden, it almost broke my heart,
We moved along quite slowly and always looked behind
For the sands and rocks of 'Dixie' kept running through my
    mind.

*   *   *

"I feel so sad and lonely now, there's nothing here to cheer,
Except prophetic sermons which we very often hear.
They will hand them out by dozens and prove them by the
    Book
I'd rather have some roasting ears to stay at home and cook.

"I feel so weak and hungry now, I think I'm nearly dead,
'Tis seven weeks next Sunday, since I have tasted bread.
Of carrot tops and lucerne greens we have enough to eat,
But I'd like to change my diet off for buckwheat cakes and
    meat.

*   *   *

"The hot winds whirl around me, and take away my breath;
I've had the chills and fever, till I'm nearly shook to death.
All earthly tribulations are but a moment here —
And oh, if I prove faithful, a righteous crown shall wear[5]."

Success of the cotton mission was assured because most of the members shared the spirit of their leader, Erastus Snow. Calling his new associates around him he said frankly, "I feel to speak encouragingly to my brethren, so far as our removal from this to the southern part of the Territory is concerned. I feel to go body and spirit, with my heart and soul, and I sincerely hope that my brethren will endeavor to do the same; for so long as we strive to promote the interests of Zion at home and abroad we shall be happy and prosperous; and what seems to be a temporary leaving and losing of present comforts that we have gathered around us, will be like bread cast upon the waters, which after many days shall be gathered like seed that brings forth much fruit. . . . To you that think you cannot bring your feelings to go upon this mission like men, so far as I am concerned I will vote to release you[6]."

Applications for release were few if any, for most of those called shared feelings as follows:

"Sunday, 19 October, 1862. . . . At the close of the meeting some 250 men were called to go to the cotton country. My name was on the list and was read off the stand. At night I went to a meeting in the Tabernacle of those that had been called. Here I learned a principle that I shant forget in a while. It showed to me that obedience is a great principle in heaven and on earth. Well, here I have worked for the past 7 years through heat and cold, hunger and adverse circumstances and at least have got me a home, a lot with fruit trees just beginning to bear and look pretty. Well, I must leave it and go and do the will of my Father in Heaven who over rules all for the good of them that love and fear him and I pray God to give me strength to accomplish that which is required of me in an acceptable manner before him.

Wednesday, 13, of November 1862. The house looks desolate. The things all sold. The wagon loaded ready for the trip. At night went to help Brother Duffin to load up his wagon as he is going to the cotton country and we have agreed to travel together.

Thursday 14th. Fine clear day. About 1 p.m. in company with Brother Duffin I left my home, friends, relations and acquaintances and started to perform my mission. Many came and wished me goodby with tears in their eyes and blessed me, wished me well and were sorry I was going to leave as I had lived amongst them and with them for over 7 years. This was the hardest trial I ever had and had it not been for the gospel and those placed over me I should never have moved a foot to go on such a trip, but then I came here not to do my own will but the will of those that are over me and I know it will be all right if I do right[7]."

In addition to those families called from Salt Lake, a company of approximately sixty newly arrived Swiss converts was kept intact and assigned to settle at the junction of the Virgin and the Santa Clara. These in fourteen wagons, continued toward their destination without the usual stop-over in the capital of the Latter-day Kingdom. But had not Brigham Young prophesied that a city would rise on the Virgin with "spires, towers, and steeples, with homes contain-ing many inhabitants."? Who were they to question the wisdom of their inspired leader? So they continued to sing as they added another three hundred arduous miles to their overland journey. If there were any in the settlements through which they passed whose grip on Zion was weaken-ing, they heard the musical testimonies of these new recruits, caught their spirit and took a fresh hold.

In November 1861, the main company composed of four hundred heavily loaded wagons, started southward. They arrived on the Virgin to witness the river in one of its most destructive moods. Both the Virgin and the Santa Clara rose angrily in early January, 1862, and soon their crumbling banks were overrun with powerful, muddy torrents that carried everything before them. The irrigation dams of the earlier settlers were torn out completely and much of the bottom land was washed away. But there were compen-sations for the disaster wrought, and no sooner had the violence passed than the "old timers" pointed out that the river had purged and straightened itself for the new work ahead[8]. "The destruction caused by the flood," reported Erastus Snow to George A. Smith, "was very extensive but the industry and perseverance of the people will soon repair and restore what was lost and damaged. They are apparently not discouraged but feel first rate and those who went there of late are well pleased with the country and of the prospects before them."

With this unconquerable spirit the cotton mission pro-ceeded to harness the Rio Virgin to serve the purposes of irrigation. For without irrigation the whole enterprise was doomed to failure. "In the first four years and eight months after St. George[10] was founded $26,611.59 was spent in repairing and replacing dams and sections of the ditch, which had thus far watered 420 acres, making a tax of over $63.00 per acre for water alone. In 1864 the water tax per acre was $10.88; in 1865, $12.00; in 1866, and 1867, $9.00. But for the fact that these taxes were largely paid in labor it would have been impossible for the settlers to meet them[11]."

Erastus Snow, upon whom the burden of the cotton mission rested, reported to Young in a letter dated March 10, 1862, " . . . The saints were busily engaged in ditching, fencing, gathering building materials, and plowing for their crops. . . . Elder Walter E. Dodge returned from California on the 28th of February; brought home five stands of bees in good condition; one hundred pounds of sweet potatoes and several choice varieties of fruit seeds and fruit trees, among which are the olive, lemon, orange, and black pepper. A part of the trees which were washed away by the flood have been recovered. A commendable zeal is manifested by our citizens to put in early fruit trees. St. George already assumes the appearance of quite a city, all but the houses. . . .

"We expect to start up some cattle for a carding machine and perhaps for a thresher next week. We are holding ourselves in readiness to send back some teams to Florence (to bring in immigrants) yet we have nothing from Salt Lake in relation to that movement.

"We need more help upon this mission. It is a big country yet to subdue. We would be glad to have a silversmith (watch cleaner & repairer), a hatter, a potter, a gunsmith, a stonecutter, a plasterer, and more stone masons, and Robert Hill the wool carder and five hundred common laborers as soon as we can get them something to eat[12]."

The next year (1863) fifty-six thousand pounds of cotton were produced. Most of the crop was distributed in the settlements in barter for food staples. But considerable quantities were exchanged beyond the borders of Zion for more sorely needed equipment and household articles. Thus eleven thousand pounds were hauled to California and four thousand, three hundred pounds transported all the way to the Missouri River by teams sent to bring in the immigrants.

With promise of success in raising cotton came plans for construction of a textile mill. President Young himself took the initiative to import the necessary machinery investing $44,000.00 of Church money in the enterprise. The factory was completed and machinery installed by 1869. "Zion's Cooperative Rio Virgin Manufacturing Company," headed by Erastus Snow, was incorporated with a capital of a hundred thousand dollars.

Ever responsive to the call of their leaders, the Saints bought stock for cash or produce, and when these were lacking paid for their shares through labor. Though the textile mill continued to operate for two decades, manufacturing large quantities of goods, it was seriously handicapped by lack of materials. Cotton production suffered in competition with more remunerative crops and finally yielded to importation.

The spirit of the gathering was too firmly rooted in the Zion builders to be forgotten even in the perplexities of new and precarious settlement. From the midst of dire local need for man power and horse power came the above announcement to Brigham Young: "We are holding ourselves in readiness to send back some teams to Florence (to bring in the immigrants,)"

This desire to share the privileges of Zion with friends and relatives in "Babylon" did not soon pass away in Dixie. Erastus Snow spoke in a conference of the southern mission held in St. George on May 3, 1868: "He expressed his satisfaction at the efforts of the people of this mission to assist the poor from foreign countries. St. George, at the present time, has paid about $1,800.00, Toquerville, $1,000.00, Santa Clara $900.00 and Cedar Wards $1,000.00 of indebtednes to the Perpetual Emigrating Fund. It is generally thought, he said, that some five or six thousand saints will be emigrated from Great Britain this year at the rate of about $100.00 per capita[13]."

Nor had the plans for a western approach to Zion been forgotten. The Gathering demanded all possible consideration of the problems of distance, delay, and physical hardships. The preliminary investigations made on the Colorado River before the contraction of the Mormon Empire in 1857 were eagerly resumed with the spread of the cotton colonies in that direction. The proximity of these settlements to the lower Colorado and reports of successful operations on the river by the "Colorado Navigation Company" and the "Union Line" determined President Young to take effective steps towards realizing his dream of a western seaport. Bishop Anson Call was appointed in November of 1864 to act as agent for the newly created "Deseret Mercantile Association," as well as immigration agent for the Church at this proposed port of entry into the United States.

Together with a party of experienced scouts, Call located a suitable place on the Colorado about fifteen miles above the present Boulder Dam and rushed a warehouse to completion by February of the following year. The Saints now had an actual port of landing on the lower Colorado within one hundred and twenty miles from St. George and four hundred and fifty miles from Salt Lake. Immigrants and supplies landed here would already be in Zion and their distribution would be one of comparative ease as Mormon settlements marked the route to Salt Lake City. Some freight arrived at "Call's Landing" and advertisements in Salt Lake newspapers by freighting companies as well as editorials in the Deseret News gave promise of the plan's fulfillment. But already forces were at work to span the gap between the Missouri River and the Salt Lake Valley and so destroy the dream of a western approach before it became a reality.

Thus did the requirements of "the Kingdom" cause the Mormon commonwealth to bulge toward the south. Iron and cotton were economic necessities and so long as the distance from sources of supply presented a greater barrier to securing them than did the problems of local production, the "Missions thrived to the glory of God." So also did the pressure of the "Gathering" keep alive plans for a western approach to Zion so long as the eastern overland route appeared to present greater risks, delays, and hardships. But slowly iron rails were creeping westward along the Mormon trail to reverse the relative advantages in each of these Mormon problems. With the arrival of the railroad in Utah, distance, delay, and hardship would be stricken from the account of the eastern route and the problems of local production would rise sharply in contrast with importation from established centers.

The "Golden Spike" celebration at Promontory Point on May 10, 1869, reverberated through the eastern capitals which hailed the transcontinental railroad as a powerful bond between east and west. But the celebration also had its repercussions in humbler places closer to the scene of the event. From Utah's Dixie came a telegram to President Young announcing: "At 12:33 our Deseret Telegraph line flashed word to St. George that the connecting rail of the Transcontinental Railroad was being laid by Governor Stanford. From information received this morning the Ecclesiastical, Civil, and Military authorities and the people were on the qui vive and immediately on receipt of the welcome intelligence greeted it by unfurling the Stars and Stripes amid the salutes of the artillery and music by the Brass and Martial Bands. After which most eloquent speeches were delivered by President Erastus Snow and Major Jacob Gates. Even while we write the concluding hearty cheers of the assembled people are making our red hills ring again." signed Richard Bentley and Joseph Birch, committee[14].

So it was that the transcontinental railroad clamped its fingers upon the Iron and Cotton Missions of Deseret and banished forever Brigham Young's ambition to establish a western approach to Zion. But the compensation of a railroad to end Mormon isolation was accepted with cheers and celebration, for now "Babylon" itself had come to the aid of the Gathering. And while the original "Missions" themselves languished and disappeared, they left the Kingdom firmly entrenched in southern Utah through the livestock and agricultural industries of Iron County and Utah's Dixie.

1   The Escalante-Dominguez party had passed through the Virgin Valley in the fall of 1776.

2   Little, James A., Jacob Hamblin, p. 44.

3   Jensen, Andrew, History of St. George Stake., November 1858. One small company sent by Brigham Young to the Virgin in 1858 returned in the fall with 575 pounds of ginned cotton, and 160 gallons of molasses which were religiously delivered to the tithing office in Salt Lake. This cotton cost $3.40 per pound to produce. Cotton production increased in one of the settlements in the upper valley so that acreage was decreased because of difficulty in disposing of the previous year's crop. More land was planted to Chinese sugar cane because molasses was in demand in exchange for breadstuffs in the neighboring settlements. Zadoc K. Judd contributed greatly to the cotton enterprise by perfecting a little machine to separate cotton lint from the seed. Necessary information for construction of such a device was gathered from southern converts and he soon produced a number of them for the Santa Clara people. It was described as "Two small rollers three-fourths of an inch in diameter, seven or eight inches long, set in two upright posts, the rollers keyed snugly together. A crank on the end of the rollers made to turn in opposite directions so as to draw the lint through while the seed would drop down on the feed side."

4   History of Brigham Young, M. S. 1861, pp. 440-451.

5   Pioneer Songs, pp. 94-95. Published by the Daughters of Utah Pioneers, 1932.

6   Bleak, James G., Annals 100 — MS.

7   Brooks, Juanita, Background for Mormon Social Security, MS. paper on file in Cedar City Public Library.

8   Report of irrigation Investigations in Utah, directed by Elwood Mead. p. 211. "The flow of both streams as well as some of the tributaries was permanently increased by the opening of springs theretofore closed."

9   History of Brigham Young. MS. p. 333.

10 St. George, named after George A. Smith, became and still is the metropolis of the Virgin valley.

11 Roberts, B. H., History of the Church, Vol. V:258. The quotation, drawing upon History of Brigham Young, MS., continues, "These figures but partially tell of the burden that had to be borne in settling the new southern wilderness. The cost of living was excessively high. Common labor cost $3.00 per day. Flour cost from $15 to $25 per hundred pounds. The price of sugar was $1.00 per pound; of molasses $4.00 per gallon; of common cotton domestic, $1.00 per yard, of coal oil, $8.00 per gallon. One hundred dollars a thousand feet was paid for lumber 50 and 75

miles away. A sheep for a pound of tea was a common bargain. Provisions of all kinds were freighted by mule teams from San Bernardino or Los Angeles, California, at 16 cents per pound. Traffic in these commodities was practically all by barter, for cash was seldom if ever in circulation. Nor was there other than a local basis for values. Prices of produce to pay for work on dams and ditches were determined in mass meetings of the owners of the land watered. Prices of produce for taxes were fixed by the county court, and it is not uncommon to find entries in the county court records such as that made Dec. 7, 1863, which states that "it was decided that molasses, at $1.75 per gallon, be paid R. L. Lloyd for 72 pounds of cotton, which is hereby appropriated to pay for the probate and county court seals."

12 Jensen, Andrew, History of St. George Stake.
13 Ibid.
14 Ibid.

18

Hand Carts

A DECADE of gathering to the mountains closed with much accomplished. But the past was to be only a preliminary to a greater future. Thousands more of the "Lord's poor" awaited deliverance from "Babylon." The Perpetual Emigrating Fund Company, however, was bogging down in financial difficulties. Not only were repayments to the fund lagging, but the cost of transportation was rising sharply. From 1853 to 1855 the estimated fare for "P. E. Emigrants" rose from ten to fifteen pounds and the price of teams from forty to fifty-five and sixty pounds. As the cost went up the number receiving help from the Fund went down and there threatened a serious decrease in the flow of immigrants to Zion. New plans must be devised either to increase the available funds of the Company or to cut the cost of transportation.

Speeding up the gathering was vital to the Mormon program on both sides of the Atlantic. In America there was an insatiable demand for laborers in the Kingdom. In Europe accumulating reserves were threatened with stagnation if not soon released to active participation in the cause which had won their allegiance. Moreover, Brigham Young recognized that stimulation of emigration would give new impetus to foreign proselyting. This he expressed to Franklin D. Richards, presiding in England.

"There are many of the really poor, and faithful, which I wish to have helped out as soon as possible. I believe it helps the cause not only by (their) coming to assist in the works of Zion; but (emigration) has a beneficial influence in the world, and aids those who go to proclaim the Gospel in obtaining hearers and believers. When the Saints remain year after year in the world it becomes so much of an old story, that it attracts less attention, and people grow indifferent about the testimony of the truth than they do by not always having the Saints of God in their midst. It works favorably therefore, in every light in which it can be presented[1]."

Already plans for cutting transportation costs had been foreshadowed in a General Epistle written to the Saints in October of 1851:

> "The voice of the good Shepherd is to all Saints, even to the ends of the earth; gather yourselves together, come home; . . . Some of the children of the world have crossed the mountains and plains from Missouri to California with a pack on their backs to worship their God — Gold! . . . Some of the Saints now in our midst came here with wagons or carts made of wood, without a particle of iron, hooping their wheels with hickory, or rawhide or ropes and had as good and safe a journey as any in the camps, with their wrought iron wagons. And can you not do the same? Yes, if you have the same desire, the same faith. Families might start from the Missouri River with Cows, handcarts, wheelbarrows, with little flour and no unnecessaries and come to this place quicker, and with less fatigue, than by following the heavy trains with their cumbrous herds which they are often obliged to drive miles to feed. Do you like this way of travelling? Do you think Salvation costs too much. If so, it is not worth having[2]."

Again, in April, 1852, the subject of walking across the plains with handcarts had been presented to the general conference in Salt Lake City. In response to the suggestion, ninety-three men volunteered to go east with teams and provisions to meet the immigrants who should adopt this mode of travel[3]. However, no serious effort was made toward hand cart migration at that time.

The financial strain upon the Emigrating Company in 1855 made continuance under the old plan impossible.

Brigham Young, as president of the Company, wrote to
Franklin D. Richards as follows:

" . . . We have not much of interest to communicate more
than you are aware of — such as meeting our heavy liabilities
constantly falling due here and in St. Louis for this year's
emigration. If I had about one hundred thousand pounds
a year to expend for that purpose there would be some
satisfaction to gather the Lord's poor, although in so doing
we might also gather some of the Devil's poor and poor
devils as well. . . .

"I have been thinking how we should operate another
year. We cannot afford to purchase wagons and teams as in
times past, I am consequently thrown back upon my old
plan — to make hand carts and let the emigration foot it,
and draw upon them the necessary supplies, having a cow
or two for every ten. They can come just as quick if not
quicker, and much cheaper — can start earlier and escape
the prevailing sickness which annually lays so many of our
brethren in the dust. A great majority of them walk now
even with the teams which are provided, and have a great
deal more care and perplexity than they would have if they
came without them. They will only need 90 days rations
from the time of their leaving the Missouri River, and as the
settlements extend up the Platte, not that much. The carts
can be made without a particle of iron, with wheels hooped,
made strong and light, and one, or if the family be large,
two of them will bring all that they will need upon the
plains.

"If it is once tried you will find that it will become the
favorite mode of crossing the plains; they will have nothing
to do but come along, and I should not be surprised if a
company of this kind should make the trip in sixty or seventy days. I do know that they can beat any ox train crossing the plains. I want to see it fairly tried and tested, at
all events, and I think we might as well begin another year
as any time and save this enormous expense of purchasing
wagons and teams — indeed we will be obliged to pursue
this course or suspend operations, for aught that I can see
at the present.

"It will become important for you to forward us a list of
their names and advise Brothers Taylor and Spencer that

they may make arrangements accordingly. If they will do this, nothing doubting, I can promise them that they will be met with provisions and friends far down on the plains, perhaps as low as Laramie if we get their names in time. You know almost everybody has friends and relatives, here now, that when they find their friends are coming will go out and meet them[4]."

The President's enthusiasm for the new plan was more than matched by the impatience of European converts who begged for the privilege of coming to "Zion" under almost any conditions. The plan was therefore announced in a letter dated October 29th. It follows in part: "Let all the Saints who can, gather up for Zion, and come while the way is open before them; let the poor also come, whether they receive aid or not from the (P. E.) Fund; let them come on foot, with hand carts, or wheelbarrows; let them gird up their loins and walk through and nothing shall hinder or stay them.

"In regard to the foreign emigration another year, let them pursue the northern route from Boston, New York, or Philadelphia, and land at Iowa City or the then terminus of the railroad; there let them be provided with hand carts on which to draw their provisions and clothing; then walk and draw them, thereby saving the immense expense every year for teams and outfit for crossing the plains.

"We propose sending men of faith and experience with suitable instructions to some proper outfitting point, to carry into effect the above suggestions; let the Saints therefore, who intend to emigrate the ensuing year, understand that they are expected to walk, and draw their luggage across the plains, and that they will be assisted by the Fund in no other way[5]."

In his letter of September, Young promised to forward instructions to the agents John Taylor and Daniel Spencer then at Iowa City, regarding the building of hand carts. These vehicles were to be completed before the arrival of the immigrants at Iowa City so that there should be no delay in continuing the journey. An early start was emphasized and there was ground for the belief expressed that the hand cart company could out-travel the ox-team train since it would be unencumbered by large numbers of cattle[6].

The carts themselves were very simple in construction. They were made of wood, and when properly selected and seasoned the material proved serviceable enough. However, experience in their use brought improvements in their construction and greater durability. The box construction was usually of Iowa hickory or oak with the shafts of the same material, but the axle was uniformly of hickory. One who had experience with them wrote, "In length the side pieces and shafts were about six or seven feet, with three or four binding crossbars from the back part to the fore part of the body of the cart. Then two or three feet space from the latter bar to the front bar or singletree for the lead horse or lead man, woman, or boy of the team. . . . Across the bars of the bed of the cart we usually sewed a strip of bed ticking or a counterpane. On this wooden cart, with thimbleless axle, having about two and one half inch shoulder and one inch point, were often loaded 400 to 500 pounds of flour, bedding, extra clothing, cooking utensils, and a tent[7]."

Another type known as the family cart was made a little heavier than the ordinary one and was provided with a top. This type was used for carrying children. Referring to the carts used by a group of missionaries travelling eastward from Salt Lake, the Florence Courier reported them to be like those used by the colored porters in eastern cities, and commented, "They had canvas covers and were better looking vehicles in every respect than we had expected to see[8]."

Acting under official instructions, the Millennial Star for February 23, 1856, announced that Iowa City had been selected as the out-fitting post for that season and that the emigrants would be forwarded from the port of landing to that point via the Chicago and Rock Island Railroad. It continued, "The P. E. Fund Emigrants will use hand carts in crossing the plains in which they will convey their provisions, tent and necessary luggage. . . . There will of course be means provided for conveyance of the aged, infirm, and those unable for any cause to walk. . . . The first two hundred miles of the journey from Iowa City will be through a settled grain growing country where it is expected that supplies of provisions can be obtained without labor of hauling them any considerable distance. By travelling this distance with carts lightly loaded the Saints will have an excellent opportunity of becoming accustomed to camp life, and walking and thereby be better prepared for starting out on the plains[9]."

The cost of transportation under the new plan for that year, was placed at nine pounds for each adult and four pounds, ten shillings for those under one year of age[10]. This practically cut the per capita cost of the previous year in half.

With New York and Boston as ports of landing the majority of the Mormon immigration proceeded from the latter city by rail via New York to Iowa City, Iowa, a distance of nearly 1,300 miles. In keeping with the aim to pare expenses the trip by rail did not permit of many comforts. One who crossed the plains in the third company of the season wrote that her ship's passengers made the railway trip in cattle cars[11]. At least one of the companies of that year slept in a New York ware house while waiting to continue the journey[12]. The fare to Iowa City was quoted at $11.00[13].

Daniel Spencer was in charge of emigration affairs at the frontier outfitting post, assisted by George D. Grant, William H. Kimball, James H. Hart and others[14]. The Agents had evidently not been very successful in providing sufficient equipment to meet the needs of the immigrants as they came. A member of the third company passing through, wrote that they were delayed for three weeks in Iowa City and the fourth company reported similar delay, both stating that the carts had to be made as well as yokes, tents, etc.[15] With the information at hand it would be difficult to place responsibility for this delay, but it was the beginning of handicaps which proved disastrous to the last two hand cart companies of the season.

The next stopping place was Florence, Nebraska, located on the old site of Winter Quarters, nearly 300 miles west of Iowa City. J. H. Latey, in a letter to John Taylor from Florence on August 14th, said of the first two companies, "They were singing as they came along, one would not think that they had come from Iowa City, a long and rough journey of 275 to 300 miles, except for their dust stained garments and sun-burned faces. The first company boasted of what they called the Birmingham Band. One of their songs, as they marched was entitled, "Some must push and some must pull,"

> "Ye Saints who dwell on Europe's shore
> Prepare yourselves for many more
> To leave behind your native land
> For sure God's judgments are at hand.
> For you must cross the raging main,
> Before the promised land you gain
> And with the faithful make a start
> To cross the plains with your hand cart.
> Chorus.
> For some must push and some must pull,
> As we go marching up the hill;
> So merrily on the way we go,
> Until we reach the valley.
> * * *
> And long before the Valley's gained
> We will be met upon the plains
> With music sweet and friends so dear
> And fresh supplies our hearts to cheer.
> And then with music and with song
> How cheerfully we'll march along,
> And thank the day we made a start
> To cross the plains with our hand cart[17]."

Latey continued in his letter: "The companies are much alike. They do not need separate description. The first Hand Cart Company left the ground on Thursday, July 16, went out three and a half miles and camped. On the 20th I went out to settle up with Captain Ellsworth and saw them start off in good earnest to the tune of 'some must pull, etc.' (Can't move without that.)" The second company left Florence on July 24th. The 3rd company, composed almost entirely of emigrants from Wales under the direction of Edward Bunker, arrived at Florence on the 19th of July and set out across the plains on the 30th. Latey's comment on the delays caused in Florence is significant as related to the two remaining companies of that season. "The companies stay here longer than they otherwise would in consequence of the carts being unfit for their journey across the plains; some requiring new axles, and the whole of them having to have a piece of iron screwed on to prevent the wheel from wearing away the wood[18]."

The optimism of those directing the hand cart movement is read in a letter from Erastus Snow to John Taylor written on September 15th. He says, "So far as is yet known the experiment with hand carts is likely to succeed quite as well as the most ardent advocate of the measure could have anticipated. At our latest advices the advance companies were in the regions of Fort Laramie and all were in excellent health and spirits, moving on finely and far outstripping the ox teams[19]."

The new experiment, however, did not always present a picnic prospect. There were those who weakened and withdrew from the ranks along the way, and those who hesitated on the borders of the plains to undertake the journey at all. An interesting contrast in the feelings of some of those who faced the prospects of a thousand mile overland journey on foot appears in current correspondence. Writes one of a family that hesitated at the sight of the hand carts, "We think it will be better to remain here or at St. Louis for a time until we are able to help ourselves to a wagon. Mother says that she must have a revelation before she can see this right. Why we would have to sell nearly all our clothes! And what shall we do for things to wear when we get to the Valley? Seventeen pounds weight each is but very little[20]."

The answer from a relative remaining in England represents the other extreme, and is sharp in its rebuke. Expressing pleasure at receiving the letter from which the foregoing was taken, the writer goes on, "But my pleasure was changed to great pain and unfeigned sorrow when I read the contents. . . . There is not one atom of the Spirit of Zion in it, but the very spirit of apostasy. You invite me and my family to stay awhile in New York . . . Brother, sister, father, or mother, when they put a stumbling block in the way of my salvation are nothing more to me than Gentiles. As for me and my house we will serve the Lord and when we start we will go right up to Zion if we go ragged and barefoot. . . . There are hundreds in England who have begged and prayed with tears for the privilege of going to Zion but have been unable to get it. And now you slight it[21]!"

A member of the third company wrote that her husband was offered many inducements to remain in Iowa City to work at his trade for as high as ten dollars a day, but concluded that money was no inducement for they were anxious to get to "Zion"[22]. "Many of the settlers along the road," she said, "made fun of us as we walked along pulling our carts, but we did not care; the weather was fine and the roads were excellent; and although I was sick and we were all tired out at night we thought it was a glorious way to come to Zion."

In contrast again is the report from J. H. Latey writing from Florence, "There are others, for I have seen both sides of the picture — who are allured by fine promises and high wages; others there are whose faith is not of that nature to stand the trials they are called upon to undergo, and back out from five to fifty in a company of three hundred[23]." No doubt the delay in Iowa City and Florence set many to serious consideration of what course to take and led to withdrawals, either temporary or permanent, from the ranks of the migrating companies.

The first two companies arrived in the Salt Lake Valley on the 26th of September. They were met near the mouth of Emigration Canyon by Presidents Young, Kimball, and Wells, with military and band escort. Captain Ellsworth's company arrived first, closely followed by Captain McArthur's. After introduction and greetings the News account says: "The line of march was scarcely taken up before it began to be met by men, women, and children, on foot, on horses, and in wagons, thronging out to see and welcome the first hand cart companies, and the numbers rapidly increased until the living tide lined and thronged South Temple Street[24]." An eye witness wrote: "As they came down the bench you could scarcely see them for the dust. When they entered the City the folks came running from every quarter to get a glimpse of the long looked-for hand carts. I shall never forget the feeling that ran through my whole system as I caught the first sight of them. The first Hand Cart was drawn by a man and his wife. They had a little flag on it, on which were the words, 'Our President, may the unity of the Saints ever show the wisdom of his counsels.' The next Hand Cart was drawn by three young women . . . The tears ran down the cheeks of many a man who you would have thought would not, could not, shed a tear[25]."

The third company soon joined the others in the valley. Summarizing the journey of these companies, the News reported that the mortality rate had been less than the average attending the ox-trains; that they had often traveled twenty-five and thirty miles a day and would have come through in a shorter time had they not been obliged to wait upon the slow progress of the ox teams carrying the tents and supplies.

The Hand Cart episode has been remembered popularly by the   tragedy that unfortunately crept into it.   The disaster that befell two of the companies must receive due attention as part of the hand cart story but the movement as a whole must not be lost sight of.   The experiment was not without success and would likely have continued over a longer period had not other developments in transportation methods brought it to a close.   It should be kept in mind also that the emigration for 1856 was not entirely made up of hand cart members.   Out of a total of 3,756 emigrants, only about half, or 1,978, were P. E. passengers listed to travel by hand cart; three hundred and eighty-five were booked to go through on their own means and the balance was to remain in the States for the season.

1   History of Brigham Young, MS, May 31, 1855.

2   Sixth General Epistle, October 1851, Millennial Star XIV:23.

3   Millennial Star, XIV:325.

4   Millennial Star, XVII:813.

5   Millennial Star, XVIII:54.

6   Millennial Star, IXX:500.   Quoting from Florence Courier, which described an east bound party of missionaries with hand carts: " . . . General impression upon the mind of the public is that the hand cart is the slowest and most laborious mode of conveyance that can be used. From the report of this party and of others we are inclined to think it exactly the reverse.   This party was but 19 days in coming from Fort Laramie, a distance of 520 miles — and average of over 27 miles per day — some days they made 25 miles. This is certainly not slow traveling and when we reflect upon the many inconveniences to which a traveller is subjected with his horses, mules, and oxen in crossing the Plains; the crossing of streams, danger of stampedes, selection of camping place for the cattle, tethering and working with them morning and night, we are inclined to think that for a California or Salt Lake Trip, we would give the hand cart the preference over any other mode, unless we had fine mule teams and so few of other traps as to enable us to take plenty of corn for the animals."

7   Latter-day Saint Journal History, November 9, 1856.

8   Millennial Star, IXX:500, From Florence Courier.

9   Millennial Star, XVIII:122.

10   Millennial Star, XVIII:713.

11   Latter-day Saints Journal History, October 2, 1856.   From Miss Priscilla Merriman Evan's Diary.

12   Latter-day Saints Journal History, November 9, 1856.   J. G. Willie's Narrative.

13 Latter-day Saints Journal History, November 9, 1856. Wm. Woodward letter.

14 Church Chronology, p. 56.

15 Latter-day Saints Journal History, October 2, 1856; November 9, 1856.

16 Millennial Star, XVIII:637.

17 Composed enroute by J. D. T. McAllister. From Pioneer Songs — 21. Pub. by Daughters of the Utah Pioneers, 1932.

18 Millennial Star, XVIII:637.

19 Latter-day Saints Journal History, September 15, 1856.

20 Millennial Star, XVIII:369.

21 Ibid.

22 Latter-day Saints Journal History, October 2, 1856.

23 Millennial Star, XVIII:637.

24 Deseret News, VI:236.

25 Latter-day Saints Journal History, September 29, 1856.

19

Tragedy

Y OU will go forward this season at your own risk."
The speaker faced a motley crowd of immigrants on the
plains of Nebraska. They were clamoring to set out across
the wilderness at once for the Great Basin. Having sounded
the warning of an experienced guide, Levi Savage turned to
kick the dust from a curious wooden cart wheel and stooped
to adjust a loosened spoke.

It was Mid-August in 1856. The immigrants were wholly
ignorant of the country ahead and unused to the rigors of
camp life. Should they attempt to cross the Rockies before winter snows set in or delay until the following spring?
Captain J. G. Willie called for a decision from the assembly.

Frank, open countenances registered impatience at this
delay in their journey to "Zion." Levi Savage's warning
went unheeded. Had not Providence brought them safely
from far-off England, Scotland, Wales and Scandinavia?
Would not a protecting hand be over them even in the
mountains? As the vote was called, these sons and daughters
of foreign lands, simply clad, travel worn, and dusty, pressed
eagerly upon their leader to render a decision in the affirmative.

Echoes of their ill fated enthusiasm had hardly died away
in the distance when members of the Martin Company began
pouring into the Florence Camp. As they emerged from
the dust clouds it was noticeable that able-bodied men were
in a minority among large numbers of aged and children.
Again there was delay, another council called, and on August
25th, seven hundred others began moving hopefully toward
the western horizon.

They formed a colorful spectacle as the winding train of vehicles, drawn by men and women moved forward between occasional supply wagons and small herds of milk cows. Many of the carts were tastefully painted to suit the fancy of the owners, while here and there appeared inscriptions such as "Truth will Prevail," "Zion's Express," "Blessings Follow Sacrifice" and "Merry Mormons." Snatches of the marching song "Some must push and some must pull" served to lighten the monotony of the daily routine. Self-imposed discipline and strict camp regulations facilitated progress, permitting an advance of from twelve to fifteen miles per day. Men, women, and children alike, tramped patiently forward. The fatigued and ill, alone, received whatever comforts were afforded by riding in the supply wagons.

Evening brought rest and recreation. Family fires smouldered after supper while the community blaze mounted as a signal for a general gathering. Young folks sang and made merry in impromptu programs. Untamed muscles strained for supremacy in wrestling, jumping, and camp stunts, for the entertainment of the gentler sex. With song and story the older ones, too, joined in the evening's diversion until the hour for retirement approached.

The noise subsided as a circle closed around the smouldering embers. Then with one accord all voices joined in singing those lines which encouraged thousands to go on when enthusiasm lagged. "Come, Come Ye Saints" had been bequeathed by the pioneers of a decade earlier to the thousands who would follow them into the west. It became the common heritage of foreign, as well as native tongues.

> "Come, Come Ye Saints, no toil nor labor fear,
> But with joy wend your way;
> Though hard to you this journey may appear,
> Grace shall be as your day.
> 'Tis better far, for us to strive
> Our useless cares from us to drive;
> Do this, and joy your hearts will swell —
> All is well! All is well!

Why should we mourn, or think our lot is hard?
'Tis not so; all is right!
Why should we think to earn a great reward,
If we now shun the fight?
Gird up your loins, fresh courage take,
Our God will never us forsake;
And soon we'll have this truth to tell —
All is well!　All is well!

We'll find the place which God for us prepared,
Far away in the West:
Where none shall come to hurt or make afraid;
There the Saints will be blessed.
We'll make the air with music ring —
Shout praises to our God and King;
Above the rest these words we'll tell
All is well!　All is well!

And should we die before our journey's through,
Happy day!　All is well!
We then are free from toil and sorrow too;
With the just we shall dwell.
But if our lives are spared again
To see the Saints, their rest obtain,
Oh how we'll make this chorus swell —
All is well!　All is well!"

With the closing words each sought his covers and when the last echoes of taps died away in the darkness the emigrants slept with the wilderness.

October came with frosty nights. Aspen groves turned yellow and crimson patches of oak held forebodings of approaching winter. Far down on the plains of Wyoming the Willie and Martin companies moved hopefully up the Platte. Emigration agents, having closed the business of the season at Iowa City hurried westward. With horse teams, they passed the Martin Company at Loupe Fork and found them in good spirits and health. Later they met two members of the Willie Company returning for thirty head of strayed cattle. Purchasing a few buffalo robes for this latter company at Platte Bridge the agents hastened on to Salt Lake City.

The morning of October first dawned upon a disappointed camp of men and women on the outskirts of Fort Laramie. Someone had blundered. Provisions of food and clothing, upon which they depended, were not awaiting them. The scant seventeen pounds of clothing permitted each member of the Willie Company gave little comfort on that frosty morning. As they gathered, shivering, around the camp fires to prepare a meager breakfast, there was lacking the usual banter and song. The consciousness of threatening storms, decreased rations, and insufficient clothing was not easily shaken.

Day after day they pushed painfully forward. A brave heart responding to a moment of sunshine brought back "Some must push and some must pull," and for a brief hour it revived their spirits as the tramp, tramp, tramp, fitted into its rhythm. The clouds grew darker and lowered. A breeze from the north rustled through the last oak leaves clinging crisply to barren twigs. Naked aspens stood in columns of somber whiteness. A coyote slunk through the under-brush and a moment later, silhouetted for an instant against a grey sky-line, howled a melancholy, unearthly challenge. Strong men cast anxious glances toward their mates. Instinctively, children trudged more closely upon parental heels. A flutter of leaves broke through the moving line and women drew their shawls a little more closely about them, bowed their heads a trifle lower, and plodded onward.

A sudden gust of wind brought a flurry of snowflakes. Their worst fears became a reality. Hour after hour the treacherous snow piled up its death trap. Shoes, worn through, exposed bare feet to its damp and chill. Scarcely a wrap was provided as a change for wet and frozen clothing. More serious still, cutting the food rations to a minimum could only preserve the supply a few days. The two scouts who had been sent to recover strayed cattle overtook the camp without them. But they had come upon the tracks of the Martin Company and reported that they led away from the main trail. It was evident that five hundred and seventy six other victims were caught in Wyoming snows with scarcely able-bodied men enough to care for the aged and children!

It was Conference Time in the Mormon settlements. The colonists had gathered in Salt Lake City to hear the message of "the Presiding Brethren." Brigham Young rose before the assembly in the Bowery and gravely addressed them;

"My subject is this: On this fifth day of October, 1856, many of our brethren and sisters are on the plains with handcarts, and probably are now 700 miles from this place; we must send them assistance. The text will be 'To get them here.' This is the salvation I am now seeking for, to save our brethren[2]."

When ox teams were volunteered he thundered:

"I do not want to send oxen. I want good horses and mules. They are in the territory and we must have them; also twelve tons of flour and forty good teamsters."

Pioneer families recounted their scanty winter stores and within three days a relief train set out with their sacrifice. The contributions up to that time included:

"Fifty-four teams, 6 horses, 51 teamsters, 14 tons of flour, 31 bushels of onions, 12 pounds dried meat, 5 bushels of oats, $8.00 cash, 106 quilts and blankets, 8 cloaks, 153 coats, 51 pairs of pants, 51 vests, 134 pairs of boots and shoes, 29 shawls, 9 pair mittens, 1 buffalo robe, 40 bundles of clothing, 2 overskirts, 2 chemises, 4 neckties, 13 hats and caps, 3 boy suits, 8 pair of drawers, 15 jackets, 12 bonnets, 7 skirts, 4 handkerchiefs, 1 rug, 5 yards linsey, 2 aprons, 1 pair of gloves[3]."

By October 31st, no less than 250 teams were on their way to relieve the sufferers. Among the first and best equipped were those sent by Young and others of his council.

Meanwhile the Willie and the Martin companies were trapped in the earliest snowfall in the experience of the Pioneers. The former made a forced encampment two miles below Rocky Ridge on the Sweetwater. The latter

found it impossible to proceed beyond Platte Bridge. Tents
and other improvised covering gave only partial shelter from
the chill of winter.

Snow continued to pile up with recurrent storms. The
cry of babies against the bitter cold drove men in desperation through the blinding sleet for firewood. Frozen feet
and frostbitten fingers maintained meager fires around
which huddled mothers with feverish children. The daily
rations were cut down again and again, each time with a
prayer that help would come on the morrow. But the morrow, instead, brought death — first one, then another, and
another. It was the men who died. They were not sick, but
chilled through, and among those who dug graves in the
morning were some who, before night had fallen, themselves
required burial. An evening came when each survivor received his portion of the remaining rations. Unaware of
approaching help they faced starvation and a frozen grave.

On October 20th, the first relief wagons hove into sight
of the Willie Company. A pathetic sight awaited them.
Already twenty had perished, of whom nineteen were men.
Messengers carried word of the serious condition to teamsters
in the rear, and others pushed on to the Martin company.
Several days still separated the victims from effective succor
and the death toll mounted higher. When at last relief
trains penetrated the snow barrier it was only to effect a
partial rescue. Over two hundred dead remained to mark
the scene of tragedy.

When the survivors arrived in Salt Lake on the ninth and
last of November, respectively, no pains were spared in Zion
for their relief and comfort. News of the latter company's
arrival came during the Sunday morning service. Brigham
Young immediately dismissed the congregation with a classic
declaration of the true principles of the Christian faith:

> "When those persons arrive I do not want to see them
> put into houses by themselves. I want to have them dis-
> tributed in this city among the families that have good,

comfortable houses; and I wish the sisters now before me, and all who know how and can, to nurse and wait upon the newcomers, and prudently administer medicine and food to them. . . . The afternoon meeting will be omitted, for I wish the sisters to go home and prepare to give those who have just arrived a mouthful of something to eat and to wash them and nurse them up. . . . Prayer is good, but when (as on this occasion) baked potatoes and pudding and milk are needed, prayer will not supply their place. Give every duty its proper time and place[4]."

Then, setting an example for them all the President issued instructions to the Presiding Bishop that any or all of the immigrants for whom accommodations were lacking should be sent to his own home.

An unfortunate mistake had been made. There were those who, it seems for personal reasons, attempted to place the blame upon Brigham Young for the disaster. They charged him, and consequently the whole emigrating agency, with disregard of life so long as emigrants were obtained in large numbers. But there is no foundation for the charge against Brigham Young[5]. He urged continually that emigration should commence early. He pointed the finger of responsibility toward the frontier agents when he stated in a letter dated October 31st, 1856: "This year's operations have eminently proved the feasibility and success of the hand cart enterprise when the business is rightly managed and the companies leave the frontiers in anything like the proper season. Those companies that left Iowa City in the forepart of July arrived in good time and were in excellent condition and spirits[6]." Franklin D. Richards wrote in November, "The President has graciously approved of our general operations in getting the Saints off by hand carts, the most important objectionable feature being 'too late,' concerning which I experienced as great or greater care last February and March than we can now entertain for their welfare[7]."

Profiting by the experience of the preceding year, particular care was taken to prevent delay in the future shipping of emigrants. The Millennial Star urged that payments be made at an early date, and announced that no ships with "through" emigrants would be chartered to leave after a safe time limit. "It is our intention," read one announcement, "to have our through emigration hereafter embark from Liverpool in the month of February so as to be able to leave the Missouri River for the plains by the middle of May or the first of June, and arrive in Utah in August[8]."

The emigration of 1856 had involved heavy financial expenditure which seriously affected operations during the following two years. Agents of the company in Liverpool announced in December, 1856, "This office will not send any P. E. Fund Emigrants to Utah during the year 1857. All the funds the company can command will be exhausted in discharging the heavy liabilities incurred in sending out over two thousand souls in the year 1856. The Saints will bear in mind that two thousand persons cannot be sent to Utah without incurring expense of about eighteen thousand pounds sterling. It will probably require nearly two years from the present time before the P. E. Fund Company will have discharged the debts contracted by last season's operations[9]." The announcement quoted the President who gave an unpromising picture of P. E. finances in Utah and instructed the agents abroad not to incur further liabilities until past debts were cleared. Nevertheless, it added, the company would continue to act as agent for those who planned to emigrate on their own means.

The total number sailing from Europe under Mormon arrangements in 1857 dropped to 1,994, of whom 567 crossed the plains with hand carts, 511 supplied their own teams, and the remainder located in the states temporarily[10].

If the hand cart could be recommended to the immigrant crowding Zionward it should be acceptable to the missionary moving out into the world. To test the benefits of the new mode of travel and reassure the gathering Saints as to its advantages, a company of seventy-four missionaries traveled eastward in the Spring of 1857 with twenty-five handcarts. The Deseret News, which announced the departure of such missionary groups at frequent intervals, made the following observation.

"All things being ready at a quarter before 10 A. M. the company started off in regular order, with as much apparent cheerfulness and unconcern as though they were going to return in the evening, whereas many of them will be gone for years, and all will probably have to pass through trials, and endure hardships, of which the pulling of their carts across the plains will be among the least.

"The company consisted of 74 men, with some twenty-five handcarts, and was made up of individuals of nearly every imaginable occupation and pursuit of life; farmers, mechanics, tradesmen, merchants and clerks — some Americans some English, Scotch, Irish, Welsh, Danes, Swedes, Norwegians, Germans, and of other nations, were to be seen in the company, which made it an unusually interesting sight. To see such a variety of men, some of them young, some in the prime, and some past the meridian of life, leave their vocations at a moment's notice, and go forth in that way to proclaim the Gospel of Salvation to the nations that have long been wandering in the darkness, bespeaks a devotion to the principles of eternal truth not often seen[11]."

The approach of Federal troops during the so-called Utah War reacted seriously upon the Mormon emigration during the next two years. The Star announced in October 1857, "In view of the difficulties now threatening the Saints we deem it wisdom to stop all emigration to the states and Utah for the Present[12]."

The fund also was inactive with the result that foreign immigration for 1858 and 1859 numbered only 179 and 809, respectively[13]. Returning missionaries made up the bulk of the number in 1858 while the total for 1859 was augmented by approximately 2,000 converts from the States. These latter included native Americans, and immigrants who had arrived in the United States in previous years[14]. In

1860, the record lists a total of 1,588 immigrants of whom 268 appear under the heading of hand carts. Thus in the period from 1856 to 1860, approximately eight thousand immigrants arrived in the United States bound for Utah. Of these 3,008 came prepared to walk the full distance from the frontier outfitting post to Salt Lake City, pushing or pulling a hand cart[15].

1 Clayton, William, Latter-day Saint Hymn, No. 194.
2 Deseret News, VI:252.
3 L.D.S. Journal History, October 7, 1856.
4 Roberts, B. H., The History of the Church, Vol. IV: 100. quoting History of Brigham Young, MS, November 30, 1856.
5 Bancroft, H. H., History of Utah, 429. Bancroft summarized the causes of the Hand Cart disaster as follows: Error in starting late, insufficient number of able-bodied men in proportion to the numbers in the company, and the winter setting in earlier and more severe than had been known in the previous experience of the Utah Colonizers. This author concludes after his survey of the situation: "Even the worst enemies of Brigham Young admit that he was in no way to blame for the disaster and that he spared no efforts to relieve." Linn, writing in 1902 and apparently drawing his conclusions from Stenhouse's "Tell it All," emphasizes the lack of preparation for emigrants when they arrived in Iowa City, the weak features of the cart construction, and the failure to have supplies in readiness at Fort Laramie as the primary causes of the disaster. (Linn, W. A., The Story of the Mormons, pp. 419-422.)
6 Deseret News, VI: p. 382 and Latter-day Saints Journal History, October 31, 1856.
7 Millennial Star, XIX:108.
8 Millennial Star, XIX:249.
9 Millennial Star, XVIII:820-821.
10 Little, James A., From Kirtland to Salt Lake City. p. 235. General Epistle of October, 1851.
11 Deseret News, April 29, 1857.
12 Millennial Star, XIX: 668.
13 Emigration MS in "Mormon" Church Historian's Office. Compiled from Millennial Star.
14 Jensen, Andrew, Contributor, XIV: 437, 440.
15 Emigration MS in "Mormon" Church Historian's Office. Compiled from Millennial Star.

20

"Church Trains"

W E are rich in cattle but do not abound in money either at home or abroad, and we desire to so operate as to use our small amount of money and large number of cattle in the best possible manner for accomplishing the most good[1]." This communication from Mormon headquarters, dated February 28, 1861, revealed that a new plan to facilitate the gathering was already under way to replace the hand cart experiment. This plan evolved in recognition of the heavy demand upon cattle in the middle west with resultant high prices as against increasing herds in Utah which might be utilized for transportation.

Already an ox team train of twenty wagons, under command of Joseph W. Young had gone east in the Spring of 1860 to bring out machinery and merchandise and returned to Salt Lake the same season. The oxen so engaged arrived in the same good condition as those purchased in the east and driven only one way. Joseph W. Young, who was accounted one of the ablest captains of the Mormon migrations, gave further impetus to the forthcoming plan by preaching a sermon on the novel, but practical, subject of "Ox-team-ology." In this he enlightened hundreds who would soon accompany "Church Trains" across the prairies on how to properly care for and preserve cattle on the plains so as to bring them back from a season's round trip in good condition. Foreign as it might have appeared in the orthodox Christian pulpit, the sermon was quite in harmony with the problems of the Gathering and of building of the Kingdom.

Wagon trains would now be dispatched eastward each

Spring to meet the Utah bound immigrants at the railway terminal. The Mormon outfitting post had moved west from Iowa City to Florence, Nebraska in 1857. Here it remained on the Missouri River until 1864. Then the railroad, creeping westward. crowded it to Wyoming, a little village seven miles north of Nebraska City. Subsequently in 1868, Benton, and later Laramie, became the railway terminal and frontier outfitting post. Under the new plan the Church teams took up the burden of freight and passengers where the railroad dropped it.

The February 28th Epistle from the Presidency continued, giving details of organization:

"It is desirable that both the oxen sent in teams and those driven for sale should be between the ages of 3 and 8 years inclusive, and be well broke. The wagons should be the best Chicago make, two inch iron axle tree and be in such condition as not to require repair, accidents excepted, during the trip, and be provided with bows and good covers unless some should provide their bows and covers at Florence. . . .

Each team should be provided with some eight light thin ox shoes, with the requisite number of nails, that oxen may be shod on the road when necessary, otherwise they would do better without shoes.

The teams wagons, loose oxen, teamsters and their outfit will be inspected by a competent person in G.S.L. City and must pass that inspection previous to being permitted to start the trip.

It is designed to organize the teams in companies of fifty each, each company to be under the charge of a responsible person, as captain, and all the companies to be under the charge of one superintendent or agent. Each company will be furnished with four mounted men, whose duty it will be to take charge of the animals when out of the yoke and see that they have the best grass and water the circumstances will permit. The guard must be assisted in their duties, when necessary, or when they require it, by the company to which they belong. When a man fits out a team to send for the poor and Church freight and then wishes to send one or more teams to freight for himself, he is at liberty to do so by paying his proportion of the expense for wagon master and mounted guard. Persons sending loose cattle for sale will also be required to pay a proportionate share of the expenses incurred in driving, guarding, and selling said cattle. Teams taking flour or other loading for the Church from here to Florence, will be allowed ten dollars a hundred, on labor tithing; and in like proportion for any distance on the route said loading is deposited, as we wish to deposit flour at different points. And for return loading they will be allowed $15. a hundred from Florence to this place, also on labor tithing.

* * *

Where there is tithing wheat, the teams from G.S.L. County are expected to haul reasonable loads of tithing wheat to G.S.L. City to be ground into flour to take toward Florence.

In addition to transporting Church freight and the poor brethren and their effects this plan furnishes an excellent opportunity for individuals to send money, teams, loose oxen, or each or all for the purchase and transportation of wagons, groceries, machinery, and other staple articles for their own use, thus supplying themselves with imported merchandise at the cheapest rate and in a way within their reach. It is expected that the train and loose oxen will start from S.L.C. as early in the spring as the snow in the mountains will permit. . . .

Outfit

"To each wagon, 1 tar can or keg and at least one gallon of wagon grease, 2 good whip lashes, with buckskin to splice and for crackers. For each teamster, 250 lbs. of flour, 40 lbs. bacon, 40 lbs. of dried beef (if to be had) as much butter as each chooses and can take safely. Ten lbs. sugar, 4 lbs. coffee, 1 lb. tea, 4 quarts beans, 1 bar soap, 4 pounds yeast cake (or its equivalent in acid or yeast powder) salt enough for teamster and team, 1 good buffalo robe and 2 good blankets, one gallon of vinegar which should be carried in a stone jug, and some pickles if to be had. 2 good pair of boots or shoes, with grease enough to keep them well greased, 2 pair of good pants, six shirts, 5 pair socks, 3 overshirts and coats enough for comfort with needles and thread for mending. 1 good gun (double barrelled shotgun preferable) with plenty of powder balls and shot, one 2 gallon water can or keg.

"It is recommended that six form a mess and that each six get together in their different neighborhoods and agree about furnishing the necessary cooking utensils for their mess also the necessary medicinal articles such as no. 6 cayenne pepper, purgative pills, or castor oil, pain killer composition, linament, etc. . . .²"

The call to supply teams for the Church trains was received early in March by the ward bishops throughout Zion. A team consisted of two or three yoke of oxen. In addition to a teamster for each outfit, an extra man to approximately every four wagons went along on horseback as "herder" and "scout." These men, selected by the bishop, were called on "missions." The mission would cover the period required to make the trip to the frontier outfitting post and return, which was usually six months. Compensation for their services came in form of labor tithing receipts. At least one middle aged bachelor received unexpected additional reward in the form of a wife selected from his immigrant train.

One season the "southern mission," which included most of present Southern Utah, was called upon to furnish fifty seven wagons with necessary equipment and provisions. Distribution of such an assignment is illustrated in the records of Harmony Ward (just over the south rim of the Basin) for 1863:

"March 16, 1863. 8 o'clock a.m. A messenger arrived with letter from Orson Pratt and Erastus Snow requesting Harmony Branch to furnish three outfits of wagons with four yoke of cattle to each to go down to Florence and assist in bringing out the poor saints. Each wagon to be outfitted for a six months journey and each team to carry one thousand pounds of flour to feed the poor on the road.

March 25. Meeting called to arrange for teams and outfits for the journey to the plains.

William, James, Harvey and Wilson D. Pace agreed to raise one team, wagon and outfit.

George W. Sevy, Lemuel H. Redd, and George Hill agreed to raise another team.

Benjamin J. Redd, a young man, volunteered to drive a team across the plains.

M. H. Darrow agreed to drive another team.

Richard Woolsey turned out the only yoke of oxen he had for the third team.

Thomas Woolsey furnished an old wagon cover, one sack and a small keg.

T. A. Woolsey furnished a sack.

H. Woolsey, a sack and helped to run out some tar.

John H. Lee, two whips value $4.00.

William Woolsey one pair of boots, $10.00 and one homespun shirt.

T. Woolsey, one pair of jeens pants.

Clarissa Woolsey one pair of pants.

Sister Susan Hill made a mat and pillow and night cap, furnished a plate, spoon, cup, needles and thread and presented them to George Woolsey as part of his outfit. May she be remembered by all good Saints.

Reuben Woolsey furnished one gallon of molasses and a keg.

John D. Lee exchanged one yoke of cattle with Thomas Woolsey and bought one yoke from James Powell. (Woolsey's cattle were too poor for the journey and Lee gave him a good yoke for them so Woolsey could contribute a good pair to the mission.)

C. Whitmer furnished one yoke of oxen and one sack.

Peter Markes made a flour box.

John D. Lee furnished a good Chicago wagon and cover, one pair of pants, one pair of shoes, three overshirts, and flour, bacon and molasses, rifle and ammunition to the amount of $122.50.

The three teams from this place were said to be the best rigs in Washington County.

March 26. In a meeting M. H. Darrow, George Woolsey and Benjamin Redd were sustained by vote to make the trip and were formally blessed and set apart for their mission. Benjamin J. Redd requested a dance before leaving which was granted and a good time had[3]."

Most of those called into the Church train service (and some were called repeatedly,) were comparatively new settlers. The growing season ahead held high promise for them and their equipment was needed badly for planting and harvesting. But the call of authority was to go with the

Church train, and without question they prepared to obey. After all the progress of the Kingdom held right of way. So while the men assembled necessary equipment, the women were busy packing food supplies which, in addition to flour and cured meats, included large slabs of hard unleavened bread. Extra cattle driven along with the train would supply the fresh meat.

The "train" usually left Salt Lake City the last week in April so it became necessary for the teams from the south to depart accordingly. Outfits from beyond the rim were soon joined by those from Kanarra, Cedar City and Parowan and the enlarged company was on its way to add still others as it proceeded northward.

Untrained oxen must be broken on the way. This was done by yoking the new animal with a dependable broken one, the yoke usually remaining unremoved from their necks for many days. In this combination the young oxen learned their places and responsibilities in the train and were kept under control at night. The wagons, except in face of grave danger, were so camped as to encircle a large grazing area, thus facilitating the morning's round up for an early start.

In like fashion teams had been assembled throughout the territory, and in the latter part of April converged upon Salt Lake City for final organization prior to departure for the east. The assemblage included, in 1861, two hundred outfits including nearly three hundred men and two thousand cattle. They represented pioneer communities distributed far and wide across the Basin and had spent weeks moving laboriously over primitive roads toward the capital. President Young appointed four seasoned men as captains[4] and the teams were accordingly divided into four companies of fifty each. They were well provisioned, carrying a total of 150,000 pounds of flour as well as other necessities. The teams required for transportation were augmented by a considerable number of extra cattle. These, in addition to serving as a supply of fresh meat, were intended for the eastern market — primarily for Mormon immigrants who would have sufficient means to purchase their own facilities.

As the required number of wagons became available, each company, under command of its captain, moved out to the eastern limits of the city for final inspection of supplies and equipment. Every man must be well armed and his pieces in good condition. Occasional children, who had been permitted to ride to this point with indulgent local fathers were kissed good bye with last-minute admonitions. Teamsters entrusted with messages for expected friends or kin among the season's immigration took inventory of their trust and climbed to their places. The signal was given and each company of fifty moved up the foothills and was soon swallowed in the shadows of Emigration Canyon. By nightfall they were far up the trail which not many years before had ushered each one of them into the Salt Lake Valley. Freely they had received of the blessings of Zion and now they were on their way to give as freely in the gathering of others who had heard the call. As they jolted along, more than one tried his hand at verse to be sung around the evening's camp fire.

> "In 1864 we started out to meet the poor,
> We left our families and our friends
> To help to gather Israel in
> Four yoke of cattle to each team
> But some of them were rather lean
> Our teams did number fifty-three
> And on we rolled so merrily."

The following days and weeks brought back the familiar scenes and campsites of the old Mormon Trail as each Englishman, Scot, Swede, or Dane, recalled his own flight to Zion. Perhaps he had passed that way as one of the original pioneers of '47, as a refugee from the flames of Nauvoo, as a Perpetual Fund Emigrant embarking from Liverpool, or as a handcarter of only yesterday. His heart quickened as he anticipated re-union with delayed members of his family, or perhaps his sweetheart was aboard the river boat which would be waiting at his journey's end. And so, as the weeks passed they put Fort Bridger, Laramie, and Camp Kearney behind them and stopped briefly at the lesser stations on the Great Western Trail. At selected points, part of the provisions were cached to be picked up on the return journey. No need to carry surplus weight and the space would be needed to accommodate freight and immigrant baggage.

At last the first company approached the little village of Florence on the Missouri River. To some of the older teamsters it was not Florence, but Winter Quarters, where in the late forties they had paused in their flight to the Rocky Mountains. At the landing a river steamer was unloading its cargo and here and there foreigners were testing the comforting security of earth again after many weeks upon the water.

Soon the Mormon frontier agent appeared. He conducted the Church train captain to the main body of the immigrants who were camped in a small grove at the edge of the village, waiting eagerly the arrival of the teams. They were a motley group of men, women, and children assembled from foreign lands and held together by one single, powerful bond — a consuming desire to participate in building the Latter-Day Kingdom. The majority were Englishmen with a colorful addition from Scandinavia. The confusing babble of tongues told its own story, but had the experienced agent heard no betraying word, he would still have recognized the lands from whence they came. National pride forbade these simple women folk to step ashore in the promised land without displaying some distinguishing garment of their country and native province. The men were less concerned about appearance; they were looking forward to Zion — not backward to Babylon.

Here and there were those who moved about with native confidence. They were missionaries returning homeward with their friends and converts. These, the "deliverers" of the migrating Saints, continued their spiritual labors among them and greatly eased their introduction to a new and strange environment. The missionaries were also useful to the frontier agent in helping to complete his inventory of the company, accounting for all who were booked to arrive, checking their baggage and ascertaining their needs for the overland journey .

Now the teamsters came up to meet their prospective "passengers." It was a happy reunion in many instances of long separated friends or relatives. There ensued a wholesale adoption of new members into the strong fellowship of the "Saints." Greetings from the old country and Zion were exchanged, letters delivered, and soon the Church Train crew turned to the problem of loading.

At the warehouse they found all the worldly belongings of these voluntary refugees who were severing connections with the old world to accept the new. The loading platform presented a miscellaneous assortment indeed, but none the less precious. Conspicuous in the heap were farmers and mechanics tools and chests bursting with implements of every craft. Occasionally one of the women edged near the wagons to inquire timidly about this or that piece of baggage. Could it be given special consideration for in it lay, carefully packed, some personal treasure from the Fatherland and it must not be broken. Perhaps it was a bit of china or a mirror from England intended to brighten some corner in Zion; or a fragile wood carving from Scandinavia, or even a musical instrument selected in tears from all that was abandoned in Babylon.

The frontier agent had the situation well in hand and in a few days the first of the "fifties" was ready for the return trip. Only the aged and infirm were allowed to ride, finding places on the driver's seat or in convenient nooks between the baggage. The thousand miles separating the immigrants from Zion held much in store for them — both of joy and sorrow. There was always the challenge of uncertainty. If the plains ahead were hot under the blistering sun, the

mountains beyond would bring chilly nights; the friendly streams which made their journey possible also had their moods and often heavy clouds ahead turned them into angry, dangerous torrents. Precarious food supplies and forced marches to watering places heightened a sense of dependency upon the Almighty. Reports of Indian depredations or actual attack upon their own cattle kept guards on the alert and tired souls awake. Tragedy, too, stalked their trail as sickness and accident took their toll of human life.

Throughout the whole distance the Captain, judiciously selected for his task, carried the responsibilty for the safety and progress of his train. He and his sturdy men provided security against man and beast and wrested whatever comforts were available from the capricious elements. His word was law in administration of justice; his counsel usually accepted by his adopted family. Riding the best horse available he scouted the country along the route in search of feed for cattle and signs of lurking danger.

Captain John R. Murdock, veteran of many trips across the plains, once found it necessary to protect the humbler ox-team train against the usurpations of the "road hog" of the sixties. A stage-coach driver overtaking the creeping caravan, yielded to an urge to have some fun. Lashing his mules into an impressive gallop he cut in on the train crowding a number of the wagons off the trail. Suddenly he found himself confronted by a tall, muscular figure on a horse. The Mormon captain said nothing but drawing his pistol he motioned for the driver to proceed. The latter did so and with due consideration for the humbler conveyances on the "Great White Way" to the West.

It was early September when the Church trains began pouring back through Emigration Canyon into Salt Lake Valley. Already an independent company had arrived and the caravans continued to move in until the last of the month. Zion absorbed 1,959 souls into its membership that year, of whom only 652 came by their own teams[5].

The Church team plan of aiding immigration to Utah also made possible the importation of much needed machinery and merchandise as well as facilitating the marketing of surplus cattle and other commodities. Among these other commodities, perhaps the least expected was a cargo of 4,300 pounds of cotton in 1863, produced in the Cotton Mission in Utah's Dixie[6]. The surplus cattle found a ready market among the Zion-bound immigrants who possessed means to travel on their own. It was estimated by Brigham Young that a saving of ten to thirty thousand dollars accrued to the people of the territory from funds which had previously been paid out for cattle and wagons to "gentiles" in the east.

Excepting the years 1865 and 1867, the Church Train pilgrimage continued throughout the sixties to meet the annual immigration at the shifting rail terminal. The yearly total of wagons and oxen varied as follows[7]: 1861, two hundred wagons; 1862, two hundred sixty wagons, 2,990 oxen and 293 men; 1863, three hundred and eighty-four wagons, 3,064 oxen, 488 men; 1864, one hundred seventy wagons, 1,717 oxen, 277 men; 1866, three hundred ninety-seven wagons, 466 teamsters, 49 mounted guards, 89 horses, 134 mules and 3,042 oxen; (in addition to these, 62 wagons, 50 oxen and 61 mules were ordered to be purchased in the States. These figures were further augmented when it became necessary to send a relief train for the last companies to replace losses of cattle due to Indian raids;) 1868, five hundred teams, together with $27,000 as a special effort to assist the foreign immigration. During that year a total of $70,000 was raised by the Latter-day Saints for the special purpose of "gathering the Lord's poor[8]."

The immigrants of 1869 rode into Zion on the railroad, enjoying its relative comforts the entire distance overland to Ogden. Their arrival, on June 25, marked the close of the Church Train operations, and the frontier outfitting post passed into history. Transportation rates varied during the next few years, ranging from 15 pounds 10 shillings in 1871, to 12 pounds, 16 shillings in 1875[9].

Summarizing the accomplishments of the Church Team period in its contribution to the cause of "the gathering," it appears that at least 1,913 wagons were sent east to receive the immigrants, employing in that service over 2,389 men and 17,543 oxen[10]. During that period a total of 20,426 European immigrants were assisted to Utah, of whom not more than 726 are recorded as coming by their own teams. These figures do not include emigrants to "Zion" from the States.

The changing fortunes of Zion's Caravan were also extended to ocean travel. Coincidently, the same year which replaced ox teams with steam engines on the prairies also witnessed the steam packet succeed the sailing vessel on the high seas. The ocean voyage formerly occupying weeks, thenceforth was reduced to as many days, with superior comfort. But, contrary to expectations, the railroad and the steamship, with all their advantages in speed and comfort, did not raise Utah's annual immigration totals. Conversely, in the eight year period preceding 1869, during which the Church Trains were in operation, the number of immigrants exceeded the number for the next eight year period by six thousand, six hundred and forty-four.

1   History of Brigham Young, MS, February 28, 1851.
2   Ibid.
3   Palmer, William R., in August 1842, Improvement Era, p. 540.
4   Joseph W. Young, Ira Eldredge, Joseph Horne and John R. Murdock.
5   Larson, Gustive O., History of the Perpetual Emigrating Fund Company, MS. p. 117.
6   Jensen, Andrew, Church Chronology, p. 69.
7   Roberts, B. H., Comprehensive History of the Church, Vol. V:109-111.
8   Jensen, Andrew, Church Chronology, p. 77.
9   Millennial Star, XXXII:408, XXXVII:266.
10 Larson, Gustive O., Story of the Perpetual Emigrating Fund Company, MS. p. 119.

21

Counting the Cost

Deseret, U. S. A.

. . . . Agent, Liverpool

W E the undersigned, do hereby agree with and bind ourselves to the Perpetual Emigrating Fund Company, in the following conditions, viz. . . .

"That in consideration of the aforesaid Company emigrating or transporting us, and our necessary luggage from Great Britain to the Valley of the Great Salt Lake, according to the rules of the Company, and general instructions of their authorized agent;

"We do severally and jointly promise and bind ourselves to continue with, and obey the instructions of, the Agent appointed to superintend our passage thither; that we will receipt for our passages previous to arriving at the several ports of New Orleans, St. Louis, and Kanesville;

"And that on our arrival in the Great Salt Lake Valley we will hold ourselves, our time and our labour, subject to the appropriation of the Perpetual Emigrating Fund Company until full cost for our emigration is paid, *with interest if required."*

Such an instrument signed by the beneficiaries of the Emigrating Fund was intended to assure its perpetuity. "The Perpetual Emigrating Fund is founded upon the principle of everlasting increase, and if the people do right, or even half right, our means will increase," announced Brigham Young on April 6, 1857.

There were years when the fund received sufficient support to allow most encouraging operations and justify considerable optimism relative to its potential "gathering" capacity. For example, during the years 1853 to 1855 an estimated $200,000 to $250,000 dollars were expended annually by the Company. Again in 1860, between $60,000 and $70,000 were used from the fund to aid the immigrants. In 1858, seventy thousand dollars were donated for emigration purposes in Utah. Again in 1872, fourteen thousand dollars were collected by special drive.

But the Gathering movement was generally curtailed by lack of finances and the harvest thereby limited. Human nature did not conform to the ideal referred to by Young. There were years when the company could give but little or no help financially to aid the emigration from Europe. For instance, in December 1856, the Millennial Star announced that the Liverpool office would not send any P. E. Emigrants to Utah during the coming year since all the funds that the company could command would be required to discharge the heavy liabilities of the previous year[2]. Similar announcements appeared from time to time indicating that the fund was not operating in harmony with the principle on which it was organized[3]. Beneficiaries of the fund were nullifying a worthy Church-aid program by failing to make good their promises to repay.

By 1855, the indebtedness to the Company had reached $56,000[4]. Brigham stormed against the debtors threatening legal procedure to collect. "I want you to understand fully," he roared from the pulpit, "that I intend to put the screws upon you, and you who have owed for years, if you do not pay up now and help us we will levy on your property and take every farthing you have on earth[5]."

It does not appear, however, that the threat of legal proceedings to collect was ever resorted to, although such was within the power of the company. The debt continued to grow and became the subject for many a tongue-lashing from company officials. Mormon periodicals, both at home and abroad, joined in the tirade against the debtors. In 1866, the Millennial Star announced: "We are inclined to believe that there are many in the Mission who look upon the Liverpool office as being in possession of exhaustless resources of wealth, and think it is optional with those who handle the funds how many they assist to emigrate . . . we wish them to understand to what extent those who have been emigrated by the Perpetual Emigrating Fund have succeeded in tying the First Presidency in Zion. It is lamentable and yet it is true that the inability of the Fund to assist to the desired extent those who anticipate going up to Zion the coming season, arises from the fact that those who were formerly emigrated by it have failed to re-imburse the amount used for their emancipation[6]."

The following appeared in the Deseret News three years later: "There are thousands of persons throughout the territory who are indebted to the Perpetual Emigrating Fund for the cost of their passage from Europe to this city. Much of their indebtedness had been due for years. Many reasons have been assigned by one and another for its non-payment, which they who made them have thought were sufficient, but which in the case of any other creditor but the P. E. F. Co., would have been declared trifling and insufficient[7]."

But the promissory note which all beneficiaries were required to sign remained, in spite of threats, a very merciful instrument.

The cost of transportation to Utah had increased in 1866 to fifteen pounds six shillings for adults. Of this, six pounds two shillings were paid for passage to New York and the remaining nine pounds, four shillings represented railroad fare to the terminal, then at Wyoming, Nebraska[8]. Advancing costs threatened further decrease in immigration and various devices were called into play both in England and in Utah to hurdle the financial barriers. In the European Mission there developed a system known variously as the Emigration Deposit Fund, the Individual Emigration Account, and the Penny Emigration Fund[9]. All of these had for their objective the encouragement of systematic saving toward future emigration to Utah[10]. Headquarters for this account was at the Mission Office in Liverpool but smaller amounts were collected by the branch officers who acted as agents for the fund.

It happened occasionally that these modest savings entrusted to the local agents were not properly accounted for and in 1867, the Millennial Star sounded a warning to send all moneys direct to the Liverpool Office[11].

Another difficulty presented itself when an occasional candidate for emigration suddenly changed his mind and, failing to appear in time for sailing, requested a refund of his deposits. In 1862, it became necessary to announce through the Mission organ that no money deposited with the Liverpool Office for emigration purposes would be returned[12].

Prospective emigrants, (and in the Gathering program that included all worthy Latter-day Saints), were strongly urged to make every effort toward paying for their own transportation to Zion. The Millennial Star announced editorially in February 1866, "There are those who are expecting to be assisted by this office to emigrate the coming season, and amongst the number are those who are really doing nothing to help themselves; while others, receiving no more wages than they, perhaps, are adding daily to the Emigration Deposit Fund, and at most will require a few pounds to free them from the yoke of bondage so universally imposed upon the working classes of this country[13]."

The following form was used by the local district officials in forwarding the names and deposits of prospective emigrants:

"Please to receive the following named persons as emigrants to Utah, and credit them with the amounts opposite their names as deposits, to secure for them sea passage in a vessel sailing about...... for the United States; and charge the same to the Individual Emigration Deposit Account of the.........Conference[14]."

In Utah the threatening decrease in immigration was met by bringing greater pressure on the Saints to assume personal responsibility in sending for friends and relatives. In the General Conference in October 1867, the President proposed to have the men of the territory confronted squarely with the question as to how many converts they could personally bring to Utah during the coming year. As a stimulus he asked three or four men in the audience how many they would send for and the report states the "willingness and numbers were a very excellent beginning[15]."

Another modification seemed expedient with reference to acceptable medium of exchange. There was strong demand that the company accept cattle and grain in lieu of cash. The following excerpt from the Star, issued in January 1868, presents the new development: "The plan proposed at the last conference for the emigration of the poor from Europe has been heartily endorsed by the people. Especially do those who have some portion of their family there feel interested in the subject . . . Numerous inquiries have been made of President Young to know whether, as President of the Perpetual Emigrating Fund, he would not take grain and stock on donations for immigration of the poor. The general response made to these inquiries has been that it would save expense and trouble for each individual, who wished to make donations, to convert his own grain and stock into money and send it.

"But in view of the difficulty there is in selling stock for cash, the president has finally concluded to take cattle on donations. Young, thrifty, neat cattle, from one to six years old, will be taken on this account, if delivered to Briant Stringham in this city, or to A. P. Harmon, Cedar Fort, Millard County. Grain — wheat, oats, barley — will also be received at cash rates on the same account. But in receiving cattle the President of the P. E. Fund Company will not be willing to bind himself to send for any particular individuals as he would if money were deposited, but will use his discretion, and, if possible, will bring the individuals whose names may be presented by those making the donations[16]."

In 1877, the year of Brigham Young's death, indebtedness to the emigrating fund exceeded two hundred thousand pounds ($1,000,000.) according to the Millennial Star. This obviously included accumulated interest. The journal emphasized how the delinquents had tied the hands of the Emigrating Company in performance of its objective, "This fund is used as a loan to those who are considered worthy, and would now be in active operation if those who received of it had not been delinquent in repayment[17]." In 1880, Albert Carrington, who had succeeded Young as president of the company, complained that there were some who claimed exemption from their debts due to the statute of limitations[18].

The year 1880 was a "Jubilee Year" for the Church of Jesus Christ of Latter-day Saints. To celebrate its fiftieth anniversary, it resolved to follow the ancient Hebrew practice of cancelling certain of its claims against debtors. Individual members were urged to do likewise and to set the example, John Taylor, Brigham's successor as President of the Church, announced in the April Conference that one half of the debtors to the Perpetual Emigrating Fund Company would be stricken from the list. The selection of those so favored was left to the judgment of the bishops of wards whose instructions were to select "worthy poor." These names were to be forwarded to the Perpetual Fund office. All others were again urged to pay up their indebtedness.

The amount of original indebtedness at this time was $704,000. Accumulated interest at ten percent over several years amounted to $900,000. making a total of $1,604,000. due the Emigration Fund. From this, one half, or $802,000. was stricken from the account. To impress the remaining debtors with their delinquency the "News" for April 9th of that year published the names of all those who had discharged their responsibility to the Emigrating Company since October 6, 1879.

While striking out one half the names on the books of the company brought relief to many conscientious poor who could not meet their obligations, this act also served to relieve the company books of many names which had been carried for years with little hope of any return. Many of them were debts long since cancelled through the law of limitations.

The grand total of Mormon European emigration from 1840 to 1887 exceeded eighty-five thousand[19]. While some of this number were able to finance all or part of their own transportation, all were aided either directly, or indirectly through the services of the Perpetual Emigrating Fund Company. The thousands of dollars expended annually in the services of the Emigrating Fund amounted in their repeated use to well over a million. The fact that its notes, due without interest, amounted to $704,000. in 1880 would indicate that the foregoing is a very modest estimate. Indeed, one writer has estimated that its revolving expenditures approached five million dollars by 1870[20].

Contemporary references to poverty among prospective emigrants are not without value in emphasizing the importance of this revolving fund. Orson Pratt, already quoted, wrote: " . . . if none were to go only such as have sufficient funds to perform the whole journey there would not be much gathering from this Island. We should hardly judge that there were a hundred families among the Saints in Great Britain who are able to go direct from this to the Salt Lake Basin[21]." Again in 1854, the Star, in computing the possible service of the fund through systematic contributions, said, "There are probably about 28,000 Saints in this Island. We will make the allowance of 13,000 who are quite destitute or can barely maintain themselves. Suppose that the remainder, or 15,000 would on an average contribute sixpence per week to the P. E. Fund it would amount in one year to 19,500 pounds and at fifteen pounds per person would emigrate to Utah thirteen thousand persons[22]."

While the fund did not operate as ideally in practice as in theory, it did accomplish a tremendous work of economic and spiritual emancipation[23].

1   Linforth, James, Route from Liverpool to Great Salt Lake Valley, p. 10.
2   Millennial Star, XVIII:820.
3   Millennial Star, XXI:9, XXXII:517, No advances were made from the Fund in 1859 or 1870. Brigham Young said in 1854 (Journal of Discourses 11:50) "With a few exceptions no man has put forth his hand to pay the debts he owes to the P. E. Fund."
4   Journal of Discourses, III:5.
5   Ibid.
6   Millennial Star, March 3, 1866.
7   Millennial Star, XXX:53, Deseret News quoted.
8   Millennial Star, XXVIII:266.
9   Millennial Star, XIX:570.
10 Millennial Star, XL:57, "As a fund (General P. E. Fund) it has also been the recipient of deposit from those seeking to extricate themselves — thousand of pounds in small amounts have passed through its books, and it has never failed to honor its drafts when needed; the Saints in Europe have had confidence in it and P. E. receipts are everywhere as good as gold."
11 Millennial Star XIX:570. Again in 1855, Brigham Young wrote as follows: "I desire to say that the Saints in various conferences (districts), who deposit in the Individual Emigration Account, should not place money, say to exceed ten shillings, in the hands of the officers of their branches, but should forward it to the Liverpool Office, and have your receipt for the amount."
12 Millennial Star, XXIV:298.
13 Millennial Star, XXVIII:121.
14 Millennial Star, XXVIII:139.
15 Millennial Star, XIX:757.
16 Millennial Star, XXX:49.
17 Deseret News, April 8, 1880.
18 Report of proceedings of the fiftieth Annual Conference, Salt Lake City, 1880. Pamphlets Volume 46. Also Roberts, B. H., History of the Mormon Church VI:175.
19 Mormon foreign immigration during the periods into which this review has been divided, appears as follows: Preceding the commencement of immigration under the direction of the Fund Company in 1852, there had already arrived ten thousand, three hundred and nineteen from Great Britain. During the period from 1852 to 1855, a total of 11,592 emigrated, of whom two thousand eight hundred and eighty-five came under the heading of "P. E." Emigrants, 1,043 came under the ten pound and thirteen pound arrangement, and the remainder provided their own means. (Linforth, James, Liverpool Route, tables 15-120.) The compiled figures for 1856 to 1860, show seventy-three listed as "P. E." Emigrants, three thousand and eight under the heading of

"Hand Cart," one thousand, two hundred and ninety-five with "Teams" and three thousand, nine hundred and fourteen "others," making a total of eight thousand, two hundred and ninety. From 1861 to 1868, out of a total of 20,426 European emigrants, 16,226 were brought over the plains by "Church Teams" and of the remaining 4,220, 229 are listed under "P. E." and 726 under "own teams." Both of these latter terms, however, occurred only at the beginning of the period and then dropped out completely. (Emigration MS in L.D.S. Historians Office compiled from Millennial Star.) Following 1868, no distinction appears in the compilation, although the Emigrating Company was still in operation. Dating from their first arrival by "through rail" in 1869, to the dissolution of the Company in 1887, a total of thirty-four thousand, five hundred and ninety-three immigrants came to Utah.

20   Todd, Rev. John D.D., The Sunset Land, 192. "Out of this fund (P.E.) they have up to the present time expended more than five million dollars in bringing emigrants over the ocean." Authority for this statement, unfortunately, is not given.

21   Todd, Rev. John D.D., The Sunset Land, p. 79.

22   Millennial Star, XVII:322.

23   Sloan, Robert W., Utah Gazetteer and Directory, 1884, p. 295. "P. E. F. Co. has been the instrument by which a large number of immigrants have been brought to Utah. Thousands, however, have paid their own way, taking advantage only, of the opportunities which association with the P. E. F. Co. in system and arrangements and cheap fares gave. Thousands also have been helped by friends and private parties who have sent money from Utah to assist persons in foreign countries to the U. S. The "Mormon" immigration so called has not been confined solely to the Latter-day Saints. Yearly reports show that persons not of the faith do emigrate from foreign nations under Latter-day Saints emigration organizations and find it safer and more profitable to do so. The statistics given below show that in the last 43 years the church immigration has helped to the U. S. from foreign countries, 78,225."

22

Zion's Melting Pot

PETER NIELSON, stone cutter, had accepted the message of the Mormon missionaries in his native Denmark. But the "spirit of gathering" apparently was not urgent in him, and it was only after much persuasion that he finally accompanied missionary J. H. Hansen to Utah. He remained in Salt Lake City where his services as a stone cutter were needed on the Temple Block. Here he caught the real spirit of Zion building as he worked in the shadows of the massive grey walls of the Mormon Temple and helped shape the stones which rose higher and higher above the city.

Hansen, in the meantime, returned to his home in San Pete Valley and three years later was freighting into Salt Lake City. Inquiring after his old friend, he found him on the temple grounds absorbed in his work. Upon seeing Hansen the Danish convert threw down his hammer and ran to embrace him with much feeling.

"Now I have a little home of my own and two cows and some chickens" he said, "I have just been over to the office and paid my tithing and I pay more tithing now than I made in wages over there."

The "spirit of the gathering" was turning the hearts of such men and women toward "Zion" by the tens of thousands. As the Perpetual Emigrating Fund Company helped them in their journey to the Great Basin, the world looked on to ask what kind of people were thus being poured into the social mould of Mormonism. The answer has been varied and until further study is made of individual family traits[a] preserved through posterity, must confine itself to such broad considerations as nationality, trade or profession, and general character of the immigrants as a group.

Great Britain early became a Mormon stronghold and contributed in numbers far in excess of the other foreign fields[1]. In fact, over ten thousand converts had already sailed from her islands when missionary work was opened on the Continent in 1850[2]. Within the United Kingdom, England contributed the bulk of the emigrants, followed by Wales and Scotland, and finally Ireland contributed a few. The latter, though in a very distressing industrial period, never became a fruitful field for the Mormon missionary, a situation obtaining more or less among all strongly Catholic peoples.

Following Great Britain, the Scandinavian Kingdoms contributed next in numbers. Of these, Denmark ranked first, Sweden, second, and lastly, Norway. A reason for the predominance of the Danes may be found in the Danish constitution in 1859, providing for religious freedom, while in Sweden, missionary activity was constantly repressed by law[3]. The Swiss-German Mission, while considerably less in numbers, came to rank third in its yield of immigrants to Utah. Late in the century the Netherlands Mission began to add considerable numbers. The Latin countries to the south were never responsive to Mormon proselyting and few converts were recruited there[4].

A survey of the Latter-day Saints membership in the three main fields from which the emigrants were drawn, follows: In 1854, British Isles, 20,441; Scandinavia, 2,447; Swiss-German, 355[5]; in 1874, British Isles, 5,423, Scandinavia, 4,519; Swiss-German, 556[6]; in 1880, British Isles, 5,112; Scandinavia, 5,363; and Swiss-German, 895[7]. These statistics reflect the rapid emigration from England during the first period, reducing the membership there to that of the Scandinavian countries. They also indicate that the annual emigration during the period covered, just about absorbed the membership increase in all of the European countries.

The reports up to 1855, when 21,911 emigrants had sailed from Liverpool, show their nationalities as follows: British, 19,535; Scandinavian, 2,000; French, 125; Italian, 125; German, 100 and one other[8]. From the commencement of proselyting on the Continent there was a gradual increase in the percentage of Scandinavian and Swiss-German. In the eight year period from 1861 to 1868, inclusive, sixty percent of the total European emigration to Utah came from the United Kingdom, thirty-five percent from Scandinavia, and two percent from the Swiss-German Mission. Later, in the three year period from 1878 to 1880, the United Kingdom had dropped to 48 percent of the total and the Scandinavian had raised to thirty-nine percent and the Swiss-German to eight percent[9].

It should be kept in mind also that all of the recruits to Mormonism were not from Europe. A statistical report for 1878, published in the Millennial Star, listed 15,000 Mormon converts in the United States, (outside of Utah Territory) 4,000 in Canada, 3,000 in the Pacific Islands and 2,000 miscellaneous[10].

The original settlers in Utah were primarily of American stock and large accessions were made in following years from the States. The Utah Gazetteer, in its summary of Utah immigration up to 1883, states, "The 78,225 (immigrants) does not show the total immigration through the instrumentality of the Church by a considerable number. Emigration to Utah from the United States and Australia and Pacific Islands are not included in the estimate[11]."

Commentators on the class of people attracted to Utah differed widely in their judgments. Some of the estimates reflected favorably upon the emigrant as being, on the average, intelligent and industrious, while in the opinion of others, he was an ignorant, superstitious creature easily led by the persuasive powers of the missionary. As a matter of fact there were representatives of each class and it would not be hard to make a case on either side. It was natural that, drawing from the masses of European industrial centers[12], the double religious-economic appeal would gather a wide variety. There was always the religious fanatic, the dissatisfied ne'er-do-well and the scheming individual ready to use the cloak of religion to further material ends.

Governor Arthur L. Thomas, in his report to the Secretary of Interior in 1889, states, "The early Mormons were mainly Americans and religious enthusiasts. Under a vigorous system of proselyting by missionaries they have been largely recruited from all parts of the world. Either by chance or from policy their missionaries have mostly been to the parts of the country where the average rate of intelligence is the lowest, and they make many converts either of American birth or from those of foreign birth who had first settled elsewhere in the United States. For a long time the bulk of their converts have come from the lower classes of England and Scandinavian countries and they are yearly brought over by the shiploads[13]." But the Governor qualifies his estimate later in the same report when he states, "They are not without intelligence sufficient to utilize their general experience in practical affairs; they are industrious in a slow plodding way, frugal and easily governed."

Bancroft summarized conditions most favorable to Mormon proselyting as well as it has been done, but the facts do not support him altogether in his estimate of the class of people gathered. He affirms: "It may be stated in general terms that the success of Mormon evangelism has been the most pronounced in countries where the climate is harsh, where wages are low, and the conditions of life severe, where there is freedom of conscience, and where there is a large class of illiterate men and women, prone to superstition and fanaticism[14]." The statement was also made in Congress, in 1887, that the menace of bringing in so large a number of immigrants by the Mormons was to be found in their continued illiteracy after arriving in Utah and their practical slavery to the Church[15].

The facts, however, in relation to illiteracy and suppression of private enterprise as revealed in official statistics, point emphatically to the contrary of these conclusions. The census reports for 1880 show that only five percent of the population of Utah over ten years of age were unable to read as compared with an average of 6.6 percent for nine of the western states surrounding Utah[16]. Delegate Cane stated on the floor of the House of Representatives in 1887, that "As yet 90 percent of all the Mormon families in Utah own their own homes[17]"

William Chandless who crossed the plains in 1855 as teamster in a cattle train, had opportunity for intimate acquaintance with a Mormon Caravan. He referred to its members as "good plain honest sort of people, simple minded, but not fools, nor yet altogether uneducated; an omnium gatherum from half a dozen nations, containing many excellent artisans and some trades people, along with a large number of mere laborers and some few men of talent and cultivation[18]."

Burton, in the City of the Saints, at least presents the objective of the Mormon Church in its emigration program when he states that the classes preferred by the fund are *agriculturists* and *mechanics* — the latter being at a premium — moral, industrious, educated people — qualified to increase and enhance the interest of the community they go among[19]. No less an observer than Charles Dickens already referred to in relation to the method of shipping the emigrants, said, after his departure from a Mormon emigrant vessel, "I should have said they were in their degree the pick and flower of England[20]."

Burton touched upon the two keys that seemed to govern the emigrating officials in their selection generally, and the two most referred to in the instructions sent out by the Church leaders. These were *character* and *industry*. James Linforth, who acted as an agent both in proselyting and in emigrating, says, "In the selection of persons to be emigrated by these donations regard is had first to integrity and moral worth, second to occupation. The selection is made largely by the conference (district) presidents who should be able to judge[21]."

Occupations represented in the immigrant list might well have varied according to demand as when President Young wrote to Orson Pratt in England:

"We want a company of woolen manufacturers to come with machinery and take our wool from the sheep, and convert it into the best clothes, and the wool is ready. We want a company of cotton manufacturers who will convert cotton into cloth and calico, etc., and we will raise the cotton before the machinery can be ready. We want a company of potters: we need them. The clay is ready and the dishes wanted. Send a company of each if possible, next spring. Silk manufacturers and all others will follow in rapid succession. We want some men to start a furnace forthwith; the coal, iron and moulders are waiting. We have a printing press, and any who can take good printing and writing paper to the valley will be blessing themselves and the Church."

With regard to the industrial classification of the emigrants, a record of the actual trades and professions represented appears following: Out of a total of 1,146 heads of families listed in the shipping books of the British Mission from 1849 to 1852, inclusive, the following appear in order of frequency[22]:

laborers	207	colliers	26	butchers	10
miners	96	shipwrights	22	boiler makers	10
farmers	68	engineers	22	painters	9
shoemakers	54	masons	21	sawyers	9
tailors	39	bakers	19	mechanics	9
ministers	38	gardeners	16	spinners	9
weavers	38	mariners	16	servants	9
blacksmiths	36	bricklayers	14	millers	9
ironworkers	36	cloth workers	13	stonemasons	9
carpenters	33	brick makers	12	plasterers	8
wheelwrights	8	cordwainers	6	shopmen	5

tin plate		clerks	6	cutters	5
workers	8	plumbers	6	cabinet makers	4
millwrights	8	grooms	6	grocers	4
drapers	8	stonecutters	5	glassmakers	4
rotters	8	dyers	5	printers	4
knitters	8	watchmakers	5		
shepherds	6				

Jules Remy estimated that from 1850 to 1854, twenty-eight percent of the emigrants to Utah were laborers, 14 percent miners, 27 percent mechanics, and among every 500 a school teacher, a dancing master, a doctor, a dentist, and a retired army officer[23]. Linn reports, "The manager of the leading shipping agents at Liverpool who furnished the ships said, 'they are principally farmers and mechanics, with some few clerks, surgeons, etc.' He found on the company's books for a period between October, 1849 and March, 1850, the names of 16 miners, 20 engineers, 19 farmers, 108 laborers, 10 joiners, 25 weavers, 15 shoemakers, 12 smiths, 19 tailors, 8 watch-makers, 25 stonemasons, 5 butchers, 4 bakers, 4 potters, 10 painters, 7 shipwrights, and five dyers[24]."

Such classifications do not suggest an ignorant class of people. Rather there seems to have been some careful selection in the emigration process; nor do the statistics above concerning the percent of home ownership indicate that the immigrant became subservient to an oppressive religious institution. The fact that so large a number, as revealed by the financial report of the emigrating company in 1880 and again in 1877, did not repay their obligations to the organization, reflects two items often overlooked: first, that the oft reported oppression exerted upon its members by the Church is without foundation; and second, that many of the beneficiaries of the fund were not so conscientious, and in some instances, not so honest as it was hoped for by the Church leaders[25].

The new arrivals were readily absorbed in the expansion of the Kingdom. It was charged by certain observers that the immigrant obeyed orders to colonize anywhere regardless of hardships involved[26]. The observation was true as affecting general obedience to counsel. But the implication of arbitrary disregard of personal welfare is hardly supported by the procedure as noted in previous chapters.

Newcomers were assigned to locations where needs were greatest but they were seldom directed into virgin fields. As previously observed, Young called experienced men, who had already accumulated necessary means, to lead the advance into new areas. Raw immigrants were then sent to strengthen these communities as conditions warranted. Here they invariably found themselves under leadership of seasoned veterans whose long service in the vanguard of the gathering movement justified confidence in their ability to protect, and utilize man power to best advantage. Many of these leaders served on so many fronts that it was not improbable that the immigrant might find himself associated with the same individual on both sides of the Atlantic. For example, a Scandinavian, brought into the fold by Erastus Snow in the early fifties might find, a few years later, the same gentleman on the Missouri frontier arranging for his outfit to cross the plains and still later serve under his direction as he supervised expansion of the Kingdom into the remote sections of Southern Utah.

However, foreigners were not always assigned to their destination. In many instances they sought out friends and relatives with whom they cast their lot. As happened so frequently on other American frontiers, there developed foreign communities where the immigrants clung tenaciously to their mother tongues and retained the characteristics of their native lands. Burton reports such persons attending services in the Tabernacle without understanding a word of the speakers[27].

It would appear from the organized immigration activities of the Mormons that Utah Territory would exceed the neighboring states in its proportion of foreign born popula-

tion. Such, however, is not the case. The United States
Census for 1880, shows the following number of foreign
born to every one hundred thousand native in Utah and
five of her neighboring states for the years 1870 and 1880:

	1870	1880
Arizona	150,922	65,798
Colorado	59,881	51,217
California	19,838	25,749
Idaho	110,838	44,062
Nevada	79,363	70,065
Utah	54,743	44,007

Utah Territory, let it be remembered, did not contain
all of the Mormon immigrants. More than half of Idaho's
population in 1890 were Latter-day Saints. Governor
Thomas in the report referred to above, said, "They have
been sending out colonies into the states and territories adjoining Utah. This is an overflow, and in this they do not
go singly, as settlers usually do, but the neighborhood where
they intend to settle, is explored, a few families sent, to be
followed by others, and a colony established and exclusive
occupation taken so far as such occupation is possible. In
this way they have colonized Utah, and with the aid of assisting immigration have acquired the agricultural lands
and appropriated the waters which can be easily reached
to irrigate them[30]."

The Utah Gazetteer, published by Robert W. Sloan in
1884, refers as follows to the Mormon colonization in Utah
Territory and beyond her borders: "The figures show —
while Utah is filled with a hardy and industrious agricultural population, to a considerable extent, the result of
immigration — that neighboring communities have been
developed to an extent through the same instrumentality
and the material interests of these adjacent commonwealths
have been assisted by the colonies planted in them and
brought to Utah through the Mormon system of immigration. Whatever may be said of the policy of bringing for-

eigners, those thus far immigrated into Utah have been of vast benefit in developing inter-territorial resources, and, as a rule are sober, industrious and thrifty[31]."

The following table shows the proportion of "Mormons" in the total Church membership of Utah and the States surrounding in 1890:

	Latter-day Saints	All Bodies
Arizona	6,500	26,972
Colorado	1,762	86,837
Idaho	14,972	24,136
Nevada	575	5,877
New Mexico	456	105,749
Utah	118,201	128,115
Wyoming	1,336	11,705

The preamble to the incorporating articles of the Perpetual Emigrating Fund Company recognized that human values would be more important in the Company's operations than the development of physical resources. And so it proved as thousands of cramped souls found release for development of their personalities in the open west. R. F. Burton, English writer who had opportunity to make comparisons, observed:

"Morally and spiritually, as well as physically, the proteges of the Perpetual Emigrating Fund gain by being transferred to the Far West. Mormonism is emphatically the faith of the poor, and those acquainted with the wretched condition of the English mechanic, collier, and agricultural laborer. . . . must be of the same opinion. Physically speaking there is no comparison between the condition of the Saints and the class from which they are mostly taken. In point of mere morality the Mormon community is perhaps purer than any other of equal numbers[33]."

While the beneficiaries of the Emigrating Fund were largely drawn from the poor the harvest of "the Gathering" generally was from the great middle class. Among the converts were many leaders of superior caliber whose contributions to the Basin, as indeed to the nation, amply justified the emigrating enterprise. There remains to be compiled a record of the men and women who have achieved prominence, whose presence in Utah and surrounding states is due to the gathering movement of the Mormon Church. In the meantime a study on "The origin of Superior Men," by Dr. F. L. Thorndike is relevant and suggests some interesting possibilities.

The survey of "comparative productivity of superior persons in the forty eight states" found Utah ranking fourth in the number appearing in 1938 "Who's Who," first among the states in number of "Men of Science" and between second and fourth in number of "Leaders in Education." Idaho also ranked high particularly relative to the first two classifications.

The report commented, "It is probable but not at all certain, that the states have differed in the production of superior artists, technicians, farmers, etc. in the same ways that they have differed in the production of superior workers in science and education. It is probable, indeed almost certain, that a state which produced relatively many high on the scale of human quality produced relatively few that were low in such a scale." Following additional statistical data the report finished, "We may conclude therefore that the production of superior men is surely not an accident, that it has only a slight affiliation with income, that it is *closely related to the kind of persons residing* in New England, and the block formed by Colorado, Idaho, North Dakota, South Dakota, Utah and Wyoming from 1870 to 1890[34]. . . . "

a   One such study including 142 converts in a localized area has already been made by R. Welling Roskelly and results recorded under title "The Missionary System in a local area." The study is revealing in relation to physical and mental qualities of the limited number of converts included and indicates the lack of any selective process on that basis.

1   Bancroft, H. H., History of Utah, p. 407.
2   Linforth, James, Route from Liverpool to Great Salt Lake Valley, p. 15.
3   Burton, R. F., The City of the Saints, 296.

4   Ibid. This author states that the strange language and a too strong attachment of the Latin peoples to the soil for interest in colonization, were causes contributing to the lack of Mormon proselyting success in Southern Europe.
5   Millennial Star, XVII: 79.
6   Millennial Star, XXXVII: 122.
7   Millennial Star, XL: 206-207.
8   Linforth, James, Route from Liverpool to Great Salt Lake Valley, 15, 120.
9   Manuscript Compilation of Emigration from Millennial Star in Latter-day Saints Church Historian's Office. Twenty years later the Scandinavian emigration increased beyond the British. The records showed for 1899, Scandinavia, 5,438; Great Britain, 4,588; Swiss-German, 2,276 and Netherlands, 1,556. (Millenial Star, December 31, 1899.)
10 Millennial Star, XLI: 110-111.
11 Sloan, Robert W., Utah Gazetteer, 295.
12 Millennial Star, XIV: 15, 318. See statistical reports. The converts came very largely from industrial centers.
13 House Executive Document, III:494. Governor's Report to Secretary of Interior, 1889.
14 Bancroft, H. H., History of Utah, 413.
15 Congressional Record House Proceedings, XVIII:584.
16 Tenth Annual Census of the United States, I:191.
17 Congressional Record House Proceedings, I: 590.
18 Chandless, quoted by Katherine Coman in "Economic Beginnings in the Far West."
19 Burton, R. F., The City of the Saints, 297.
20 Dickens, Charles, Uncommercial Traveller, 205.
21 Linforth, James, Route from Liverpool to Great Salt Lake Valley, p. 9.
22 Compiled from original records in Latter-day Saints Church Historian's Office. The remaining 110 represented a wide miscellaneous group of occupations.
23 Remy, Jules and Brenchley, Julius, A Journey to the Great Salt Lake City, 224-225.
24 Linn, W. A., The Story of the Mormons, 416.
25 Young, Brigham, Journal of Discourses, III:2-3.
26 Tullidge, E. W., History of Salt Lake City, 100. And Brockett, L. P., Our Western Empire, 1185-1186.
27 Burton, R. F., The City of the Saints, 296.
28 Tenth Annual Census of the United States, (1880) page XXXIX.
29 Thomas, Governor Arthur L., Report to Secretary of Interior, 1889, House Executive Document, Volume III: 494.
30 Thomas, Governor Arthur L., Report to Secretary of Interior, 1889, House Executive Document, Volume III: 494.
31 Sloan, Robert W., Utah Gazetteer, 295.
32 Linn, W. A., Story of the Mormons, 611. Taken from United States Census, 1880.
33 Burton, R. F., City of the Saints, 198.
34 Dr. Thorndike, E. L., "The Origin of Superior Men," Scientific Monthly, May, 1943. pp. 424-433.

23

Defensive Economy

WHILE the Mormons were concentrating on building the Kingdom through agricultural expansion and immigration aid to converts, commerce and trade drifted into "gentile" hands. Already in the fifties protests were heard against "outside" exploration. By 1860 the pinch of high prices became serious and business heads among the Mormons urged the adoption of defensive measures. Their plans included cooperative buying and selling. They would have the Saints do their own importing of goods in sufficient quantities to relieve the price situation. But Brigham Young in 1860 was so intent upon promoting home manufacture that he was unwilling to let that program play second fiddle to any importation schemes. By 1865, however, the rapacity of the gentile trade had persuaded him to give the commercial experiments an equal share of attention with home industry. The sixties thereupon presented a double line of experimentation in cooperative economy.

I

In 1864, a unique cooperative program began in Brigham City under direction of Lorenzo Snow. Launched originally as a mercantile establishment, it grew to include numerous industrial units which came to be known as the "Brigham City Mercantile and Manufacturing Association." They included a cooperative store, a woolen mill, lumber mill, blacksmith shop, tannery, a hat factory, a dairy of five hundred cows, sheep and cattle herds, and agricultural and professional trades departments. The venture which introduced a spirit of cooperation and "consecration" into the practice of a stock corporation, enjoyed more than a decade of high success.

"As this enterprise prospered," wrote Snow, "We continued to receive capital stock, also adding new names to the list of stockholders, until we had a surplus of capital, or means, and succeeding in uniting the interests of the people and securing their patronage. We resolved then to commence home industries and receive our dividends, if any, in the articles produced[1]." Capital stock was represented by cash, land, livestock or labor. Four enterprising men including Snow had started the movement with a capital of about $3,000. The new stockholders were added largely through labor in the construction of buildings, equipment, etc. for which shares of stock were issued. If in need the laborer received part of his wages in merchandise. Finally when livestock herds were needed to support the factories and mills, individual members pooled as many head as they could spare to form the cooperative herd and thereby became shareholders in proportion to their contribution. Just as the livestock units supported the woolen mills and tanneries, so the tanneries made possible the leather industry with its manufacture of harnesses, saddles, boots and shoes.

Wages were generally paid in stock dividends or goods produced. In 1876, it was reported, "The past two or three years we have paid our employees five sixths in home products, one sixth in imported merchandise, amounting in aggregate, at trade rates, to about $160,000. In the year 1875, the value of products in trade rates from all industries reached about $260,000[2].

The various departments were carefully supervised with the superintendents seeking the best available workmanship in each craft. In this connection the harvest of "the Gathering" was studied in order to select colonists according to needs of the labor market. Where needed representatives of any particular craft were lacking the Perpetual Emigrating Fund Company was appealed to for aid in supplying the deficiency. In this way many a skilled tanner, shoe-maker, iron monger, etc., was "sent for" through the Fund.

In a sense the Brigham City enterprise proved to be a fore-runner of a number of "United Order[3]" experiments through-out Mormondom in the seventies. It was frequently pointed out by the Church leaders and the Deseret News in this con-nection. "The people of Brigham City have clearly mani-fested that any people who will cooperate on correct prin-ciples will increase in material wealth and prosperity."

Home industry was the popular theme as Brigham Young and his associates moved about the Territory. A new foun-dation of security was promised "if you will start here (in each community) and operate together in farming, in making cheese, in herding sheep and cattle and every kind of work, and get a factory here and a cooperative store . . . and operate together in sheep raising, storekeeping, manufacturing and everything[4]. . . . "

As the years passed the pioneer leaders had the satisfaction of seeing the fruits of their exhortations in the form of woolen mills, cotton mills, paper mills, broom manufacture, hat manufactories, tanneries, saw and grist mills, silk worm culture and considerable home made cloth. Of this latter, Cedar City alone boasted of having spun and woven three thousand yards of cloth from the fleeces of seven hundred sheep.

Ezra T. Benson presented the case for home industry at the Fall Conference in 1865: "We have got to learn how to take care of ourselves, and to organize the elements around us for our own comfort and cease going to New York, Boston, and other places for supplies."

Establishment of woolen factories and tanneries was en-couraged in order to stimulate the sheep and cattle indus-tries. George Q. Cannon argued the fallacy of importing articles simply because they could be brought in cheaper than they could be manufactured locally. "That which is manufactured here, though it cost ten times the amount it would cost in the east, is the cheaper, for that is the commencement of independence."

George A. Smith preached many sermons in the same vein: To build factories with outside capital was to invite bondage "but if, by your own efforts and exertions you cooperate together and build a factory it is your own. . . . The profits are divided among those who labored to produce it and will be used to build up the country." To send money away for imported goods meant continued dependence upon others. "If, on the other hand, we devise means to produce them from the elements by our own labor we can keep our money at home, and it can be used for other and more noble purposes, and we become independent." He summarized the Mormon objectives as follows: "Seek after the Lord with all your hearts. Cooperate in building factories, importing merchandise and machinery, taking care of your cattle, and in every kind of business. Remember that 'United we stand, divided we fall[5].' "

This was the philosophy which dictated the establishment of the first woolen mill west of the Rocky Mountains on the Jordan River in 1853. It was the same philosophy which maintained the largest woolen mill west of the Mississippi, at Provo, for many years following its construction in 1872. This mill was built entirely on the Mormon cooperative plan, the people contributing their money and labor in return for shares of stock in the enterprise.

Manufacturing is seldom profitable in new regions even from resources native to them. But in spite of the absence of materials needed in the manufacturing process and of the high cost of importing them, numerous tanneries operated at a modest profit in Mormondom. It was this eagerness for economic independence which led Bancroft to eulogize:

"Under such disadvantages it was greatly to the credit of the settlers that they undertook to compete to any considerable extent with eastern manufacturers, and that the production of goods should increase steadily from year to year with occasional set-backs caused by dull markets or over-production[6]."

At the time of Brigham Young's death in 1877 Utah's volume of manufacture approached five million dollars annually[7].

The livestock industry responded with profit to the co-operative formula and felt the indirect benefits from promotion of tanneries and wool manufactories. The herd boy of the Mormon village drove his animals at sunrise toward the grazing lands. His herd increased as every corral gate opened to add freshly milked cows and unruly heifers. The herd grazed far and wide under careful watch until evening urged them homeward to waiting calves and milk pails. Cows which once supplied milk to emigrant caravans upon the plains now mingled in the community herd as the Mormons solved their grazing problems in the cooperative way.

The California-bound emigration added greatly to the pioneer stock as thousands of worn out steers and cows of good breed were traded in the Mormon settlements. Increasing herds soon caused over-grazing and presented a problem of trespass upon cultivated areas. Legislative enactment came to the farmer's rescue: "When two-thirds of the citizens of any settlement vote to remove the surplus stock from grass needed for milk cows and work animals . . . any person having care of surplus stock of said settlement is hereby authorized and required to remove and take care of stock. . . . " When livestock reached such numbers the next step was the organization of the community herd into cooperative companies. A general movement in this direction was formally launched in 1868. Considerable numbers of church-owned cattle acquired through tithing were included in these widely distributed herds. Under good management such cooperatives continued for many years yielding good returns to the share holders. Cattle in the territory increased from twelve thousand head in 1850, to 190,934 in 1870.

One of the largest of such livestock cooperatives was known widely in Southern Utah by its brand consisting of a cross in a circle. Organized in St. George in 1870 under personal guidance of Brigham Young, it was known as the Canaan Co-operative Stock Company. It secured lands and water rights at Pipe Springs, Arizona and was empowered to own dairies, meat markets and to issue its own scrip. The company was capitalized at one hundred thousand dollars with shares acquired through both cash and contributions of cattle.

Sheep men organized similarly and in some communities very thoroughly: "The principles of cooperation are gaining ground among the Saints in Weber County. Our sheep owners have organized a cooperative herd which includes nearly all the sheep in the county." From the southern end of the state came the encouraging report, "On the 12th Inst. (Nov. 1871) the annual meeting of the Stockholders of the Kane County wool producing institution was held at this place (Toquerville). A dividend of 25% of wool and 20% of lambs was declared."

The Cedar City sheep owners formally incorporated their herds in 1869 with the Church acquiring shares of stock through contributing a considerable number of tithing sheep to its herd of twelve thousand.

When the wool industry lagged, the Territorial Government came to the aid of sheep raising by exempting all sheep within the Territory from taxation. Further the Deseret Agricultural and Manufacturing Society appropriated a five thousand dollar revolving fund to be used for importation and improvement of sheep.

But lack of winter feed definitely limited livestock possibilities in the Basin until "the Gathering" came to the rescue with a new resource from half way around the world. In 1853 a shipload of converts arrived from Australia and

settled in the Mormon Colony at San Bernardino. At least
one of the party brought with him a supply of alfalfa seed[9]
After proving itself in southern California the seed appeared
in various parts of Utah. The town of Lehi boasted the
first stack of alfalfa hay in 1867. This new crop, so vital to
the livestock industry of western America, was introduced
incident to the Mormon immigration activities. It spread
through Utah Territory as a part of the program to lay a
sound economic foundation for "the Kingdom."

II

Important as Home Industry became in Mormon economy
it nevertheless failed to curb the exploitation of the "Saints"
by outside capitalists and some of their own merchants. As
a result Brigham Young gave his support to defensive commercial measures. In righteous wrath he declared:

"We propose to the bishops, presiding elders and leading
members of the Church, who are here assembled to represent the Kingdom of God upon earth . . . to do their own
merchandizing and cease to give the wealth which the Lord
has given us to those who would destroy the Kingdom of
God and scatter us to the four winds . . . means that we
should have to bring the poor here, to build our temples,
our towers, ornament our public grounds and buildings,
and to beautify our cities. For as merchandizing has been
generally conducted here, instead of having our means to
perform these public works, it has been borne away by our
enemies by the millions.

"I wish the brethren in all our settlements, to buy the
goods they must have, and freight them with their own
teams; and then let every one of the Latter day Saints, male
and female, decree in their hearts that they will buy of no-
body else but their own faithful brethren, who will do
good with the money they will thus obtain[10]."

Already in 1864, a Price Convention had sought to stabi-
lize the market for farm products — to establish a uniform
rate of higher prices and to curb middleman profiteering.
But the plan did not achieve its objective. So the Mormons

launched an experiment in cooperative buying and selling, which after a few years of success was followed by cooperative merchandising.

A collective buying and marketing plan sought (1) to import goods to the consumer at lower prices and (2) to promote agencies for marketing agricultural commodities. The first objective was achieved through buying organizations usually including members of separate "wards" or settlements. The members were encouraged to sell their farm commodities for cash which was then pooled and entrusted to reliable business men who acted as agents in collective purchasing. The ward units cooperated in sending teams to the commercial centers where they bought direct in large quantities. Thus the annual Church Trains which brought in the immigrants to the Kingdom often included wagons loaded with freight to be distributed in competition with gentile merchants.

The second phase of the program was an experiment in cooperative marketing. The objective was to secure fair prices for farm products through collective selling. The Utah Produce Company with offices in Salt Lake City, operated "freight trains" from that city to outlying markets. One such train, typical of its service, left for the mining centers in Montana in May, 1866. Southern Utah also adopted cooperative selling to good advantage. When individuals from Cedar City hauled their grain, eggs, dairy products, etc. to the Nevada mining towns, they found themselves at the mercy of unscrupulous dealers. Robber prices were forced upon them and if they resorted to door to door peddling they often did so at the risk of personal safety. The mining settlements needed the Iron County produce, and so long as they dealt with individuals they secured it on their own terms. Then the Mormons organized for cooperative marketing. Agents were appointed to conduct all transactions. Representatives from the mining towns now came to Cedar City and there paid in advance for goods to be delivered by the Mormon freighters. Often the prices were two and three times as high as formerly forced upon individual peddlers[11].

Similar organizations were recommended for wards and stakes generally throughout the territory. Results from this movement are reflected in Young's sermon of February 3, 1867. "With regard to the wealth of this people I can say that they would get immensely rich if they would take the counsel that is given them. For instance, here is one little circumstance: we have quite an outlet for our grain; our oats, barley and flour are very much wanted in the neighboring territories. Who raised this grain? The Latter-day Saints. Suppose they were perfectly united, do you think they could get a suitable price for it? They could. We required Brother Hunter to counsel the Bishops to take measures to bring about union in this direction and we saved the Territory two or three hundred thousand dollars a year for two or three years. Then business slackened; but I was satisfied; we had shown the people what could be done; they have become comparatively well off, and if they have a mind to pursue a proper policy, they have matters in their own hands. Many will not, however, do this[12]."

Thus the Mormons in the sixties and seventies sought greater economic security through a system of cooperative buying and marketing which has become so important in recent years in many countries and in rural America[13].

But the rapacity of the merchants continued and after the experiments of a milder nature failed to bring desired relief, the Mormon leaders turned to cooperative mercantilism. Cooperative stores were adopted as a last resort. Powerful sermons on economic independence in the Fall Conference of 1868 were followed by incorporation of Zion's Cooperative Association. It was organized for wholesale and retail service "to supply the wants of the people of the territory." Brigham Young was elected President and about $10,000. was subscribed. Capital stock was fixed at $3,000,-

000. with the privilege of raising it to $5,000,000. Stockholders were apportioned one vote for each share owned. "Holiness to the Lord" appearing on the company letterhead signalled the usual Mormon blending of the spiritual with temporal engagements, as did the constitution itself. The preamble announced the unity of Utah's population in cooperative transaction of its own business as against leaving it to be "conducted by strangers." Membership was limited to tithe payers in the Church and even the net profits of the institution were tithed before declaration of dividends.

While Latter-day Saint merchants in Salt Lake hesitated to take the plunge into cooperative waters, the movement made rapid headway in Provo. Here Brigham himself spurred the enterprise in 1869 by becoming a stockholder and urging Provo Cooperatives to purchase direct from the east until the Z. C. Wholesale Association in Salt Lake bestirred itself. Almost at once the reluctant Salt Lake merchants won for themselves the following Deseret News benediction by becoming absorbed into the cooperative movement:

"We have never witnessed in peaceful times among us a more willing, unselfish and magnanimous spirit, than has been exhibited by many of our merchants in aiding in the establishment of this cooperative institution. They have been ready and desirous to do all that could be asked of them. What might be looked upon as their own personal interests, viewed from the standpoint generally occupied by men, have not been considered, but when it was fully decided that it was wisdom to establish this institution, they arranged their own business in such a manner that it would not interfere in the least with the successful carrying out of the proposed plan. This change, to those who do not understand the principles in which the Latter-day Saints believe, and upon which they act, must, to say the least, have been surprising. To see men in the full tide of success perfectly willing to invest largely in the cooperative institution, to change their business, or even retire from it altogether, and rent their buildings, and to do all in their power to make a plan a success, which according to the ideas which prevail in the world, if successful, must inevitably result in injury to their business, is something so remarkable that it cannot escape comment[14]." . . .

While reduction in commodity prices was the immediate objective of the cooperative stores, it was hoped that further advantage would come through wide investment opportunity for people of modest means. Said Young, "If the people called Latter-day Saints do not become one in temporal things as they are in spiritual things they will not redeem and build up the Zion of God on the earth. This cooperative movement is a stepping stone. We say to the people take advantage of it, it is your privilege. Instead of giving it into the hands of a few individuals to make hundreds and thousands, let the people generally enjoy the benefits arising from the sale of merchandise[15]."

Cooperatives on a small scale sprouted throughout the territory as well as in various "wards" in Salt Lake City. And for a time they paid good dividends as illustrated in 1870 when the Twentieth Ward "Coop" paid ten percent on six months business. The "Lehi Union Exchange" starting with only $357.50 worth of goods, which it replaced as rapidly as necessary from Salt Lake merchants, declared a dividend of $28.55 in six months on shares costing originally only $25.00. Such instances gave support to Brigham's campaign for wide participation in the program: "What I have in mind in regard to this cooperative business is this: There are very few people who cannot get twenty-five dollars to put into one of these cooperative stores. There are hundreds and thousands of women, who by prudence and industry, can obtain this sum. And we say to you put your capital into one of these stores. What for? To bring you interest for your money. Put your time and talents to usury. We have the parable before us. If we have one, two, three, or five talents, of what advantage will they be if we wrap them in a napkin and lay them away? None at all. Put them out to usury. These cooperative stores are instituted to give the poor a little advantage as well as the rich[16]."

Cooperative stores appeared in every town and village in the Territory. Everyone who could buy or earn a share of stock contributed of his means or labor. The stores bought their goods through the Z. C. M. I. (Zion's cooperative mercantile institution) and through it disposed of the produce they received in barter. The system presented a powerful competitor to the "gentile" stores and a decade after its inception was estimated to command the patronage of two thirds of the Mormon population. Abut that time the Z. C. M. I., with its branches at Ogden and Logan, "imported at least one third of all the merchandise consumed in Utah[17]."

While cooperative mercantilism worked no miracles in the distribution of wealth among the Mormons it did achieve much in the direction of its objective. Commodity prices were forced down from twenty to thirty percent[18] and values were stabilized in face of scarcity of articles. Before the cooperatives sounded their warning note the sky had been the limit for articles much in demand.

The mortality rate of the cooperatives proved heavy. After some years of initial success they disappeared either through failure or through transformation into joint stock companies or corporations. Among the reasons for this trend the following are most obvious. First, some succumbed to developments beyond personal control as illustrated by the temporarily successful Cooperative Association at Brigham City. Here a series of unfortunate events proved too much for the otherwise promising venture: A thirty thousand dollar fire destroyed its woolen mills, successive years of drought and grasshoppers ruined the crops, and a ten thousand dollar tax (belatedly reversed as illegal) was levied upon its medium of exchange. Especially during the commercial panic of 1873 did many of the cooperatives close their doors.

Secondly, human instability contributed heavily toward dissolution of the unseasoned cooperatives. The zeal to join the movement through investment was not matched by the will to see it through. There was no control of stock transfers. Reasons, both personal and otherwise, led to sale of once coveted shares of stock. These, together with voting power, gradually concentrated into the more interested hands and eventually the cooperative feature gave way to private control. And even at this stage some of the remaining owners, without business experience, completed the process of dissolution through mismanagement.

Among the mercantile institutions which survived the transformation from cooperative to corporation, the Z. C. M. I. was most prominent. Launched as the world's first department store with the avowed humanitarian purpose of bringing relief from grasping profiteers, it served also as an investment opportunity for hundreds of small share holders. Within two decades it paid about two million dollars in dividends and its total sales rose to nearly seventy million. Gradually as enthusiasm for cooperatives subsided, the Z. C. M. I. lost much of its original character. The inner circle of management acquired most of the stock and the idealistic plan for wide distribution was defeated. The Z. C. M. I., however remains today one of the largest commercial institutions in the intermountain west.

A third weakness contributing to the decline of the cooperative movement was its considerable dependence upon patriotic support from church membership rather than upon real economic advantage. Patriotic sentiment ebbed with the downward readjustment of gentile prices and many Latter-day Saints lost their enthusiasm for exclusive support of the cooperatives.

The movement had much to commend it as a community program but it could not ignore economic principles. High purpose can never be a substitute for the operation of economic law and cooperative enterprise, if it is to continue, must succeed first of all on a sound business basis[19]. It is unfortunate that the Mormons did not continue their experiments and expand their cooperative organizations. The present-day rise of consumer, producer, and marketing cooperatives in America to billion dollar proportions should challenge descendants of the pioneers to greater participation.

1 Snow, Eliza R., Biography of Lorenzo Snow, p. 291.
2 Snow, Eliza R., Biography of Lorenzo Snow, p. 295.
3 The term United Order was generally applied to the several communal attempts in Utah to revive the Law of Consecration. The economic experiments launched in widely scattered rural communities in 1874 varied considerably in practice as well as in degree of success. They were most promising in Southern Utah. The Orders generally originated through consecrating of, or at least pooling, of property for management purposes, and operated on a cooperative basis. All produce was distributed in proportion to the work contributed. In Orderville the people not only pooled their properties but they lived together in some degree of moral and spiritual unity; they ate together in a common dining hall and met mornings and evenings in community prayer. A Board of Directors supervised their entire social and economic activity. The fruits of their labors went into a common storehouse from which all shared alike. Most of the United Orders lasted only a year or two, but in Orderville the experiment continued more than a decade. For further reading, see footnote 1, Chapter II.
4 Journal of Discourses, Volume 16, p. 169.
5 Neff, Andrew L., History of Utah, p. 841.
6 Bancroft, History of Utah, p. 734.
7 Bancroft, History of Utah, p. 733.
8 The Deseret Agricultural and Manufacturing Society was organized in 1856. Its purpose was to promote local industries and stimulate improvements through exhibitions of industrial and farm products. It served effectively as a clearing house for new ideas and practices.
9 Neff, Andrew L., History of Utah, pp. 770-771, is authority for report of Australian origin of alfalfa as it came to the Mormon colonies. After recounting Spanish introduction of alfalfa in America, he quotes the following from "Ingersoll's Century Annals of San Bernardino County," "In the winter of 1852-3 a party of Mormons arrived in San Bernardino from Australia. At least one of the party, Mr. John Metcalf, brought with him some alfalfa seed." This agrees with general acceptance that alfalfa did not come into western United States until between 1850-1860. (Encyclopedia Americana)
10 Journal of Discourses, Volume II, p. 139.
11 Palmer, William R., Improvement Era, January, 1943.
12 Neff, Andrew L., History of Utah, p. 804.
13 Bakker & Shares, Economics of Cooperative Marketing. Christian Century. LXIII, 364.
14 Deseret News, April 21, 1869.
15 Journal of Discourses, Volume XIII, p. 3.
16 Journal of Discourses, Volume XIV, p. 169.
17 Bancroft, History of Utah, pp. 761-762.
18 Journal of Discourses, Volume XII, p. 373.

19 The Mormons in cooperative merchandizing were experimenting in a
field that has more recently been explored considerably and has developed
sound legal and economic principles of successful operation. Among
these, two would have been particularly useful to the Mormon cooperative movement, namely: A limit of one share of voting stock per
member, and "restrictions upon alienation of voting stock or membership interests thus preserving the dispersion of control and keeping the
control within the class affected."   (Evans & Stokdyk, The Law of Cooperative Marketing, pp. 3-4.)

24

Public Works

NEARLY a century ago a Public Works program was in full swing in the Mormon commonwealth west of the Rocky Mountains. It was not a program to rescue an economic system bogged down in industrial complexities. Instead, it was a simple program designed to absorb an endless stream of man power pouring into a virgin country where, as Brigham Young had predicted, "A good living would require hard labor."

The responsibility of the Perpetual Emigrating Fund Company ceased with the delivery of its beneficiaries in the Salt Lake Valley. But the story of the Mormon caravan would hardly be complete without a glance at the agencies set up to absorb its annual returns. The large majority of recruits were wholly unaccustomed to frontier life. Without proper attention to the receiving end of the emigrating stream many of the new comers would have become disheartened, ready to return at the first opportunity. Indeed such disappointments were not altogether avoided.

The reception awaiting immigrants is reflected in snatches of correspondence. The following is from the Presidency to Orson Hyde at Kanesville, dated July 28, 1850:

"The Emigration poured in here to such numbers that they raised provisions to a very high price. Flour sold for one dollar per pound, which was sufficient to induce some of our speculators to sell the last morsel and go without. Harvest commenced on the 4th of July and has continued until the present. It is a general time of health with the Saints, and peace, and plenty of hard work, as every one has been so busy that they can hardly get time to eat or sleep. You speak about hurry and bustle at Kanesville;

but if you were here to see, feel and realize, the burdens,
labors and responsibilities which are daily, hourly, momen-
tarily, rolling, piling, tumbling and thundering about us,
you would at least conclude that there was no danger of
our getting the gout from idleness or too much jollity[1]."
A news item reprinted in the Millenial Star brought the
following picture to waiting Mormons in Britain:

" . . . the Bishops and their assistants have had a stirring
time since Captain Hyde's train got in, enormous quantities
of meat, pies, bread, potatoes, and other consumables having been 'taken up' through the wards and 'put down' with
considerable gusto by the arrivals on emigration square.
Such material comforts are very acceptable after 'enjoying'
a trip over the plains and through the mountains and arriving with the thermometer ranging downward with chilling
celebrity.   We paid a visit to the 'square' yesterday afternoon and found Col. Little and 'everybody' busy ministering to the wants and comforts of a few emigrants who still
remain there, waiting opportunities of leaving for other
parts of the Territory.   Comfortable tents are ranged in
goodly order and the occupants seem pleased with, and
appreciative of, the care bestowed upon them.   Great credit
is due to Bishop Hunter and his counsellors, and the Bishops
generally, who have participated in the affair[2]."

Such temporary care was necessary but it could not continue long with the same group. Most of those pouring
into the Basin were not prepared to establish themselves
immediately on their own resources. Especially was this
true of those who came with the aid of the Emigrating Fund.
They must either be passed on to the outlying colonies or
be put to work near at hand. After so great an expense in
transporting the immigrants to Utah, and that expenditure
made in order to promote the building of the Kingdom,
it would not do to let new-comers remain idle.

The situation demanded constant vigilance on the part
of the bishops. Wrote the First Presidency in 1854: "Bishops, we have a word of counsel to you. You are the fathers
of the poor, and stewards in Israel. Lend your efficient aid
in collecting the tithing and consecrations of the Saints;

and see that all is preserved and taken care of and faithfully deposited in the Storehouse of the Lord, and not diverted from its legitimate use. True charity to a poor family or person consists in placing them in a situation in which they can support themselves. In this country there is no person possessing an ordinary degree of health and strength, but can earn a support for himself and family. But many of our brethren have been raised at some particular trade or employment in the old country, and have not tact and ingenuity to turn their hand to anything, which forms a strong feature in American character. It therefore becomes our duty to teach them how to live. They are generally good citizens of industrious habits, and with a little teaching will soon be able to support themselves. We desire bishops to give them employment which they can perform, and exercise a little patience in instructing them; and it will soon be found that they will no longer prove a burden upon the public funds[3]."

The manner in which the Bishops in the Salt Lake Area proceeded to absorb the immigrants into local industry excited the admiration of an early visitor:

"Last Sunday, after service at the Tabernacle, Brigham Young sent for us to the raised dais on which he and the dignitaries had been seated, to see a private meeting of the bishops and to hear what kind of work these reverend fathers had met to do . . . The old men gathered in a ring; and Edward Hunter, their presiding bishop, questioned each and all, as to the work going on in his ward, the building, painting, draining, gardening; also as to what this man needed, and that man needed in the way of help. An emigrant train had just come in, and the bishops had to put six hundred persons in the way of growing their cabbages and building their homes. One bishop said he could take five bricklayers, another two carpenters, a third a tinman, a fourth, seven or eight farm-servants, and so on through the whole bench. In a few minutes I saw that two hundred of these poor emigrants had been placed in a way of earning their daily bread[4]."

The plan for industrial absorption of the immigrants stirred varied comment from both friendly and unfriendly observers. Said one, "It is in the organization of this emigration and of its labor after coming here that the great ability has been displayed in the creation and maintenance of this state[5]." Another witness concluded that whatever else might be said of Mormonism, "As a business enterprise it is conceded to be a marvel[6]."

Practically every writer who visited the Territory had something to say about the "fate" of the immigrants on their arrival in Utah. Burton stated that the immigrant "works out his debt in the public ateliers of the Tithing Office Department under the superintendence of the third President. He is supplied with food from the 'Deseret Store' and receives half the value of his labor besides which a tithe of his time is toil free[6]." No authority is given for these details, but the facts with regard to laxity in enforcing payment of debts to the Perpetual Emigrating Fund Company seriously question the strict disciplining implied.

The same objection holds true of other statements relative to the subject which otherwise have merit in them. Benjamin Ferris wrote: "Many were poor and unable to defray expenses of so great a journey without aid from the Church. This gave rise to two institutions, 'The Perpetual Emigrating Company' and 'The Public Works,' which, in connection with the 'Tithing Office,' are now engines of state in the hands of the ecclesiastical despotism existing in Utah[7]." It is significant that such charges of "despotism" invariably originated from without the Church.

The "Public Works" program was another expression of the spirit of Zion building. It was a happy fusion of the spiritual and temporal. The tree of the Kingdom must root itself firmly in temporal earth in order that its branches might reach heavenward to bear spiritual fruit. Brigham Young expressed it thus:

"I have Zion in my view constantly. We are not going to wait for angels, or for Enoch and his company to come and build up Zion, but we are going to build it. We will raise our wheat, build our houses, fence our farms, plant our vineyards and orchards, and produce everything that will make our bodies comfortable and happy, and in this manner we intend to build up Zion on earth and purify it and cleanse it from all pollutions. Let there be an hallowed influence go from us over all things over which we have any power; over the soil we cultivate, over the houses we build, and over everything we possess; and if we cease to hold fellowship with that which is corrupt, and establish the Zion of God in our hearts, in our own houses, in our cities, and throughout our country, we shall ultimately overcome the earth, for we are the Lords of the earth; and instead of thorns and thistles, every useful plant that is good for the food of man and to beautify and adorn will spring from its bosom[8]."

The "Works" included all such enterprises as were undertaken in public interest including construction of buildings, walls, mills, roads, bridges, canals, and in spirit at least, a railroad. Among the buildings which rose out of the public works program were the original forts, houses of public worship and school buildings, the Social Hall, Counsel House, the Bowery and Tithing Office.

The president exemplified the spirit of public works in his personal affairs as well as those of the Church and Territory. Said he:

"Some have wished me to explain why we built an adobe wall around this city. Are there any Saints who stumble at such things? Oh, slow of heart to understand, believe. I build walls, dig ditches, make bridges, and do a great amount and variety of labor that is of but little consequence only to provide ways and means for sustaining and preserving the destitute. I annually expend hundreds and thousands of dollars almost solely to furnish employment to those in want of labour. Why? I have potatoes, flour, beef, and other articles of food, which I wish my brethren to have; and it is better for them to labour for those articles, so far as they are able and have opportunity, than to have them given to them. They work, and I deal out provisions, often when the work does not profit me[9]."

The Public Works were supported by Church as well as Territorial funds. Tithe paying had succeeded the earlier Law of Consecration. Under the new law the convert upon entry into the Church paid one tenth of his annual increase thereafter. In addition he was also subject to the property tax which applied to all citizens of the Territory, Mormon and non-Mormon alike. From these two sources came the necessary operating capital of the Public Works enterprises. Probably as in no other community in America, Church funds were applied freely to the development of temporal improvements. And yet, from the Mormon point of view, they were not wholly temporal, for in the building of the Kingdom, temporal and spiritual were inseparable.

One of Young's first important decisions in the Salt Lake Valley related to a Temple location. Striking his cane upon the ground where a sparkling stream issued from the North canyon, he said, "Here we shall build our Temple." It was as if a miracle had happened for the spot suddenly became the center of Mormon activity. Not only did the Temple gradually rise above the surrounding walls during a forty-year period of construction, but the "Temple lot" accommodated the principal workshops of the Public Works Program. Here, within a ten-acre walled enclosure were located the blacksmith shop, machine shop, carpenter shop, and painters establishment.

The Temple Block indeed symbolized the spirit of the building of the Kingdom. Let the following announcement from the Deseret News supply a mental picture of workmen converging upon the gates of the historic wall to be admitted for participation in one of the most unique work projects in history.

"The bishops are requested to come with the brethren of the respective wards, to work on the public works the coming week as follows: Bishop C. Williams of the 3rd; J.

Reese of the 4th, and Wm. N. Nickenlooper of the 6th Ward
on Monday. — Bishop S. Taft of the 9th and A. F. Farr
of the 17th on Tuesday. — Bishop D. Pettigrew of the 10th
and J. Lytle of the 11th on Wednesday. — Bishop B. Covey
of the 12th on Thursday. — Bishop T. Lewis of the 13th
Ward on Friday, and Bishop J. Murdock of the 14th on
Saturday.

— D. H. Wells, Superintendent[10]."

Some came to work out their indebtedness to the Perpetual Emigrating Fund, while others came to donate a
tenth of their time for the upbuilding of the Kingdom of
God.

While many were thus absorbed by industry in and around
Salt Lake City the majority of newcomers were dispersed
throughout the settlements. In many instances "standing
orders" for certain classes of tradesmen determined assignments to specific localities. At other times personal choice
of communities was influenced by nationality or family ties.
Where no such factors of distribution operated, Young
spread the immigrants over the Territory according to its
developing needs. In 1854 for example, he sent Anson Call
to locate a sizeable farm about eight miles from Brigham
City to which he directed a company of Emigration Fund
converts. Under Call's direction they planted fifty acres
of wheat immediately upon arrival. As already noted, one
whole company of Swiss Saints were sent to Utah's "Dixie"
where they located on the Santa Clara.

Transportation development afforded many opportunities
for remunerative service. Expansion demanded new roads
and bridges. First the Jordan and nearby streams were
spanned. Gradually the engineers extended the avenues
of traffic throughout Salt Lake Valley and beyond into all
parts of the Territory. Other beneficiaries of the Fund
made use of these roads by hauling timber from the mountains or freighting tithing grain from the remote settlements
to the granaries of the Presiding Bishop.

The spirit of Zion building was never stronger on a public

works program than when a railroad was built from Ogden
to Salt Lake City. The Mormons had followed the proposal
for a transcontinental railroad with interest, petitioning Congress in 1852 to aid the project in every way possible. On
January 14, 1854, after the survey had commenced, another
memorial from the Utah Territorial Legislature urged that
it be located so as to pass through Provo Canyon, instead of
the Weber, thus bringing the railroad around the south end
of the Great Salt Lake. It was a keen disappointment to
the Mormon leaders when the route finally chosen left Salt
Lake City "out in the cold," as Brigham Young put it.
However the Mormons did not withhold their support.
Early in 1869, when bids were received for building the
western end of the Union Pacific, Young personally took
the contract for construction of fifty-four miles of the most
difficult portion of the road.

Even before the golden spike was driven at Promontory
Point on March 10th, the Utah Legislature took steps to
bridge the gap between Salt Lake City and Ogden by passing
"an act providing for the incorporation of Railroad companies and the management of the affairs thereof." This
act provided that the incorporating body, which must not
be less than ten in number, must include two thirds residents
of the Territory. One thousand dollars per mile must be
subscribed by the stockholders and ten percent paid in cash
to the treasurer. Subscriptions exceeded the requirements
of the territorial act and on March 8, 1869, the Utah Central Railroad Company was organized. Brigham Young was
elected president, William Jennings, vice president; Joseph
A. Young, general superintendent; John Sharp, assistant superintendent; Jesse W. Fox, chief engineer; John W. Young,
secretary; and D. H. Wells, treasurer.

Had it not been for the experience of the Mormons in
assisting with the construction of the Union Pacific and for
the credit established in connection therewith, the incorporation of the Utah Central might well have remained

only a paper transaction. Large sums were owing from the Union Pacific and a committee went to Boston to press their claims upon the company. An important feature of the settlement was the acceptance by the Utah men of $600,000 in rail and rolling stock. These men recognized the importance of such material in affecting the rail connection between the Mormon capital and Ogden.

When ground was broken for the Utah Central at Ogden on May 17, the Deseret News received the following message over the Deseret Telegraph line:

> "Ogden, May 17. At 10 o'clock this morning President Brigham Young broke the first ground for the Utah Central Railroad near Weber River immediately below Ogden City. . . . After a few remarks President Young cut the first sod, observing that it was customary to use a pick in breaking the first ground, but he believes in using a tool the best adapted to the soil. President George A. Smith then dedicated the ground for a railroad, praying that nothing might be wanting to complete it; asking blessings on the President and the officers. . . . that the work might be speedily accomplished. President Young then removed the first sod, followed by President Smith and D. H. Wells, W. Jennings, esq., and others cutting sod[11]."

The method of locating the thirty-seven miles of rail road was as unique as the enterprise itself. The Deseret News commented editorially:

> "President Young, before fully deciding upon this point for the depot called upon Bishop Staker and the people of Bountiful to express their feelings. From Bountiful the party proceeded to Centerville where a point about a quarter of a mile from the town was chosen for the depot in the same manner as at Bountiful; the people's wishes, as well as those of the owners of the land, being consulted."

The concluding paragraph summarized the spirit of the whole enterprise:

> "President Young and the other officers of the U. C. R. R. have taken the right method to secure good feelings. Probably their course is unexampled in the history of railroad building. But the U. C. R. R. is not being built by a

company solely to make money for its own benefit, but for the good of the people and country. And it is desirable that whatever is necessary to make that scheme a success shall be done by the common consent of all concerned."

Community interest kept pace with progress of the road itself. Ogden members were promised that they should ride by train to attend the Conference of the Church in October and all summer the people watched announcements appearing under the caption "Progress of the U. C. R. R." Plans for construction of the road bed included community participation as far as possible. Small contracts for grading local sections distributed the work quite uniformly along the line and injected a spirit of competition. Reflecting this rivalry the News reported:

"We learn that Captain Green Taylor of the fourth district "Weber County" established his grading camp on the line of the Utah Central Railroad about noon yesterday. He claims that his was the first camp on the ground and confidently told our informant that he and his stalwart party would finish their contract this week."

In the fall when preparations were being made for track laying, another News item stated:

"P. Barton, esq., just returned from Kaysville, informs us that the enterprising bishop and citizens of that settlement are pushing the work ahead with a vim on the three miles of grading they have contracted to do for the Utah Central Railroad, and are determined that no one shall have to say that they had to wait for Kaysville."

Among those who labored on the grading contracts, and received an early baptism in the spirit of "Zion building," were hundreds of Perpetual Fund immigrants. Having felt the helping hand of the revolving fund it was now their privilege to pass its blessings along to others. And what more fitting channel of service than the building of a railroad upon which thousands more would ride into Zion in the decades to come! The Utah Central project not only made it possible for them to repay through honest labor, but to add to the comforts of friends and relatives who would follow. Brigham, as president of the company, gladly made provision for assuming their indebtedness to the Emigration Fund in return for labor on the railroad. Fathers and sons worked together to pay off the transportation expenses of many an immigrant family and often, when giving service beyond their indebtedness, received as pay some of the tools with which they labored. Thus their first worldly assets in Zion came in the form of shovels, wheelbarrows, and wagons.

At last track-laying commenced. On October 14th, Young and other officials watched the first locomotive take the switch at Ogden, and cross the newly constructed bridge on the Weber River. It proceeded slowly along the tracks, dragging fifteen carloads of iron and ties to be distributed as needed. Again the News reported: "President Young and the other gentlemen who returned with him, speak with much pleasure of the gratification the sight of the first locomotive on the first road, built and owned by the people of this territory, gave them, which argued so much for the future well being of Israel."

Interest of Salt Lake residents in their new railroad increased as the line crept ever nearer. When it approached the outskirts of the city crowds began to gather, arriving in every conceivable vehicle to witness the art of track-laying. This shifting crowd escorted the enterprise to its terminal.

Church, Territorial, and Railroad officials gathered in Salt Lake to celebrate the completion of the Utah Central on January 10, 1870. Among others, Colonel Carr, representing the Union Pacific, said approvingly: "The U. C. R. R., although only thirty-seven miles in length, is perhaps the only railroad west of the Mississippi that has been built entirely without government subsidies; built solely by money wrung from the soil which we used to consider a desert."

The last spike was driven by President Brigham Young. Both the spike and the mallet, products of the Temple Block blacksmith shop, were inscribed with "Holiness to the Lord" and "U. C. R. R." "We are in debt to none but our own people," said the pioneer leader, and after expressing appreciation to the Union Pacific and Central Pacific companies, he added, "If they had paid us according to agreement this road would not have been graded and this track not laid today." His concluding assurance that the road was "not for individual benefit but an aid to the development of the whole country," was followed by a cannon salute for each of the thirty-seven miles of community track.

But the people scattered throughout the Territory must not be forgotten! The same evening the great pioneer warmed the hearts of devoted disciples in every Mormon hamlet with a homely telegram[12]: "To all Saints throughout the Territory — we congratulate you on the completion of the U. C. R. R. The last rail laid and the last spike driven at 2. P. M. today. Many thousand were present to witness the ceremonies. Two engines and a number of cars, including two palace cars from the Union and Central Pacific railroads, were in attendance. Fine celebration. No accident. Grand ball will be given at the theatre tonight. Love and peace abide with you. — Brigham Young."

1   Little, James A., From Kirtland to Salt Lake City, pp. 225-227. Also Stansbury, Howard, Exploration and Survey of the Valley of the Great Salt Lake, p. 139.
2   Millennial Star, XXVI: 813.
3   Fox, F. Y., Deseret News.
4   Bowles, Samuel M., Our New West, p. 212.
5   Thayer, William M., Marvels of the New West, p. 404.
6   Burton, R. F., City of the Saints, p. 296.
7   Ferris, Benjamin C., Utah and the Mormons, p. 163.
8   Brigham Young, Journal of Discourses, Volume 18:356.
9   Brigham Young, Journal of Discourses, Volume 9:284.
10 Deseret News, September 28, 1850.
11 Improvement Era, February, 1925. This and following quotations from article by the writer.
12 The Deseret Telegraph Company (1865) was another cooperative victory of the Mormons in which money, poles and labor were contributed by the settlements along its five hundred mile line extending from Logan to St. George.

25

Dissolution of the P. E. F.

AN undertaking of such nature and proportion as the Perpetual Emigrating Fund Company soon challenged the attention of sources outside the Latter-day Saint Church. From the beginning it suffered the antipathy of those who viewed the Mormon program with suspicion. To such it was an organization effected to expedite all sorts of questionable ends, including rapid immigration of sufficient colonists to set up an independent empire and to bring in women to supply the needs of a polygamous social structure. Material is lacking however to make a good case for either of these charges. The conduct of the Mormons in their westward movements as well as statements of their leaders did not indicate a desire for independence from the United States[2]. Further the records reveal nothing of instruction from the Church leadership to the missionaries to serve as a basis for the charge that women were in special demand.

A more plausible interpretation of the Latter-day Saint immigration activities was that they hoped to bring in, as rapidly as possible, sufficient colonists to enable Utah to enter the union as a new state in which Mormon ideals and practices might be preserved. Such an objective would be understandable in light of repeated Mormon expulsions from former locations as soon as they became outnumbered by the "gentiles[3]." However the Mormon leaders' own announcement that they were literally engaged in building the Kingdom of God, spiritually and temporally, and gathering its scattered membership, offers the most satisfactory explanation of the whole movement. State recognition and other motives, if there were any, could only have been secondary to the main spring of Zion building. A deep spiritual incentive undergirded the whole early-day Mormon structure.

Whatever the motives behind it, official opposition soon developed against the immigration movement as carried forward through the Perpetual Emigrating Fund Company. Secretary William M. Evarts of the State Department at Washington felt the matter of sufficient consequence to be called to the attention of several European Powers. On August 9, 1879, he instructed American Diplomatic and Consular agents[4] to keep in close touch with Mormon emigration activities. Also to acquaint officials of the respective countries with United States anti-polygamy laws in an effort to discourage what he regarded as polygamy-motivated emigration from Europe.

Foreign official response was unenthusiastic and the press critical of such diplomatic procedure. The London Times ridiculed the idea of prohibiting emigration of those who had broken no law[5] and the London Examiner commented, "finding themselves powerless to cope with the Mormon pest in the U. S. the authorities have issued a plaintive appeal to the governments of England, Germany, Norway, Sweden and Denmark begging aid in their troubles. The morality of this Circular is admirable; the logic is lamentable[6]."

President Grover Cleveland, also persuaded that Mormon immigration was linked with the practice of polygamy, made recommendations for restraining measures in his first message to Congress. "Since the people upholding polygamy in our Territories are reenforced by immigration from other lands I recommend that a law be passed to prevent the importation of Mormons into the country[7]."

On September 16, 1883, Governor Eli H. Murray, of Utah Territory, in his report to the Secretary of Interior, entered a protest against special legal privileges under which the Emigrating Fund Company operated. He wrote, "By this act the whole system of Emigration is handed over by the

Legislature to a corporation under the control of the Church. No other system has by law been authorized or permitted in Utah, and this rich corporation continues as a part of the "Church & State" machinery to gather converts from all parts of the world[8]."

The facts hardly supported the Governor in all particulars of the above, and his further charges against the immigration movement. His recommendations nevertheless prompted the framing of an amendment to the Edmunds-Tucker Bill in Congress aiming to annul the laws creating the Perpetual Fund Company. In its original form this bill which appeared in December of 1883, had little direct bearing upon the emigration company but represented an effort to strengthen the anti-polygamy law of 1862. After four years of varied appearances in Congress the bill finally became law in 1887. It included provisions disincorporating the Perpetual Emigrating Fund Company as a part of a similar action against the Mormon Church itself.

Subsequently, after lengthy and bitter court proceedings the company was dissolved and a receiver appointed to assume charge of its assets. On November 18, 1887, United States Marshal Frank H. Dyer proceeded to take over the property which was found to consist of the following: a safe, desk, records, account books, promissory notes, paper of various kinds, and $2.25 in defaced silver coins[9].

The $50,000 bond required of the receiver was hardly necessary in view of what the safe marked "P. E. F." yielded when unlocked. The company's statement as of November 10, 1887, read:

Assets and Disbursements	$585,832.84
Liabilities	167,874.34
Total amount of assets	$417,968.50

Practically all of the assets represented were in the form of promissory notes, uncollectable and of no value.

So passed one of the most unique cooperative devices of

the American frontier. While tangible assets were found to be meager at its expiration they by no means represented the strength of the organization or that it had already ceased its operations. As pointed out by defense counsel in the disincorporation proceedings, it was not the practice of the company to keep idle funds on hand. While thousands of dollars passed through the Emigrating Agency annually, amounting to a total of millions, it is doubtful if the safe marked "P. E. F." ever contained any considerable sums of money. It was a revolving fund whose successful service depended upon constant use. But promissory notes acknowledging its helping hand to tens of thousands were there in abundance.

In these days when economic necessity, military exigency, race conflicts, and nationalistic urges are creating irresistible pressures toward large scale evacuations and population shifts throughout the world, the Perpetual Emigrating Fund Company challenges review of its operations and achievements. During thirty-seven years of corporate existence it was the mainspring in the machinery which colonized the vast reaches of the Great Basin. Its accomplishments reflected the colonizing genius of Brigham Young as well as the practical nature of Mormon Zion building. Through its services, direct and indirect, no less than a hundred thousand men and women were snatched from the hopeless treadmill of economic distress and set free to build life anew on the physical and spiritual frontiers of America. At least three fourths of these were brought overseas from Europe.

It is doubtful if more recent agencies set up to assist large scale evacuations, or colonization of new frontiers, have purchased as much in human relief and happiness per dollar expended as did the dollars administered through the Perpetual Emigrating Fund. The contribution of this organization to American frontier development has not only been a permanent one but one which expands as the descendants of P. E. F. immigrants increase in numbers and influence in the west.   Time continues to enlarge upon the achievements of the Perpetual Emigrating Fund Company.

1 Brockett, L. P., Our Western Empire, pp. 1185-1186.   Tucker, John Randolph, House Proceedings, XVIII: p. 594.
2 McClintock, James, Mormon Settlement, Vol. V:48.
3 Stansbury, Howard, Exploration & Survey of the Valley of the Great Salt Lake, page 39.
4 Evarts, Wm. H., Circular to American Diplomatic & Consular Officers, Vol. II, Circulars, Dept. of State, August 8, 1879.
5 Roberts, B. H., History of Mormon Church, Vol. VI: pp. 142-143.
6 Millennial Star XLI:545.
7 Richardson, James D., Messages and Papers of Our Presidents, VIII: p. 362.
8 Murray, Eli H., Report to Secretary of Interior, September 16, 1883, p. 10.
9 Deseret News, November 18, 1887.

26

Desert Conquest

ALL our labor will be concentrated in the salvation
of the children of men and the establishment of the Kingdom
of God on the earth. This is cooperation on a very large
scale[1]." The Mormon project to build the Kingdom was
indeed a large scale cooperative movement. It proceeded
under a sense of divine vocation and of responsibility in administering the factors of production. Said Brigham Young,
"Time and ability to labor are the capital stock of the whole
world of mankind, and we are all indebted to God for the
ability to use time to advantage, and he will require of us
a strict account of the disposition we make of this ability[2]."

Young placed primary emphasis upon the human factor in
production: "All the capital there is upon earth is the
bone and sinew of workingmen and women. Were it not
for that the gold and silver and precious stones would remain
in the mountains . . . but it is the activity and labor of the
inhabitants of the earth, that bring forth the wealth[3] . . . "

To emphasize the perfect blending of temporalities with
spiritualities, he said, "Is not the building of the Kingdom
of God on earth a temporal labor all the time? . . . The
Lord has done his share of the work. He has surrounded
us with the elements containing wheat, meat, flax, wool,
milk, fruit, and everything with which to build up, beautify
and glorify the Zion of the last days, and it is our business
to mold these elements to our wants and necessities according to the knowledge we now have and the wisdom we can
attain from the heavens through our faithfulness. In this
way will the Lord bring Zion again upon the earth, and in
no other[4]."

It was this conviction that their work was God's work, together with the exigencies of nature, which dictated the cooperative spirit among the Mormons in the Great Basin. As the Kingdom rose from its desert foundation it became a great regenerating force in the lives of tens of thousands of people. It opened the doors of opportunity to many who escaped a world of spiritual and economic frustration to participate in a challenging enterprise. These lost themselves in the Kingdom and found a new hope in productive labor.

The first lesson in cooperative action in the Basin involved utilization of land and water. It was an arid, forbidding region which the Mormons chose for their home — a region rejected by other homeseekers as "not one mile from hell[5]." Nothing else so confirms their faith in supernatural guidance as the fact that they dared plant their families in the midst of such a barren wasteland. Added to the uncertainties of productive values in the land were the harshness of the elements and the famine threatening insect pests. Small wonder that predictions of Mormon failure in the Basin were popular. Yet a decade of successful irrigation and hard work transformed the scene into fields of waving grain, flowering orchards and extensive gardens. Economists have been unstinted in their praise.

"The Mormon pioneers possess the honor of having founded modern irrigation in America, not because of the initial irrigation on July 24, 1847, but because the Mormon people continued the work, dug extensive canals, brought thousands of acres under irrigation, devised methods of irrigation, established laws, and rules for the government of populous settlements living 'under the ditch,' — in short, because they developed permanent irrigation on a community scale, under the conditions and with knowledge of modern civilization. Irrigation, knowledge and inspiration have been drawn by the whole world from the work of the first American irrigation pioneers[6]."

Dr. Herbert E. Bolton added, "Irrigation was one of the signal contributions of the Mormons to the upbuilding of the Great West. Without it starvation was as certain as death in old age. So the Mormons built reservoirs in the mountains, ran ditches and great canals across the valleys, and poured the life giving waters of the Wasatch upon the thirsty soil of the sunbaked desert, causing it to bloom like the rose[7]."

Development of principles and practice of irrigation proceeded on a basis of community rather than individual benefit. (Chapter VIII). Group action made possible the victory over obstacles which individual effort could never have surmounted. Regulated distribution of available land on the basis of utility and community fencing of the "big fields" instead of individual enclosures eliminated waste of both resources and manpower.

The abandonment of the principle of riparian rights in favor of the theory that the waters of streams and lakes belong to the public and are subject to appropriation on the basis of beneficial use was clearly indicative of community as against private interest. The development of rules, regulations and practices in the use of that water was equally expressive of the will and capacity for cooperative effort. Even when control of streams was sometimes legally vested in one individual it proved to be for group interest rather than for private monopoly[8].

New water projects such as canal or reservoir construction might be formally launched in a Sabbath Meeting when the Bishop announced: "Tomorrow we shall need every available man (or a specified number) in this ward, together with teams and tools, to begin canal construction. Brothers Jones and Brown have been appointed foremen of the laborers and teamsters respectively and you are asked to report to them." Usually a time-keeper kept record of each man's contribution for in that way only did he acquire capital stock in the community owned water project.

The ingenuity of the pioneering Saints was forever taxed by the perplexing problems of irrigation, land contours, storage, tunneling and distribution. By pooling their labor and available equipment they faced each challenge with the strength of cooperative effort. Sometimes on particularly difficult undertakings the Church furnished such essentials as blasting powder.

Repairs to leaky bank emplacements, puddling where seepage stole the precious water, and annual canal and ditch cleanings demanded continued labor. The total expense was apportioned according to shares of water owned. Each spring before the onrush of melting snows, cleaning crews moved along the ditches and canals in preparation for the irrigating season. During the summer the Water-master assumed command to direct the life-giving streams through proper channels to be apportioned equitably and in rotation among the share holders.

The building and maintenance of these extensive canals and reservoirs imposed tremendous labor burdens upon the settlers. During the first two decades in the Basin they built over a thousand miles of canals at an approximate cost of one thousand seven hundred dollars per mile. Sub canals, dams, etc. went far toward doubling the expense. Labor was the only answer to such demands in those days and canal building afforded many a work project for newly arrived P. E. immigrants who had scarcely heard of irrigation in their homelands. " . . . the farmers supplied the labor themselves," says George Thomas in "Development of Institutions Under Irrigation," "to build the canals and reclaim the land. So that the thousands of miles of canals of early Utah were built without indebtedness of any kind. They were built by the farmers, owned by the farmers, and operated by the farmers. In fact they constitute one of the greatest and most successful community or cooperative undertakings in the history of America."

Irrigation statistics filed by the Deseret Agricultural and Manufacturing Society in 1866, showed the following progress: "There has been constructed 277 main canals in

length amounting to 1,043 miles and 102 rods, which water
153,949 acres of land at a cost of $1,766,939; and there is in
course of construction canals at an estimated cost of $900,-
000[9]." A half century later Dr. Thomas reported a total of
7,709 miles of irrigation canals and found that out of a total
irrigated area of approximately one million acres in Utah
"individual and partnership canals irrigated 222,448 acres
and cooperative canals 687,260 or 91.1 per cent . . . at a cost
of $11.22 per acre[10]." The farms averaged 32.9 acres.

Upon canal building fell some of the editorial blessings
of the Deseret News. This organ of the Church did much
to stimulate community morale by its frequent spiritualiz-
ing of temporal drudgery. In Sevier Valley "A canal from
6 to 10 feet wide, 2 or more feet deep and 11 miles long was
located and pushed to completion in about 40 days, 123 men
being engaged in the labor[11]." Commented the News:
"Everything speaks well for the enterprising laborers under
the direction of President Orson Hyde. The pioneers of the
Sevier were going along merrily, and the prospects for permanent and beneficial extensions were very encouraging.
That's right. Labor is wealth, and Industry the first virtue.
Without them come poverty and crime. Go ahead and
God bless your efforts[12]."

The "gathering" of converts from widely scattered places
introduced many foreign articles and practices to Mormondom. Among seeds of varied origin France contributed that
of the sugar beet. This new product became the basis of
one of the most important industries in the West — an industry wholly dependent upon irrigation.

An important element of cooperation in the Kingdom was
church support of individual enterprise. This appeared
variously as intangible encouragement or as substantial financial backing as circumstances dictated. It might express
itself through organization of societies to foster new industries, legislative action, sermons from the pulpit, Church
News editorials, etc. Such was the manifold cooperative

nature of the development of the intermountain sugar industry.

Leaders of the Mormon missionary invasion of Europe in 1849 carried with them Brigham Young's counsel to be on the lookout for any industries or enterprises which might profitably be adapted to the new State of Deseret. John Taylor, assigned to France, brought back with him in 1852 not only a promising idea but an organization and machinery to launch it. Together with a young convert, an engineer of means, he investigated sugar production in Northern France, became convinced that it could be applied to conditions in the Basin and proceeded to organize the "Deseret Manufacturing Company." A shoe manufacturer in England, a salt dealer, a shipbuilder, converts all and men of wealth, together with the French engineer, subscribed $60,-000. to create the manufacturing company. The best available machinery was purchased for $12,500. and shipped to America. During five months in 1852, the "sugar train" of two hundred yoke of oxen struggled over the 1,200 miles of wilderness to arrive in Zion in heavy November snows.

Five hundred bushels of beet seed[13] had preceded arrival of the equipment and the next season all Mormondom looked forward expectantly to a good crop and subsequent sugar manufacturing at Provo. But insurmountable difficulties due to lack of experience brought bitter disappointment and temporary defeat. The Company's assets were exhausted and in face of dissolution the Church stepped in to take over the whole enterprise. The machinery was moved to Salt Lake and the Deseret News continued to support the movement with frequent announcements as on October 29, 1853: "Beet Sugar Factory: We understand from the Superintendent of Public Works that next week said factory will be ready to receive beets to be made into molasses on short notice. We know that some were disappointed last fall in not getting sugar, and some in poor molasses. But brethren don't be discouraged; we have different workmen this year and if we cannot give you sugar as you desire, no effort will be wanting to give you good molasses. Bring your beets and try."

Experimentation under church sponsorship continued each year until 1855 but a good grade of molasses was all the operating officials would point to with any degree of satisfaction. It appeared that a hundred thousand dollars had been expended in vain.

Interest in sugar manufacture slumbered for twenty-five years only to be reawakened by enterprising men in scattered areas. Again came public support — this time through encouragement from the Territorial Legislature. By action of 1880, two thousand dollars were "to be given as a premium to be paid to the party or parties who shall produce subject to inspection 7,000 pounds of merchantable brown sugar manufactured in Utah Territory and of material produced in Utah Territory in the year 1880." The premium was raised to five thousand dollars two years later. Particularly zealous in the cause of sugar manufacture was Arthur Stayner who after years of futile effort with sorghum cane, turned to the sugar beet and thereby won coveted Church support.

That support came when President Wilford Woodruff who had been skeptical about Stayner's sorghum experiments, about-faced to espouse the sugar cause. Committees were sent to study operating plans in California. Their reports were discouraging but Woodruff persisted even to the extent of over-ruling decisions of his trusted advisors. The result was the formation of a sugar syndicate in 1889, followed by formal organization of the Utah Sugar Company. On November 14, 1890, the First Presidency addressed a circular to all Stake Presidents and Bishops: "A company for the manufacture of sugar has been organized and steps have been taken for the erection of a factory . . . That this business can be successfully carried on in the Territory and meet all reasonable expectations has been made clear as it is possible under the circumstances, by actual investigation of prudent and judicious men — brethren of ours. . . . The determination of those interested is to have the management of this manufacture in the most reliable hands. . . .

"One half of the stock has already been subscribed for by a comparatively few of the brethren; but it is desirable in a factory of this kind that the stock should be widely distributed among the people, and we wish you to bring this to the attention of the Latter-day Saints in your Ward. If there be any who cannot subscribe a large amount, let them take some stock and have some interest in the enterprise. We believe it will be a great benefit to our Territory; and as it is the largest industry of the kind that has been attempted among us, and one requiring the greatest amount of capital, we trust that this appeal will be met by a general response from all parts of the Territory[14]. . . . "

Public support which would normally have been generous in response to such an invitation, was checked by the financial panic of the following year. But Woodruff was determined to carry on and at this point Heber J. Grant, (recent head of the Mormon Church) came into prominence through his successful efforts to procure eastern financial backing.

The factory costing $400,000 was erected at Lehi by the Dyer Company of Califronia. It was the fourth in the country and the first all American plant — built by American workmen and equipped entirely with American made machinery. October 1891, saw the plant in action. As samples of the first real white sugar produced in the Territory passed among the onlookers, skeptics were forced to acknowledge the power of men who knew how to work together.

This was the beginning of an enterprise which joined the outcome of two lines of cooperative endeavor — experimentation with sugar manufacture and the development of irrigation to support sugar beet production. From this point forward obstacles yielded more readily before the corporate strength of an industry which was to bring tens of thousands of acres into profitable use, putting thousands of men to work producing millions of bags of sugar. When the Lehi factory was dedicated President Woodruff's words proved truly prophetic: "This our Father, is one of the many like institutions that we will build in these valleys of the mountains to bring material blessings to our people."

1   Discourses of Brigham Young, Volume 15, p. 63.
2   Discourses of Brigham Young, Volume 18, p. 73.
3   Discourses of Brigham Young, Volume 16, p. 66.
4   Discourses of Brigham Young, Volume 9, p. 283.
5   Alter, J. Cecil, Utah, p. 44.
6   Widtsoe, Dr. John A., Principles of Irrigation Practice, p. 455.
7   Bolton, Herbert E., "The Mormons in the Opening of the Great West." The Utah Genealogical and Historical Magazine, XVII:69.
8   Two such legislative grants were made on September 9, 1850. The first awarded "sole control of City Creek and Canyon" to Brigham Young and the second granted to Ezra T. Benson "Exclusive privilege of controlling the waters in Tooele Valley, Tooele County, known as Twin Springs . . . for mills and irrigating purposes." Subsequent awards of this nature carried the clause "nothing herein contained shall prevent the waters aforesaid from being used whenever and wherever it is necessary for irrigating."
9   Neff, Andrew L., History of Utah, p. 739.
10 Neff, Andrew L., History of Utah, pp. 27-28.
11 Sevier Stake Historical Record.
12 Deseret News, March 30, 1854.
13 Millennial Star, XV:105. Taylor, Fred G., A Saga of Sugar, p. 33 gives reference to 1,200 pounds of seed.
14 Taylor, Fred G., A Saga of Sugar, pp. 78-79.

27

Challenge

DURING the Mormon expulsion from Missouri in 1839, Joseph Smith wrote an unusual letter to the baffled exiles from his prison cell. Among the items of that extended communication he suggested with reference to past failures, "We have reason to believe that many things were introduced among the Saints before God had signified the time; and notwithstanding the principles and plans may have been good, yet aspiring men, or in other words, men who had not the substance of Godliness about them, perhaps undertook to handle edged tools. Children you know are fond of tools while they are not yet able to use them." Smith refused to place responsibility for early Mormon difficulties on external factors much as these entered into the picture. His diagnosis of their troubles discovered the usual symptoms of social maladjustment:

"Behold I say unto you there were jarrings, and contentions, and envyings, and strifes, and lustful and covetous desires among them; therefore by these things they poluted their inheritance. They were slow to hearken unto the voice of the Lord their God, therefore the Lord their God was slow to hearken unto their prayers, to answer them in the day of their troubles[2]."

These human weaknesses awaited eradication in the experience of "Zion building." In their stead there gradually emerged a group consciousness, a sense of mission and a spirit of cooperation. These virtues which became the strength of the Kingdom, grew in proportion to the pressure of circumstances. In the middle west it was social conflict which drove these Latter-day Saints closely together; in the

Great Basin, where the clash of social ideals was reduced to a minimum, the exigencies of nature continued the process. Brigham Young understood the value of stern necessity in the development of social virtues. When others urged the pioneers to push on to California, he looked upon the character building laboratory about him and replied, "We are just where the Lord wants his people to gather."

As the Mormons poured in from the nations to establish Zion in the west, the words of their prophet challenged their preparation to "use the tools" which had been given them. Could they qualify as God's engineers in building His Latter-day Kingdom? Could they bridge the gulf which separated the rich man from Lazarus? Could they apply the plumb bob of righteousness to the walls of Zion? The spread of "the Kingdom" to absorb "the Gathering" into prosperous and contented villages throughout the west affirmed a high degree of preparation. A half century of Mormonism in the Basin saw the development of a compact, cooperative Christian brotherhood.

Then came a new century with increased non-Mormon penetration of Zion. While the Latter-day Saints retained a majority in the Mormon State, the population balance of its capital city gradually shifted to the "Gentiles." Converts from Europe arrived in decreasing numbers until, during the first World War the doors to immigration were practically closed[3].

Not only did "Babylon" come to "Zion," but Zion began to move out into the world. In 1900 approximately ninety percent of its quarter million members were located in Utah, Idaho and Arizona. At present only about sixty-five percent of its near million remain in these original Mormon strongholds. The balance have become "Mormons of the dispersion" with strong colonies on the Pacific Coast, Chicago, New York, and Washington, D. C.[3a] Within the past two decades "Stakes of Zion" have followed these colonies to provide the advantages of organized religious life.

As the Latter-day Saints moved out into "the world" they began to play a part in its affairs. Mormon names have appeared increasingly on the roster of American public service. Among them are many who formerly served as missionaries in the States or in foreign lands. In all the Church has sent out more than 50,000 such missionaries since the days of Joseph Smith. Relative to these, a former Utah Governor[4] wrote in 1937:

"For upwards of fifty years I have seen these missionaries by the thousands leave their homes. They have served in every country of the eastern hemisphere; they have labored in the lands of the two Americas and on the islands of the sea. They have learned to know the culture of the old world capitals, they have walked along the green plains of Britain, Holland and Scandinavia, France and Germany . . . They know the real life of the real people in the countries where they labour and they have learned to respect and to love them. I have never known a Mormon missionary that did not praise the people with whom he laboured. This great Mormon missionary system wields a powerful influence for good. Almost immediately after their arrival at home these young men take the front rank in civic, educational and religious affairs. They become the mayors of our cities, the governors of our states, the judges on the bench and influential and powerful national congressmen and senators. They hold professorships in our seats of learning and become distinguished men of science. Today returned missionaries are scattered in every state of the Union. Wherever they are they are Ambassadors of Goodwill from the nations where, in their youth, they became so intimately acquainted with the people[5]."

Thus the tree of the Kingdom was fed by the Gathering until it became firmly rooted in the Great Basin and began to spread its branches abroad. Does the spirit of Zion building survive this twentieth century emergence from isolation? Is the fourth generation of Mormons still willing to keep the covenant "to take the poor with them?" Is it able to carry on a public works program successfully and labor in the spirit of cooperative brotherhood? The answer is in the making.

Costly chapels, schoolhouses and other public buildings now cast more impressive shadows where once stood the old fort with its liberty pole and bishop's store-house. But the proceedings within these modern walls do not always present the Kingdom so impressively real and urgent as was done two generations ago. Service clubs and Chambers of Commerce have outwardly substituted Main Street for the old "Meeting House" where the bishops held court, planned work projects, and counselled their flocks for the general welfare. This shift from ecclesiastical to civil domination of local affairs has been accompanied by divorcement of spiritual from temporal matters. These two once so happily blended in the building of the Kingdom, seldom meet in some quarters now, and religion has shrunk to the measure of a begrudged Sabbath. Where this holds true little remains of the once stimulating urge to Zion building and "the Gathering" has already lost its meaning.

However, beyond real and apparent worldliness, in which some heirs to the Kingdom have been lost and others have fallen asleep, the spirit of Zion building continues strong in the faithful. The Gathering is still bearing fruit through sons of pioneers and grandsons of immigrants from many lands. Persistence of early qualities of personal sacrifice and cooperation which made the Gathering possible, is conspicuous in missionary labor and in the Church Welfare Plan as developed during the depression years. The latter, which now receives major emphasis in the Church will be reviewed in the succeeding chapter.

The missionary "call" remains a coveted honor among the faithful in Mormondom. Multiplied sacrifices in thousands of Latter-day Saint homes bear witness that the spirit of consecration is still alive. The message of "the restoration" is still vital; responsibility for its dissemination continues to weigh heavily upon the Church. The measure of the

present generation's will to missionary service is read in
the Annual Report for 1940, before the war temporarily
absorbed available manpower into its channels:

Total number of selfsupporting missionaries
in the missions of the Church   2,150
Total estimated contributions of the mission-
aries and their families for preaching the
gospel during the year $2,822,740.67

Post war activity has sought replacement of missionary
forces as rapidly as possible and hundreds of Latter-day
Saint ex-service men have responded to give additional service to the Church. The missionaries are strictly lay in
character. They include in the main, young men from all
walks of life who leave their professions or schools temporarily to devote themselves exclusively to "carrying the message
of the Gospel" to the world. Length of service varies from
two years in English speaking countries to thirty months
where foreign languages must be learned. Young women,
in lesser numbers, also serve their church in similar capacity.
Two years after the close of World War II approximately
three thousand missionaries were out in the nations delivering the message of the restoration. They were "thrusting
in the sickle" to reap as did their forefathers a century ago.
Both carried the message of the Kingdom to a confused world
looking for security. In Europe the industrial breakdown
of the nineteenth century had been replaced by the explosion
and social displacement of the middle twentieth. Comparison of "the harvest" will present an interesting study.

The proselyting program under Brigham Young was
more truly world wide than that of the present century.
(See Chapter XII, p. 126). Following abortive missions in
Asia, Mormon activities became restricted to the Christian
world and the South Pacific Islands. The "Gathering" issued
from responsive Christian countries while converts in the
Islands remained to build local Mormon communities. Today "the Gathering" has been largely divorced from mis-

sionary activity and the tendency is toward emphasis upon Zion as a standard of righteousness, instead of location. Hence foreign colonies of Latter-day Saints are urged to become self sustaining and thus spread the Kingdom abroad.

This decline in the "Spirit of the Gathering" which was formerly a mainspring to conversion, as well as an important factor in Zion building, presents the missionary system with a challenge of adjustment. Can it succeed apart from the Gathering? If it does it must make the building of the Kingdom just as realistic in foreign homelands as it did when the path of conversion led away to a distant ideal. The blessings of the Kingdom must find the people where they are. And the Kingdom of God can have no exclusion acts against race or creed.

Now that the fruits of proselyting no longer ride the wave of American immigration can the Mormon formula which has proved successful in the Basin be made to apply in foreign communities? Will it work in Mormon swarms outside the Beehive State? Approximately thirty thousand Latter-day Saints in Europe and strong colonies in the United States from California to New York will give the final answer. Already some of the "dispersion" groups give affirmative promise through cooperative effort incident to the Church Welfare Program. Perhaps other tangible "blessings of the Kingdom" will follow the dispersion and find root in foreign lands.

1   Roberts, B. H., History of L. D. S. Church, Vol. III: 301.
2   Doctrine & Covenants, Section 101:6-7.
3   Approximately 20,000 L. D. S. arrived from Europe during the 20th Century before immigration restrictions closed the doors to further entry. Thirty thousand remain in the various missions of Europe.
3a Under title of "Migration a Problem of Youth in Utah" Dr. Joseph A. Geddes makes an interesting study of this reversal from gathering to dispersion.
4   Governor Charles R. Mabey.
5   The Missionary System of the Mormon Church as a Factor in the Peace of the World, World Fellowship of Faiths Report — London, 1937, pp. 297-298.
6   L. D. S. Conference Report, April 1940, p. 8.

28

The Welfare Plan

"For thus shall my church be called in the last days, even the Church of Jesus Christ of Latter-day Saints. Verily, I say unto you all, arise and shine forth that thy light may be a standard for the nations.

"And that the Gathering together upon the Land of Zion, and upon her Stakes, may be for a defense and for a refuge from the storm, and from wrath when it shall be poured out without mixture upon the whole earth[1]."

T HAT was the rallying cry of "the Kingdom" a century ago — escape impending worldly chaos by gathering to the security of Zion! After a hundred years, was there still security in Zion?

The economic crisis of the thirties challenged the continued values of Latter-day Saint cooperative experience. Was there anything in the Mormon formula which could be brought to bear successfully on the problems of the depression? As if in answer the Church Welfare Movement came into being as an application of certain "Law of Consecration" principles to modern economic and social conditions. As it developed, the Welfare Plan proved to be a gesture of cooperation with the Federal Government in its emergency program, but registered a protest against some of its methods. The spirit of Zion building could not be reconciled with any suggestion of a dole. The prophets of Mormonism had always taught that to receive without giving honest value in return was ruinous to human character. Joseph Smith admonished:

"Thou shalt not be idle; for he that is idle shall not eat the bread nor wear the garment of the laborer.

"The idler shall not be had in remembrance before the Lord. . . . Now I the Lord am not well pleased with the inhabitants of Zion, for there are idlers among them, and their children are growing up in wickedness; they also seek not earnestly the riches of eternity, but their eyes are full of greediness[2]."

Brigham Young warned repeatedly against the evils of charity which encouraged idleness:

"My experience has taught me and it has become a principle with me, that it is never any benefit to give out and out, to man or woman, money, food, clothing, or anything else, if they are able-bodied and can work and earn what they need, when there is anything on earth for them to do. This is my principle and I try to act upon it. To pursue a contrary course would ruin any community in the world and make them idlers."

"Set the poor to work — setting out orchards, splitting rails, digging ditches, making fences, or anything useful, and so enable them to buy meal and flour and the necessities of life[3]."

The present century Mormon leaders, committed solidly to the work creed of their predecessors, viewed the effect of the depression upon their people with grave concern. The slump in agriculture, cattle raising, and mining, chief sources of income in Utah and surrounding states, left nearly eighteen percent of the Church membership on partial or total relief. A survey prior to 1936 further revealed that 13,455 were on relief due to unemployment and that many thousands received relief "who either did not need it or who had farms that might, if farmed, have kept them off relief[4]."

The late President Heber J. Grant attacked the problem in true Brigham Young fashion. After first considering immediate relief for those in distress, his committee asked,

"Could not something of a more enduring character be accomplished — something by which the presently distressed might make a permanent recovery, become self supporting

again, and resume their normal life with a full measure of
self respect?

"The question found answer in one of the basic features of
'Mormonism,' a principle by which nearly a hundred years
before, the pioneer members of the Church built thriving
settlements on the shores of the Great Salt Lake, and made
the deserts blossom as the rose. It was the Gospel of work.

"Realizing that idleness is a curse, and that self support
is a necessary element of self respect, officials of the Church
made their plans with this second objective in mind:

"Our primary purpose is to set up, insofar as possible, a
system in which the curse of idleness will be done away with,
the evils of the dole abolished, and individual thrift and
self respect once more established among the people. The
aim of the Church is to help the people to help themselves.
Work is to be re-enthroned as the ruling principle in the
lives of the Church membership.

"Then remunerative work — not a free dole — must be
provided. Projects must be conceived and developed.
Funds must be raised and an orderly system of distributing
work to unemployed must be devised[5]."

Significantly this introduction to the Welfare Plan added:

"To carry on this ambitious program, no new principles
..need be applied nor need a new organization be set up. The
Church is so organized that through channels and principles already in use, the entire plan may be carried on."

The organization and principles here referred to had their
origins early in the development of the Church. They include basically the "Ward" and "Stake" units with their
"priesthood quorums" and womens relief societies. In
rural districts a Stake averages the size of a county while
several Stakes exist in populated centers like Salt Lake City.
A Ward corresponds to a parish. There are upwards of 165
Stakes, each including an average of eight wards. Each
ward is presided over by a Bishop and the Stake by a President. The Bishop is the key man in relation to the "temporal welfare" of the people for upon him devolves full
responsibility for collecting and disbursing funds for the
care of the needy. In discharging this responsibility he is

assisted by the Womens Relief Society and by the Priesthood
Quorums which he may call to his aid. The Priesthood
Quorums consist of three teen-age gradations known as
Deacons, Teachers and Priests and three adult units known
as Elders, Seventies and High Priests. The former are organized on a Ward basis while the latter appear as Stake units,
but function generally as Ward groups. All worthy male
members over twelve years of age are ordained to, and advance in, the priesthood so that practically all are subject
to service at the Bishop's call.

The chief sources of income in the Church are the "tithes"
and "fast offerings." Every faithful member pays one tenth
of his income voluntarily. These funds are forwarded by
the local bishops to the "Presiding Bishop's Office" from
which center they are returned to the Wards, Stakes and
Missions as needed. In recent years there have been expended annually from such funds between four and six
million dollars for "the maintenance and operation of the
Stakes and Wards, Mission activities, for the maintenance
and operation of Church schools and temples, for hospital
buildings and relief assistance[6].

In addition to tithe paying, each member in his degree
of adherence to the faith abstains from two meals on the first
Sunday of each month and pays the price (in modest reckon-
ing) as a "fast offering" to his Ward. The contributions
received from this source are reserved specifically for direct
relief of the poor. These funds, which are administered by
the Ward Bishop, working in cooperation with the local Relief Society, amount annually to over a half million dollars[7].
In addition Relief Society funds are applied similarly to
assist those in need.

These were the sources of revenue and the general organization already developed in the Church to safeguard the
welfare of its members. But the depression in the 30's
brought about conditions which demanded that the machinery be speeded up. It was not a bread and butter prob-

lem alone which menaced Zion. Loss of self respect resulting
from continued unemployment and the demoralizing effect
of the dole presented evils more sinister and far reaching.
In face of threatened confusion, David O. McKay, of the
First Presidency addressed a group of welfare workers in
1936 in phrases not inappropriate on the eve of another
world conflict:

> "Brothers and Sisters, you are in the front trenches to-
> night ready to go over the top and I trust you have in your
> hearts and your hands the ammunition necessary to wage
> a successful battle. Some of you may not like my comparing
> the Welfare Plan to a war but we are in a war against idle-
> ness, against depression, a war against social enmity and to
> establish brotherhood and fraternalism among the member-
> ship of the Church."

This three front warfare required adaptation of old organization and methods to new conditions. A production and
distribution program called into being "Regional" groupings
of the Stakes, an annual production "Budget" originating
in a General Committee and broken down to Regional,
Stake and Ward units, manufacturing and canning centers,
thousands of acres of "Church" owned or rented land, and a
system of ninety Bishops storehouses[8].

"Welfare Square," containing the Bishops Central Storehouse, developed in Salt Lake City. It consisted of an administration building, storage rooms, a root cellar with
normal capacity for thirty carloads, a grain elevator capable
of storing 30,000 bushels. This "Central" unit served the
entire church. Its trucks, under direction of the Central
Committee, reached the farthest points in the West with
commodities in demand. They returned with regional surpluses for distribution elsewhere. Thus in the process
citrus fruits were supplied from the Salt River Valley in
Arizona to northern centers; Salmon from Portland exchanged for sugar from Utah; Idaho potatoes for California

oranges, nuts, and prunes. Tuna fish from Los Angeles came to the same central storehouse as cloth in large quantities from New York City.

The Bishops Storehouse in the Salt Lake Region served the needs of 160 Wards. It included a modern cannery with capacity of 30,000 cans daily. A sewing center which trained young women for employment in industrial plants, produced large quantities of overalls, dresses, underwear, etc. A milk processing plant had a daily capacity of 200 cases. This combined center employing 250 people was operated by those in need of assistance and by Priesthood Quorum members working odd hours, apart from regular employment. In addition, the Region operated a poultry farm, a hog farm, a soap plant and a cereal and pancake-flour mill. The Bishops Storehouse in Salt Lake City, while on a larger scale, was representative of many others located throughout the Church.

The machinery of the Welfare Plan was impressive but what of its capacity to meet the challenge of the triple enemy — idleness, depression, and social enmity? On the assumption that charity begins at home and that self conquest is a logical approach to participation in a larger social program, the Mormon plan proved a promising venture into the Co-operative Kingdom. While still functioning as a "depression" program, it had successfully completed fifteen hundred work projects, stored a half million bushels of wheat, and given economic assistance to nearly 300,000 persons in need[9]. A million dollar annual expenditure for direct assistance to the needy, for preservation of health, and hospitalization, was a fair measure of its scope. The rehabilitation of a thousand families that became self supporting through welfare assistance was evidence of its strong regenerating power within the Mormon group.

The Stakes and Wards continued as the essential operating units of the Welfare Movement and within these the Priesthood Quorums and the Relief Society the chief functional groups[10]. The Bishop continued as the key man in the system, now having the facilities of the Welfare Plan to aid him in caring for church members in need. Working closely with him was his Ward Welfare Committee and the Relief Society.

The production budget originated in the General Committee and was based upon regional reports of need and capacity to produce. Factors influencing preparation of that Budget were current needs, storage capacity, distribution facilities, and surplus from previous years. Specified portions of the Budget were then recommended to each of the Regional Councils which in turn proceeded to divide them among the Stakes within their jurisdiction. Here determining factors included natural productivity, existing permanent projects, anticipated needs and the overall requirements of the Church Program. The Stake allocated a portion of its assignment to each of the wards and the local ward and priesthood units went into action. All production under the Budget accrued to the Bishops Storehouse for distribution under the Welfare Plan.

During the production season vacant lots were turned to use by "Deacons," "Teachers," and "Priests," involving boys in their teens who competed in raising beans, carrots, corn or whatever their assignment. Some of the "gang" always found it possible to spend an evening irrigating, thinning, or weeding, though reminders were sometimes necessary. Others undertook to raise rabbits or chickens in lieu of garden produce. The "Elders," "Seventies" and "High Priests" usually assumed assignments for production of meat, fruit, potatoes, hay, grain, wool, etc., involving larger acreage and more capital. The land areas were often donated or rented, but Welfare projects rapidly assumed a more permanent aspect as more and more Church units acquired and operated their own properties. This was in harmony with the objective to make the movement self supporting.

So, in various ways and in every nook and corner of Mormondom, the Welfare Plan produced and gathered its relief stores. The press reflected a wide miscellany of projects:

19 TRACTORS PREPARE 300 ACRES FOR PLANTING. Montpelier, Idaho.

WELFARE SAVES DAVIS COUNTY (Utah) CROPS — 4000 PEOPLE RESPOND TO CALL.

HEBER CITY (Utah) SCENE OF DAIRY PROJECT. 123 ACRES STOCKED TO GRAZING CAPACITY.

MT. SHASTA (California) PRIESTHOOD GROUP RAISES POTATOES.

HILL CUMORAH (New York) BEAN CROP — 2½ TONS CANNED IN PRIESTHOOD PROJECT.

MT. TABOR (Oregon) PICKING ON SHARES — WOOD-CHOPPING PROJECT TO RAISE MONEY FOR STOREHOUSE.

PORTLAND (Oregon) STAKE LAUNCHES NEW WELFARE SALMON CANNERY.

TEACHERS GROW SOYBEANS — Salt Lake.

CARBON STAKE (Utah) GROWS SUGAR BEETS.

FOURTEEN FAMILIES PROSPER ON IDAHO CHURCH WELFARE PROJECT.

INDUSTRY — UNITY — FRIENDSHIP CHARACTERIZE DAVIS STAKE (Utah) DEHYDRATING PROJECT.

UP EARLY IN THE MORNING TO HARVEST CHURCH WELFARE PEAS.

WALL STREET JOURNAL TELLS OF CHURCH WELFARE — MORMONS PRODUCING AND CONSERVING ACTIVITIES IN CALIFORNIA.

One annual report summarized:

"To produce the Welfare Budget there were 1,015 crop projects, 669 livestock projects, and 55 manufacturing projects carried on. The crop project utilized 3,089 acres of land. The livestock projects produced 2,649 head of livestock, 12,200 chickens and rabbits, and 204 stands of bees[11]."

The same year sixty-five canneries and processing plants produced over a million and a half cans of milk, fruits, vegetables, meats and fish for the Welfare Program. Also thousands of pounds of spices, flavorings, etc. and hundreds of tons of flour and cereals.

Cooperative labor brought an unconscious development of fraternalism. Farmers, bankers, janitors, and professional men, tradesmen and office workers met on a common level engaged in common projects. "Bishops" picked turkeys with the humblest "elders" late into the night; the bank executive felt the spirit of the struggling young farmer as they hoed corn together at sun-up; deacons laughed loudest when the professor appeared in his "farmer's outfit"; and bake ovens sizzled over outdoor fires to provide breakfast for "early birds" soon due at their respective offices.

Frequently "quorum" socials brought wives into the circle and at least one zealous High Priest was brought to judgment for breaking the Sabbath. Having irrigated corn when the "water turn" came on Sunday he faced a Kangaroo Court. "Not guilty" was the verdict when wilting corn was placed by the defense in the same category as the ox in the mire.

In the fall when accounting showed that most of the assignments had been met, and no one remembered having made any special effort or contribution toward the reserves on hand, a local bishop devoted a Sunday Service to hearing reports from the "Quorums." The casual visitor who happened in for a worship service was undoubtedly puzzled as he listened to the "Priesthood" activity reports. But he could hardly deny that they represented a practical, if extraordinary, turn to religion. Visitors to early Utah who questioned the propriety of discussing irrigation projects or industrial plans in the "meeting houses" of Mormondom, or of a sermon on "oxteamology" in a General Church Conference, would find much to ponder over in the sermons of present-day Bishops, and in the temporal engagements of priesthood quorums. But herein lies the genius of Mormon Zion Building. Sermons most acceptable to heaven, say the Latter-day Saints, are those most firmly rooted in human need on earth.

It was more than a century ago that the Latter-day Saints attempted to found "the Kingdom" in Ohio and Missouri upon the "Law of Consecration." Ruthless expulsion resulted in abandonment of the movement as an "unfinished experiment." While the system itself was discontinued, some of its fundamental principles persisted through the entire Mormon experience. In this generation, though no claim is made to restoration of the Law of Consecration, at least four of its basic features inhere in the Welfare Plan. First of all it rests upon the principle of private ownership of property as did the original system. Further, in place of "surpluses" from properties and production which were formerly turned to the Bishops Storehouse for relief of the poor, the present Plan has at its disposal Welfare donations, fast offerings, and part of the tithes. A third common feature in the two systems is the Bishops Storehouse devoted to the same end — of storing and distributing supplies to the poor. Finally, the undistributed properties held by the Church in former days were administered under the Law for the benefit of the needy. The same is true today of the increasing acreage owned by Wards or other Church units for production purposes under the Welfare Plan[12].

So Mormonism declared war at home on the triple enemy of idleness, depression and social enmity. It was a war to establish the conditions of peace. But scarcely were the wheels of Welfare machinery turning smoothly before World War II presented a new challenge. Machinery designed to cope with problems of unemployment and depression must be adjusted to the needs of production and conservation. Something new appeared in the original Welfare Program. Neighborhood groups, priesthood quorums, Ward or other organized units, including both men and women, responded to an invitation to cooperative effort in planting and harvesting crops and canning, processing and storing foods. These activities had no connection with the Welfare Plan itself except that in many localities Welfare owned equipment and facilities were made available.

Thus in the war years there was a rush by Latter-day

Saints, as individuals, to cooperate with the Government in producing and conserving food. At least twenty-seven well equipped canneries were made available for these "independent groups" for the purpose of preserving the harvest of their Victory Gardens. Many of the canneries operated day and night during the canning season. This development brought hundreds of independent cooperative groups close to the Welfare Project.

Total production by individual groups using Welfare canneries in one war year amounted to 8,808,800 cans bringing the combined "independent" and "Welfare" canning output for the year to more than ten million[13]. It was estimated that this figure, added to total canning output of the Latter-day Saints in their homes, amounted to fifty million cans of preserved food representing a billion ration points. Commented the Salt Lake Tribune in this connection:

> "While learned economists and celebrated experts were orating, explaining, and citing statistics to prove pros and cons concerning the food situation . . . the Mormon Church leaders converted machinery already provided in the depression as an aid to unemployment, into a smoothly running food production industry. . . . The Mormon people are setting an example for their fellow countrymen with this noteworthy project. They have proceeded to solve the food problem in a democratic manner — the American way."

Not only in canning but in other fields of production did this cooperative spirit manifest itself. The figures relative to Welfare agricultural enterprise given above were increased as follows by group activity not connected with Bishops Storehouse operation:

> "Five hundred eighty-two crop projects, 221 livestock projects, and 34 manufacturing projects. . . . These enterprises utilized 2,100 acres of land and produced 1,010 head of livestock and 2,740 chickens and rabbits."

The Welfare Plan faced new problems at the close of the war. The Storehouses of Mormondom were full, but thirty thousand Latter-day Saints were starving in devastated Europe. A century ago Mormonism invaded the European countries to bring the "elect out of Babylon" in order that they might labor productively in the building of the Kingdom. Such escape is impossible in this generation, but grandsons of the past-century immigrants are returning to the lands of their fathers as missionaries and a most auspicious agency of service is the Welfare Plan. In the same European harbors where once converts embarked as eager Perpetual Emigration Fund passengers, modern ships now unload surpluses of the Bishops Storehouses for distribution among descendants of the "Saints" who remained to build Zion in their homelands. In this contribution to the well being of thousands beyond her borders lies one of the most promising opportunities for development of the Kingdom.

"The Gathering" still offers a "refuge from the storm" and the century old Mormon formula continues to provide security to its members. But the security of "Zion," like that of America itself, cannot be maintained by walls of self interest. The greatness of her storehouses will be measured in part by the length of the life lines cast to those caught in the storm outside.

1 Doctrine & Covenants 115:4-6.
2 Doctrine & Covenants 42:42; 68:30-31.
3 Widtsoe, John A., Discourses of Brigham Young.
4 An Important Message on Relief — by the First Presidency. Pamphlet, April, 1936.
5 "What is the Mormon Welfare Plan?" Pamphlet. Also "An Official Statement on the Church Security Program, October 2, 1936.
6 Annual Conference Reports of the Church of Jesus Christ of Latter-day Saints.
7 Ibid.
8 Welfare Report in April 1944 L. D. S. Conference Report —
     Fixed assets of the Welfare Plan, amounting to two and a half million dollars, consist of: "Deseret Industries; Deseret Mills and Elevators; Welfare Square Buildings, (elevators, canneries, milk processing plants, root cellar, etc.); Deseret Clothing Factory; Emery Coal Mine; and the housing and other projects. Ninety Bishops Storehouses which have a total floor area of 230,000 square feet — including in connection therewith sixty-five canneries. Farms, ranches, dairies, and other

Regional and Stake properties made up of 3,033 acres of land together with buildings, improvements, and livestock."

9 L. D. S. Annual Conference Reports — 1944-1945.

10 The Chief Functions of the Welfare Plan are listed as follows in the Church Welfare Handbook:

1. To determine the needs of the people.
2. To gather and properly control cash and commodity contributions.
3. To render needed assistance and to provide employment through work projects.
4. To manage the storage and distribution of commodities.
5. To meet the cash needs of ward members requiring assistance.
6. To promote Welfare work in Melchizedek and Aaronic priesthood units.
7. To guide agricultural and other rehabilitation.
8. To provide hospitalization for church cases.

11 L. D. S. Annual Conference Report, April, 1944.
12 L. D. S. Semi Annual Conference Report, October, 1942, p. 57.
13 L. D. S. Annual Conference Report, April, 1944, p. 24.

29

Stepping Stones

COUNT Leo Tolstoi, statesman philosopher, referred to Mormonism as "The American Religion." "The Mormons," he told U. S. Ambassador Andrew D. White, "teach the people not only of heaven . . . but how to live so that their social and economic relations with each other are placed on a sound basis[1]."

Particularly in its origins and as an important factor in the development of the West, Mormonism was, and is, a truly American religion. Conceived and cradled in an Utopian era it survived many contemporary offspring because of inherent principles of enduring value. It gave the spiritual Kingdom of God a temporal counterpart, so that ministry in His service became realistic both temporally and spiritually. It identified religion with life so closely that material engagements assumed a sense of divine vocation. It not only pointed the way to heaven — it built heavenward.

The Latter-day Saints concentrated on the American frontier vibrant with energy. Their plans were positive and comprehensive. They were commissioned to build the Kingdom of God; they held the blue prints to the City of Zion. They were irrepressible. The source of their power was the conviction that God had a work for them to do.

The Mormons needed elbow room for their far reaching plans. They crowded their neighbors not only in acreage but in ideas. Conflict developed and the old order expelled the new. Three times the Mormons yielded before the wrath of orthodoxy and the abuses of mobocracy. Each recovery found them stronger than before. Three times the "Saints" paid for the presumption of laying claim to divine dispensation by wiping clean their accounts of material possessions. These they could afford to lose; physical suffering and death they could endure. But their sense of mission could not be blacked out.

So to survive and continue their assigned task they learned to work together. Through cooperation they overcame obstacles. They found individual salvation through group solidarity. They endured because they had something to endure for. The Kingdom depended upon their building. People with a purpose will not down.

They passed through the fire and came into the Great Basin tempered for the task ahead. At last they had elbow room. They had resources with which to build. They needed builders. So they conserved their resources and called for a general "gathering." They supported the call through organized assistance to the poor who were helped to escape the economic treadmill of their homelands and given new life on the American frontiers. It was the most effective system of organized immigration in United States history[2].

So "the Kingdom" found social and economic expression in the wilderness. The result was a widespread pattern of towns and villages representing a thriving cooperative brotherhood.

Today, when serious problems of social adjustment demand the best that men can produce in the art of human relations, the past is searched for the contributions of experience. What can America learn from an organized movement which rescued tens of thousands from social and economic confusion to absorb them in productive, regenerating activity? What can bewildered humanity, seeking security in a world of uncertainty, learn from a successful cooperative enterprise which transformed a desolate frontier waste into a thriving commonwealth. Perhaps the collective quest for security pursued by the Mormons may be the key to cooperative action on a larger scale. At least three factors have served as stepping stones to whatever degree of success they have enjoyed. These included, (1) the conservation of wealth, (2) the conservation of man power, and (3) a religious basis for a sound social and economic order.

I

CONSERVATION OF WEALTH

The glory of America as a land of opportunity has reflected from her generous response to individual initiative. Freedom seekers in America have found their object abundantly in economic channels. But "rugged individualism" with its competitive private ownership has been accompanied by wasteful exploitation of natural resources. Inequalities of wealth have resulted and poverty exists in the midst of prosperity. Diminishing raw materials and conflict between selfish and community advantage have become serious American problems.

In this connection the Mormon experience is worthy of consideration. Its "law of consecration" and spirit of stewardship offered a satisfactory balance between individual enterprise and community good. This balance resulted from (a) restriction of private ownership to the limits of profitable use, (b) return to the community of surpluses beyond reasonable need and comfort. (c) Property ownership was coupled with definite social responsibility. Application of these principles to the western situation prevented land grabbing by the Mormons on the plains of Iowa and by the first comers in the Salt Lake Valley. "Every man should have his land measured off to him for city and farming purposes, what he could till. He might till it as he pleased, but he should be industrious and take care of it." They applied to the use of irrigation water, preventing the few from robbing the many. They brought into being a new law and practice which affords the widest possible use of a limited water supply. The results have been vitally important in a state with little more than ten percent of its total land area available for any kind of agriculture and only about two percent subject to reclamation through irrigation. In the words of a leading American economist, "We have a marvelous combination of physiographic conditions and social organization in the development of Utah under the guidance of Mormonism. The Agriculture pursued was irrigation agriculture, which for its success is dependent upon a compact society, well knit together. Individualism was out of the question under these conditions, and in Mormonism we find precisely the cohesive strength of religion needed at that junction to secure economic success[2a]." What has been accomplished in Utah with its limited agricultural possibilities is a tribute to the cooperative spirit of the founders of modern irrigation[3].

II

CONSERVATION OF MAN POWER

Dr. Thomas Nixon Carver found Mormon success to rest largely upon "economy of man-power:" "They not only began with desert land . . . they had to start with relatively uneducated people. The double task of developing both land and people could never have been performed except by economizing such man power as there was and utilizing it to the nth degree. The results were a marvel of statesmanship[4]."

Dr. Carver found man power conserved in the Mormon group through (1) cultivation of sound personal habits among the people, (2) discovery of hidden talents and giving them a chance to function, and (3) by cooperation and by working together harmoniously.

(1) Cultivation of sound personal habits: payment of tithes, fast offerings, welfare donations, maintenance of missionaries, etc., are a constant test of Mormon faith. They reflect individual acceptance of the philosophy of divine ownership and human trusteeship. They afford an exact-

ing test of self conquest in obedience to divine will. To
return to God one tenth of one's income regularly, and to
maintain a son or a daughter in the mission field for two
or more years out of the family budget, represents no empty
gestures to relieve the conscience but established practice in
the life of regular Latter-day Saints. The financial drain
upon many Mormon homes sometimes raises the question
of economic consequences[5] but generally the effect on church
membership is to promote habits of thrift and a feeling of
"spiritual investment."

Embedded in Latter-day Saint philosophy is a health code
known as the Word of Wisdom. It includes: no tea, coffee,
tobacco or alcoholics; little meat and plenty of grain products,
vegetables and fruit. Promised rewards include physical
and mental health. Specific results are difficult to measure
but the Word of Wisdom is generally accepted as chief contributor toward a high Mormon standard of health[6]. In
Utah the Mormons with circa sixty-five percent of the population in 1936 had a death rate of 8.1 per thousand as against
13.8 for the "gentiles" in the same state — a difference of
seventy percent. Currently the pull exerted by narcotic
interests upon Mormon youth is scarcely offset by the influence of the Church to hold them to its standards.

Additional conserving forces at work in Mormondom are
reflected through comparison of L. D. S. social statistics
with those of the United States at large. Taking the average
of the five year period from 1936 to 1940 as a basis, the comparison reveals[7]:

	U. S.	L. D. S.
Birth rate per 1,000	17.34	31.16
Death rate per 1,000	10.96	6.78
Marriage rate per 1,000	10.9	17.78

(2) The lay nature of Mormonism finds more than two
hundred and fifty thousand of its near million members
engaged in Church service[9]. A popular Latter-day Saint
slogan is "Growth through Activity." Such a practice is

naturally conducive to "discovery of hidden talent and giving it a chance to function." This process of discovery and of providing opportunity for practice demands toleration of untrained workers in responsible positions in order to encourage a minority upward toward effective leadership. Unfortunately this indulgence of mass mediocrity is the inescapable price of lay participation. However, the system seems to be paying good dividends. It is undoubtedly a contributing factor towards Utah's high rank in the scale of "leadership productivity" as presented in the Thorndike report[10]. (Chapter XXII p. 247).

The Mormon philosophy of salvation contributes to the urge for talent development. As pointed out by Dr. M. Lynn Bennion in "Mormonism and Education," "The Mormons have always held that salvation is an individual matter. The Church is but a vehicle to aid them in saving themselves. Every man to be saved . . . must rise above the power of all his enemies not the least of which is ignorance." Excerpts from Latter-day Saint scripture illustrate how basic education is in the Mormon plan of salvation:

"We are saved no faster than we gain knowledge."

"It is impossible for a man to be saved in ignorance."

"Seek ye diligently and teach one another words of wisdom."

" . . . and I give unto you a commandment that you shall teach one another the doctrine of the kingdom . . . teach . . . of things both in heaven and in the earth and under the earth; things which have been, things which are, things which must shortly come to pass; things which are at home, things which are abroad[11]. . . . "

Continues Dr. Bennion, "Mormon education embraces secular learning as a constituent part of universal truth, which emanates from a divine source. All education therefore is religious and essential to progress[12]."

Such identification of education with the doctrine of eternal progress has been a real stimulus in Mormondom[12a].

It will continue to send an above average number of youth
to college and develop leaders in educational fields in the
degree that genuine scholarship and real freedom of research
is encouraged. This will require cooperation based upon
full confidence between men of the pulpit and men of
science.

(3) Mormonism has been a cooperative adventure from
the beginning. The earliest attempts to conserve resources
and man-power through the "law of consecration" were but
preliminaries to a long series of cooperative experiences.
These included mutual assistance in escaping as a body from
Missouri to Illinois, building Nauvoo to a frontier center
of prominence and prosperity, the "Nauvoo Covenant" to
bring the poor Saints into the west, expansion of the covenant into the Perpetual Emigrating Fund Company which
assisted a hundred thousand Saints to "gather to Zion,"
effective organization which prevented the usual dissolution
of emigrant companies on the plains, founding of colonies
in the Great Basin after the pattern of the "City of Zion,"
supporting these communities under a system of irrigation,
economic experiments in buying and selling, and promoting
industries as group ventures representing unity of will and
effort. A system of tithing and fast offerings has continued
the cooperative thread in the Church enlarging currently into the Welfare Plan with its numerous ramifications.

These and other activities have represented a general
willingness to work together for common ends more than
they have the organization of formal cooperative societies.
The organizations of this latter nature which appeared in the
sixties and seventies were church encouraged, and often
church initiated, private enterprises. They were the beginnings of a movement which current success outside Mormondom suggests might well have been continued with profit
to "the Kingdom." The cooperative formula used by the
Mormons in the sixties and seventies might well offer the
solution to one of Utah's major economic problems today —

the decline of her sheep industry due to the lack of control of the factors of production and marketing.

The genius of Mormon cooperation has been unity of purpose which has grown out of the sharing of a common ideal and having a sense of mission relative to it[12b]. This was reflected in the Iron and Cotton Missions: There was general interest in their progress because the whole community would be affected by the outcome. The building of the Utah Central Railroad was equally a peoples affair. The progress of the Sugar Industry reflected the same basis of cooperation as the church, the territory, the press and every local settlement participated vicariously in the shifting fortunes of the sugar pioneers. When the factory was finally erected and sugar manufacture became a reality, it was a community victory[13].

Dr. Carver defined it as the "highest order of statesmanship" to get tens of thousands and millions working in cooperation. "I do not think," he concluded, "that the Mormons have quite achieved that result, but they have at least done something in that direction. The rest of the country can at least learn something by observing them."

III

A Religious Basis For Sound Social and Economic Order

In Mormon philosophy the "Kingdom of God" is not only a condition of righteousness but a temporal organization assigned to achieve His purposes in the earth. The Church of Jesus Christ of Latter-day Saints is the channel through which God will ultimately establish His rule among men. Imperfect as it may be in membership and practice, it is nevertheless Divine in assignment and aspiration. Its task is to seek the Kingdom of God on earth as well as in Heaven. The earthly Kingdom will be realized as eternal principles are successfully applied in the social and economic life of

God's children.   Hence temporalities and spiritualities are
often inseparable in Mormon experience.

The dual nature of the Kingdom was frequently on the
lips of Brigham Young. "The Lord designs to build up a
Kingdom that will be both a spiritual and a temporal Kingdom upon the earth. . . . When this Kingdom is organized
in any age the spirit of it dwells in the hearts of the faithful,
while its visible department exists among the people, with
laws, ordinances, helps, governments, officers, administrators
and every other appendage necessary for its complete operation to the attainment of the end in view[14]."   Again he said,
"The Kingdom we are talking about, preaching about and
trying to build up is the Kingdom of God on earth, not in
the starry heavens, nor in the sun. We are trying to establish the Kingdom of God on earth to which really and properly everything that pertains to men — their feelings, their
faith, their affections, their desires, and every act of their
lives — belong, that they may be ruled by it spiritually and
temporally[15]."

More recently Joseph F. Smith, nephew of the Mormon
founder and sixth president of the Church made this revealing statement: "It has always been a cardinal principle
with the Latter-day Saints that a religion that has not the
power to save men temporally and make them prosperous
and happy here, cannot be depended upon to save them
spiritually and exalt them in the life to come."

It was in this light and with this feeling that thousands
of converts from many lands converged upon the Great
Basin to engage in a literal building of God's Kingdom.
The conviction that they were participating in the realiza-
tion of this ideal was the source of their power and the key
to their success. It gave impetus to thousands of missionaries
who shared with the Church a deep sense of mission in the
world. It gave hope to tens of thousands who "gathered to
Zion." It gave purpose to the labor of those who felt responsibility for the progress of the Kingdom. Their daily labors

in factory and field assumed the nature of co-partnership with God. It was upon this religious basis that the Mormons built — and built successfully.

The Mormon experience is worthy of study in relation to conservation, cooperation, and inspiration. It is doubtful if any people ever accomplished more with equally limited resurces; none have understood and voluntarily applied the principles of united effort more effectively; and few have drawn such strength and staying power from the inspiration of a great ideal. The Mormon contribution to western development has been substantial; but it has been doubly important because its economic system enriched the human personality and fostered self dependence. Mormonism built men while it built an empire. Its message to America is that social and economic progress cannot ignore human values, nor can it continue long apart from spiritual ideals. Its voice is raised legitimately in the Christian chorus which pleads for return from the way of gross materialism to the surer spiritual road leading to the abundant life. Social responsibility must attach to economic power. America at her best has been the defender of Christian idealism; her influence most wholesome under the conviction that her destiny was linked with divine will. She was never more empty than when she was content with overflowing treasuries and smug security.

In this connection none of her offspring have greater faith in or deeper concern for America's future than have the Latter-day Saints. To them America is the "Land of Zion" — a refuge for the oppressed of the earth — "a land favored above all others." In Mormon philosophy America's discovery, her settlement, and finally her constitution, were divinely inspired to the end of preserving human liberty and the final establishment of the Messianic reign. A favorite quotation is the following from their Prophet:

" . . . The Constitution of the United States is a glorious standard; it is founded in the wisdom of God. It is a heaven-

ly banner; it is to all those who are privileged with the
sweets of its liberty, like the cooling shades and refreshing
waters of a great rock in a weary and thirsty land. It is like
a great tree under whose branches men from every clime
can be shielded from the burning rays of the sun[16]."

But America's destiny as "land of Zion" is conditioned
upon performance. "Zion," as interpreted by the Mormons,
means not only a favored land, but a people "pure in heart."
No land can rise in divine favor above the moral and spiritual
level of its people. Institutions and constitutions are but
means to an end. If the instruments are badly handled the
ends may be lost. Therefore the Latter-day Saints are keen-
ly alive to national and international political trends, for in
them they see either acceleration or retardation of millennial
foundations. The Mormons look with eager expectancy
toward America's leadership in the New World. To them
such ascendency is in the divine scheme of things and pertinent to their own God given responsibility.

Echoing the original announcement of "the restoration"
made more than a century ago, Dr. John A. Widtsoe, apostle
of the present generation, said in a recent Mormon Conference:

"It is our destiny to purify the world; to lead men from
evil to good; to win the nations to the realm of everlasting
truth; to prepare the earth for the coming of the Lord. We
are called to establish the Kingdom of God on earth[17]."

Presumptuous as such a declaration might appear generally, to the Mormons it represents a sense of mission. Heirs
to a pioneer conviction that the building of the Kingdom
is their seven day week assignment, the faithful still labor
to justify their claim to being a "chosen people." To do less
would be treason to the ideals and convictions of their
fathers. To believe less would be to lose the source of inspiration and strength which made past achievements possible. In the degree that "chosen" is identified with a call
to service it will continue as a stimulus in Mormondom. But

if service yields to the illusion of divine preference, then a force for good will already have spent itself. The world owes much to men and women who have felt that God had a work for them to do. The strength of America lies in such tributaries of faith which have flowed into her national stream of progress.

1 Improvement Era, Volume 42:94.
2 Comen, Katherine, Economic Beginnings of the Far West, Volume II:184.
2a Ely, Richard T., Harper's Magazine 106, p. 667.
3 U. S. Agricultural Census, 1940: World Almanac, 1944.
   At the beginning of the present decade there were 2,401 irrigation enterprises in the state; there were 22,612 irrigated farms including nearly a million and a half acres under primary and supplemental water rights. The total invested capital in the irrigation projects was over forty million dollars.
4 Carver, Thomas Nixon, A Positive Religion, The Westerner, April 9, 1930.
5 Widtsoe, John A., Evidences and Reconciliations, pp. 225-228.
   A high percentage of farm loan delinquency in certain Utah areas afforded a joint study of the problem by federal bank officials and the Utah State Agricultural College, with support from the Church. Six hundred and seventy-five cases were studied. One interesting conclusion: "The investigation showed that tithing had no depressing economic influence, but rather that the qualities in a man that led him to pay tithing also enabled him to win more success in his economic life." Another interesting study is that of R. Welling Roskelly called "The L. D. S. Missionary System in A Local Area." In pages 13-14 he considers the missionary system in connection with economic conditions in three wards selected and suggests a relation between missionary expenditures and slow development of rural village economy.
6 Vitality Records, Volume I, Number I, p. 4. Dr. Irving Fisher, after making a study of these Latter-day Saint health statistics in 1937, commented:
   "Why then are the Mormons so peculiarly free from tuberculosis, maternity death, cancer, nervous disease, and so forth? The only important reason in sight is that the Mormons are peculiarly hygienic. "If we would all make a religion of health and practice hygiene as faithfully as the Mormons do, we would doubtless, with our modern knowledge, attain an even higher level of vitality."
7 World Almanac (1944) and L. D. S. Conference Reports for years covered.
8 Huntington & Whitney, The Builders of America, pp. 195-200.
   The "Builders of America" studies found the Mormons in 1926 far ahead of other American religious groups in population increase. Their conclusion: "At the present rate of reproduction the great grandchildren of the leading Mormon families are likely to be seven or eight times as numerous as the present generation." (Mormon birth rate for 1926 was 32 per thousand as against 33.8 in 1946.)
9 Widtsoe, John A., L. D. S. Church Statistics, January, 1944.

10 Thorndike, E. L., The Origin of Superior Men, Scientific Monthly, May, 1943.

11 Doctrine & Covenants, Section 131:6 and Section 88:78.

12 Bennion, M. Lynn, Mormonism and Education, pp. 121-123.

12a R. M. Hughes and W. H. Lancelot, Education, America's Magic (1946) page 40:

> "Utah has first place among the states by a wide margin . . . . While ranking 32 in ability to support education with an income of only $1680 per child, and 4 in effort, it still ranks first in educational accomplishment, in the degree in which accomplishment is commensurate with ability, in efficiency, and in the level of adult education.
>
> "This appears to be due almost wholly to the high value placed on education by the people of Utah, coupled with high efficiency in the expenditure of funds devoted to school purposes. Indeed this combination of great effort and high efficiency in the utilization of school funds seems to have operated in a remarkable manner to overcome the handicap of relatively low ability.
>
> "Utah easily outclasses all other states in over-all performance in education."

12b Ely, Richard T., Harper's Magazine 106:667.

> "We find in Mormonism to a larger degree than I have ever seen in any other body of people, an illustration of the individual who is willing to sacrifice himself for the whole, and it is a religious sanction which impels him to do so. On the other hand the interests of the future are ever in mind and to them the present is subordinated, the final goal being the millennium, and the setting up of the Kingdom. . . . "

13 Something of its public nature is revealed in cold statistics of the Utah-Idaho Sugar Company. To date it has expended over $34,000,000.00 in erection of factories, equipment, etc., and has produced an average of a million and half 100 pound bags of sugar annually totalling over seventy-five million. Its net receipts have amounted to $325,000,000.00 of which the beet growers have received fifty-one percent or $166,000,-000.00. Total dividends to investors have amounted to nearly $22,000,-000.00. The present annual harvest is over a million tons of beets from 80,000 irrigated acres.

14 Brigham Young Discourses, Volume 10:28.

15 Brigham Young Discourses, Volume 10:328.

16 Joseph Smith, History of L. D. S. Church, Volume III: 304.

17 L. D. S. Conference Report, April, 1942, p. 34.

BIBLIOGRAPHY

PRIMARY SOURCES

MANUSCRIPTS

History of Brigham Young, MS 1844-1877.
A manuscript history of Brigham Young compiled by contemporary secretaries. In Latter-day Saints Church Library, Salt Lake City, Utah.
Journals of Discourses, 26 volumes. Liverpool, 1854-1886. L.D.S. Church Library, Salt Lake City, Utah.
Journal History, MS.
A compilation of original letters, journals, minutes, etc., from 1845 to present. L.D.S. Church Library, Salt Lake City, Utah.
Manuscript Compilation from Millennial Star of immigration statistics. L.D.S. Church Library, Salt Lake City, Utah.

NEWSPAPERS AND PERIODICALS

Contributor. A monthly publication of the Mutual Improvement Association of the Church of Jesus Christ of Latter-day Saints. Salt Lake City, Utah, 1880-1897.
Deseret News. Salt Lake City, Weekly, 1850-1867; Daily 1867 —.
Edinburg Review, London, April, 1854.
Evening and Morning Star, Independence, Mo., 1832-1834.
Frontier Guardian, Kanesville (Council Bluffs), Iowa, 1849-1851.
Improvement Era, Salt Lake City, Utah.
Iron County Record, Cedar City, Utah.
The Luminary, St. Louis, Missouri.
London Examiner, London, August 16, 1878.
Millennial Star. Weekly organ of the L.D.S. Church, Liverpool, 1840-1883. London, 1833 —.
Nauvoo Neighbor, Nauvoo, Illinois, 1843-1845.
Peoria Daily Transcript, on file in Peoria Public Library.
Salt Lake Tribune, Salt Lake City, Utah.
Scientific Monthly, Washington, May, 1943.
Times and Seasons, Bi-weekly Church publication, Nauvoo, Illinois, 1837-1846.

CONTEMPORARY PUBLICATIONS

Book of Mormon, translated by Joseph Smith, Palmyra, New York, 1830. Latest Edition, Salt Lake City, Utah, 1921.
Bowles, Samuel, Our New West, Hartford, Conn., 1869.
Brocket, L. P., Our Western Empire, Philadelphia, Pa., 1881.
Burton, Richard F., The City of the Saints, London, 1861.
Cheney, Edward P., Readings in English History. Collection of original sources. Boston, 1908.
Dickens, Charles, Uncommercial Traveler, Chicago, Illinois.
Doctrine & Covenants, Containing the Revelations given to Joseph Smith. Latest Edition, Salt Lake City, 1921.
Ferris, Benjamin G., Utah and the Mormons, New York, 1854.
Ford, Governor Thomas, History of Illinois, Chicago, Ill., 1854.
Gunnison, John W., The Mormons of the Latter-day Saints in the Valley of the Great Salt Lake, Philadelphia, 1860.
Linforth, James, Route from Liverpool to Salt Lake Valley, London, 1855.
Little, James A., Jacob Hamblin, Salt Lake City, Utah, 1881.
Lunt, Henry, MS, Dairy, Parowan, Utah.
Pratt, Parley P., Autobiography, New York, 1874.

Remy, Jules and Brenchley, Jules, A Journey to Great Salt Lake City, London, 1861.
Report of Proceedings of Annual and Semi-annual L.D.S. Conferences, Salt Lake City, Utah.
Sloan, Robert W., Utah Gazetteer and Directory, Salt Lake City, Utah, 1881.
Smith, Joseph, History of the Church of Jesus Christ of Latter-day Saints. Written by Joseph Smith, edited by B. H. Roberts. Six volumes, Salt Lake City, 1902.
Smucker, Samuel M., History of the Mormons, New York, 1881.
Stansbury, Captain J. Howard, An Expedition to the Valley of the Great Salt Lake, Philadelphia, 1855.
Sullivan, Maurice S., The Travels of Jedediah Smith. A Documentary Outline, Santa Anna, 1934.
Todd, Rev. John D.D., Sunset Land, Boston, 1870.
Tullidge, Edward W., History of Salt Lake City, 1886.

DOCUMENTS — FEDERAL & TERRITORIAL

Acts, Resolutions, and Memorials passed by the Legislative Assembly of the Territory of Utah, Salt Lake City, 1876.
Congressional Record, Volume XVIII, 1887.
Evarts, William M., Circular to American Diplomats and Consular Officers, Volume II. Circulars Department of State, 1879.
House and Senate Executive Documents. Containing reports of Utah Territorial Governors. Eli H. Murray, 1883 and Arthur L. Thomas, 1889.
Laws and Ordinances of the State of Deseret. Compilation of 1851. Salt Lake City, 1919.
Mead, Ellwood, Report of Irrigation Investigations in Utah.
Richardson, James D., Messages and Papers of our Presidents, Washington, 1898.
United States Census Reports, 1850-1860-1870-1880.
United States Statutes at Large. 49th Congress, 1855-1887.

SECONDARY SOURCES

Alter, J. Cecil, Utah, Chicago—New York, 1932
Bakker & Shaars, Economics of Cooperative Marketing, New York, 1937.
Bancroft, Hubert Howe, History of Utah, San Francisco, 1890.
Bennion, M. Lynn, Mormonism and Education, Salt Lake City, 1939.
Brown, John Z., Autobiography of John Brown, Salt Lake City, 1941.
Cannon, George Q., Life of Joseph Smith, Salt Lake City, 1888.
Calverton, V. F., Where Angels Dared to Tread, New York, 1941.
Coman, Katherine, Economic Beginnings of the Far West, New York, 1925.
Church Welfare Plan (L.D.S.) publications, Salt Lake City, Utah.
Church Welfare Handbook — Salt Lake City, 1944.
Cowley, Mathias F., Life of Wilford Woodruff, Salt Lake City, 1909.
Creer, Leland H., Utah and the Nation, Seattle, 1929.
Emigration Manuscript, Compiled from Millennial Star. L.D.S. Church Library, Salt Lake City, Utah.
Evans, John Henry, Joseph Smith, An American Prophet, New York, 1933.
Evans and Stokdyk, The Law of Cooperative Marketing, Rochester, New York, 1937.
Geddes, Joseph A., The United Order Among the Mormons, Salt Lake City, 1924.

Geddes, Joseph A., Migration, a problem of youth in Utah, Bulletin 323. Utah Agricultural College Experiment Station, 1946.

Hughes, R. M. and Lancelot, W. H., Education, America's Magic, Iowa State College Press, Ames, Iowa, 1946.

Hunter, Milton R., Brigham Young, the Colonizer, Salt Lake City, Utah, 1940.

Hunter, Milton R., American Historical Review XLIV.

Huntington, E. and Whitney, L. F., The Builders of America, New York, 1927.

Jensen, Andrew, Church Chronology, Salt Lake City, 1914 edition.

Jensen, Andrew, Manuscript histories of various wards ad stakes of the Church. L.D.S. Church Library, Salt Lake City, Utah.

Kaufman, Ruth and Kaufman, Reginald W., The Latter-day Saints, London, 1912.

Larson, Gustive O., History of Perpetual Emigrating Fund Company, MS. Salt Lake City, 1926.

Linn, W. A., The Story of the Mormons, New York, 1902.

Little, James A., From Kirtland to Salt Lake City, Salt Lake City, 1890.

McClintock, James H., Mormon Settlement in Arizona, Phoenix, 1921.

Neff, Andrew Love, History of Utah, 1847-1869, Salt Lake City, 1940.

Nelson, Lowry, The Mormon Village, Proceedings of Utah Academy of Sciences, Salt Lake City, Utah.

Palmer, William R., History of Iron Manufacturing. MS, Cedar City, Utah.

Pioneer Songs, Published by Daughters of Utah Pioneers, Salt Lake City, 1932.

Reports of L.D.S. Conferences (annual and semi-annual) Salt Lake City, Utah.

Roberts, Brigham H., Comprehensive History of the Church of Jesus Christ of Latter-day Saints. 6 volumes. Salt Lake City, 1930.

Roberts, Brigham H., Rise and Fall of Nauvoo, Salt Lake City, 1900.

Roskelly, R. Welling, The L. D. S. Missionary System in a Local Area. M. S. Utah State Agricultural College Library, Logan, Utah.

Smith, Joseph Fielding, Origin of the Reorganized Church, Salt Lake City, 1907.

Snow, William James, The Great Basin Before the Coming of the Mormons, MS, Provo, Utah.

Snow, Eliza R., Biography of Lorenzo Snow, Salt Lake City, 1884.

Talmage, James E., Articles of Faith of the Church of Jesus Christ of Latter-day Saints, Salt Lake City, 1899.

Taylor, Fred G., A Saga of Sugar, Salt Lake City, 1944.

Thayer, William M., Marvels of the New West, Norwich, Conn., 1888.

Thomas, George, Development of Institutions Under Irrigation, New York, 1914.

Werner, Robert M., Brigham Young, New York, 1925.

West, Franklin L., Life of Franklin Dewey Richards, Salt Lake City, 1924.

Westerner, The.

What is the Mormon Welfare Plan? Pamphlet, Salt Lake City, 1936.

Whitney, Orson F., Popular History of Utah, Salt Lake City, 1916.

Widtsoe, John A., Principles of Irrigation Practice, New York, 1914.

Widtsoe, John A., Discourses of Brigham Young, Salt Lake City, 1925.

Widtsoe, John A., Priesthood and Church Government, Salt Lake City, Utah, 1939.

World Fellowship of Faiths Report, London, 1917.